D060246

Fighter

A History of Fighter Aircraft

John Batchelor and Bryan Cooper

Copyright © 1973 Bryan Cooper and John Batchelor

CHARLES SCRIBNER'S SONS
NEW YORK

1 **Voisin.** Joseph Frantz makes the first known kill in
aerial combat, October 5th 1914.

**Dedicated: To the Pilots
and to DAVID**

Contents

This book published simultaneously in the United States of America and in Canada—Copyright under the Berne Convention

All rights reserved. No part of this book may be reproduced in any form without the permission of Charles Scribner's Sons.

3 5 7 9 11 13 15 17 19 I/C 20 18 16 14 12 10 8 6 4 2

Printed in the United States of America
Library of Congress Catalog Card Number 73-7211
SBN 684-13549-3 (cloth)

Foreword

by Air Commodore P. M. Brothers, CBE, DSO, DFC.

"Fighter" – a word which conjures in the mind a picture of speed and skill, of youth and daring, of freedom and loneliness. To those of us who had the good fortune to be fighter pilots, the word evokes memories of the thrill of formation aerobatics, of keyed-up periods of readiness – when the mildest of amusing remarks provoked convulsions of laughter – of solitary flights in the smooth air of sunset when all the world seemed at peace.

It was these memories which flooded my mind when Bryan Cooper invited me to write this foreword and they were such happy ones that I was delighted to accept. His book, so painstakingly researched, traces the development of fighter aircraft from those days when but a handful of enthusiasts had the vision and imagination to foresee the potential that use of the air offered and the radical impact that this would have on warfare. This was the scene and it is against this backdrop that the story of the fighter unfolds. The inevitably apathetic interest so characteristic in times of peace was short-lived and the demands of war compelled the infant aircraft industry rapidly to develop and expand; the pilots for their part were ingenious and inventive in the development of tactics and equipment and for an aviation enthusiast since early childhood such as myself I was glad to be reminded of the contribution made by such men as Immelmann, Guynemer and Hawker.

It was inevitable that many of the lessons learnt and the experience gained in the First War should have been forgotten during the years of peace which followed. However, the Second World War was to demonstrate that although the fighter alone could not win a war it could lose one, for had it failed Britain in 1940 the whole course of world history indisputably would have been changed. That air battle was certainly the first and could well be the last to be fought in isolation from other forces. Certainly the issues at stake were such that the consequences would have been catastrophic had the fighter failed us then.

What of the future? Few will question the continuing need for fighter aircraft to police our airspace in peace and contribute to the deterrent forces by their ability to defend in war. Their inherent flexibility of operation and role and speed of reaction could well provide the means by which to impose at the outset of hostilities that vital "pause" for thought and effort in a last ditch attempt to avoid nuclear war. The fighter could thus again prove to be successful in saving mankind from another "Dark Age".

One of three D.F.W. two-seaters brought down behind British lines on the Italian Front after a raid on Istrana Aerodrome on December 26th, 1917. *Imperial War Museum*

Fire was the most feared hazard in the days before parachutes were carried. The pilot of this German airplane brought down near Contalmaison during the Battle of the·Somme in September 1916 was burned to death. *Imperial War Museum*

The Need for Fighters

The fighter airplane was born in the First World War, over the trenches of the Western Front. It was in those un-sullied skies, high above the grim struggle taking place on the ground, that the frail reconnaissance aircraft with which the major powers went to war fought their first aerial battles, leading to the development of the true fighter. As the weapons carried in airplanes became more sophisticated, from mere pistols and rifles to machine-guns, shell-guns and even the first crude firework-type rockets, so new roles were found for fighters. Beginning as interceptors, their uses were extended to include infantry support, ground attack, bomber escort and night fighting. Before the war was over all the basic tactics had been devised that were to govern aerial combat for the next fifty years, until the arrival of modern supersonic fighters equipped with automatic weapons systems reduced the pilot's role to little more than that of a passenger during actual engagements, when because of the sheer speeds involved he now has to rely on electronic devices to detect, identify and open fire on an enemy.

The First World War also created the ace fighter pilot. Aviation was in its infancy in 1914 and many of those who went to war in the air, fighting for the first time in a new element, had been among the pioneers of flight before the war began. Flying alone in open, unheated and un-armoured cockpits, constantly at the mercy of mechanical or structural failures, they felt a 'brotherhood of the air' that transcended frontiers. It was not unusual for German and Allied pilots to wave to one another when they met during reconnaissance flights, which was all their aircraft were at first considered good for. Even when battles between opposing aircraft inevitably became a grim life-and-death struggle, to the point where the life expectancy of a combat pilot on the Western Front was no more than a few weeks, there still remained a tradition of chivalry and respect for the enemy that never entirely vanished. The 'aces' were those who learned the arts of flying and man-oeuvring into position better than others, even against superior aircraft on occasion, and their deaths were honoured by friend and foe alike. But in general, air supremacy went to the side possessing the best aircraft. Throughout the war, this balance shifted continually between the German and Allied air services, favouring one side or the other at any given time.

A few designers and enthusiasts had foreseen before the war that aircraft would meet and fight one another in the air, but this was not a view officially held by any of the belligerent powers. Aircraft had been used in war as a means of dropping small bombs and grenades, first by the Italians in Libya during the Italo-Turkish War of 1911-12, after Glen Curtiss had pioneered the technique on an experimental basis in the United States. A number of countries, France and Germany in particular, carried out bombing experiments as a prelude to the possibility of bombers being employed in the European war that was threatening. By 1913 two distinct types of military aircraft were being developed, one of inherently stable design that would enable the pilot to perform other duties such as bombing and another that could carry out deliberate aero-batics for it was seen that airplanes might well be employed in combat manoeuvres against airships. But for the most part the military authorities of all nations saw the use of aircraft in war as being limited to locating enemy troop con-centrations and spotting for the artillery, an extension of the observation balloon in fact or the reconnaissance functions of light cavalry. Given that most of the aircraft then in service were clumsy two-seater biplanes with underpowered and unreliable engines that limited speed to about 60 m.p.h. and ceiling fully laden to about 5,000 feet, there was perhaps some excuse for that attitude. And although some outstand-ing airplanes of the period had shown by their performances a hint of what was to come – the Sopwith Tabloid could climb to 1,200 feet in one minute for instance, a Deper-dussin monoplane had achieved 126 mph in level flight, and Germany held the altitude record at 27,000 feet and the endurance record at 24 hours, it was generally agreed on both sides that the war would be over in a few months and it was not really worth spending a great deal of time and effort on improving military aircraft.

Although it was only eleven years since the Wright brothers had made their first successful flight and only five since Louis Blériot had crossed the English Channel, the com-batant powers had a total of some 767 aircraft in opera-tional use early in August 1914 when war broke out. The numbers for individual countries, not indicative of quality or effectiveness as the first months of the war were to prove, were Germany 232, Russia 224, France 138, Britain 113, Austro-Hungary 36 and Belgium 24. Two basic types of aircraft were predominant at that time, the tractor airplane with the engine and propeller in front and the pusher type in which the engine and propeller were mounted behind a tub-like nacelle seating the pilot and passenger, the tail being carried on booms. Both were made in biplane and monoplane form, biplanes being the most prevalent. The tractor type was usually the fastest but the pusher offered a far less obstructed view to the observer in the front cockpit. This was to become a vital factor in the development of aerial combat.

France possessed the widest range of flying machines as a result of being the first European country to take up aviation. Pioneer designers such as Charles and Gabriel Voisin, Henri Farman, Blériot, and the brothers Robert and Leon Morane with their associate Raymond Saulnier had experimented with many different types, helped by considerable financial backing from the French govern-ment. The French Army was the first to appreciate the military potential of aircraft, both for bombing and fighting but especially for reconnaissance although operations in the early days of the war were hampered by a bureaucratic chain of command which delayed the passing on of information to the commanders who most needed it. By the end of August 1914 the *Service d'Aeronautique* had twenty-nine squadrons (*escadrilles*) in service with many more building up. Most of the aircraft were two-seater pusher biplanes such as the Voisin and Henri and Maurice Farmans (3), suitable for bombing missions in addition to their reconnaissance duties. But they also included the first of the Nieuport tractor biplane scouts with their distinctive vee-shaped struts and sesquiplane wing arrangement – the upper wing being exactly twice the area of the lower – which were to become one of the most successful aircraft of the war, and the Morane-Saulnier monoplanes, the Type L 'Parasol' two-seater (6) and Type N single-seater (14), which were effectively to be the world's first fighter aircraft.

The main effort in Germany before the war had been concentrated on designing and building airships as a result of Count Zeppelin's pioneering efforts in this field, and the intention was to use these for bombing missions rather than aircraft. A fleet of seven Zeppelins and six smaller airships was in service at the outbreak of war. Aircraft had by no means been neglected but the military and naval authorities saw their duties as being confined

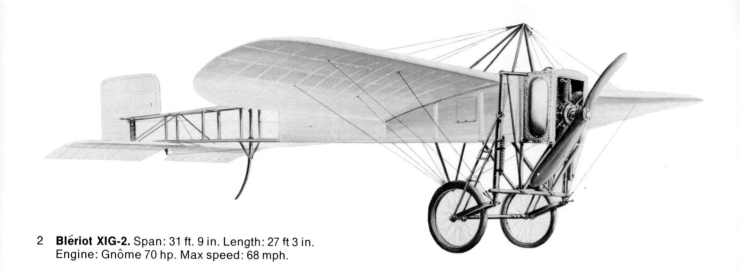

2 **Blériot XIG-2.** Span: 31 ft. 9 in. Length: 27 ft 3 in.
Engine: Gnôme 70 hp. Max speed: 68 mph.

to reconnaissance and went so far as to restrict the development of fast aircraft in case speed should interfere with careful observation. By 1914 two main types had become standardized, monoplanes known as *Tauben* (doves) such as the Rumpler, and the more predominant biplanes known as *Pfeil* (arrows), of which the L.V.G. and D.F.W. 'Flying Banana' were in widest use. These were all tractor airplanes and the Germans did not in fact possess any pusher types. While the army and navy squadrons possessed nearly as many airplanes between them as the French and British combined, over a hundred of these were reserved for training purposes. However, the military squadrons were operating from the beginning at Corps level and the German armies were able to make more immediate use of the information brought back from reconnaissance.

Britain had lagged behind both France and Germany in aircraft development, due to government neglect and uncertainty whether to concentrate on heavier-than-air machines or lighter-than-air airships. When the Royal Flying Corps was formed in 1912 with military and naval wings (the later to become the independent Royal Naval Air Service two years later), it first had to rely entirely on airplanes bought from France until the products of the newly established government-owned aircraft factory at Farnborough became available. The research effort at Farnborough, where Geoffrey de Havilland had been given the job of designer and test pilot, was primarily focused on the achievement of inherent stability so that the pilot of an airplane could devote much of his attention to reconnaissance duties. The B.E.2, first of a series of two-seater tractor biplanes which was given military trials in 1912, fulfilled this demand admirably and the B.E.2c version was ordered in large numbers. But its very stability held the seeds of its own destruction when later in the war it came up against the more manoeuvrable fighters developed by the Germans. While the RFC primarily patronised the Army (later Royal) Aircraft Factory, the RNAS preferred to encourage private constructors such as Avro, Sopwith and Short Brothers, which did much to help the embryo British aircraft industry. The result was that at the outbreak of war, most of the airplanes in service with the RFC and RNAS consisted of a mixed bag of two-seaters; French types such as Farman pusher biplanes and Blériot and Morane-Saulnier 'Parasol' monoplanes, as well as British B.E.2s and Avro 504s. None of these formed a homogeneous squadron, making fitting and

maintenance even more difficult. Included in both the RFC and RNAS were a very few single-seat scouts whose numbers were increased as quickly as production allowed. These were the Bristol Scout, the Sopwith Tabloid and the Martinsyde S.1. The first true scout was the S.E.2a (Scouting Experimental) built at Farnborough in 1913 to basic designs provided earlier by Geoffrey de Havilland, but it did not get past the prototype stage as later production was concentrated on the S.E.4 biplane. Together with the French Nieuport and Morane Type N monoplane, the scouts were the nearest thing at that time to a true fighter aircraft. They were single-seaters and in comparison to other airplanes they were fast, between 90-100 mph, and highly manoeuvrable. They were the first aircraft to engage in air combat, although their only armament was a service revolver (5) or rifle, and one or two were attached to each of the British and French squadrons to protect the slower two-seater reconnaissance machines. Had they been armed from the beginning with machine-guns, the basic weapon of a fighter, they would have made a much greater impact than they did. As it was, the slow pusher types, the least suited to air combat, were the first to carry machine-guns.

Most of the airplanes in the Russian Imperial Air Service were of French and German design, built under licence, and as the war progressed further aircraft were imported from France, Britain and the United States. The Russians favoured the heavy bomber type for the relatively few aircraft they built at this time but one small tractor biplane, the S-16 designed by Igor Ivanovich Sikorsky, was possibly the first to be armed with a synchronised machine-gun. It could have made a considerable contribution early in the war had greater numbers been produced quickly. But by the time deliveries began, it had been outclassed by its German counterparts. The Belgian Air Force relied entirely on French aircraft while the Austro-Hungarian *Luftfahrtruppen* was supplied with a variety of types such as Etrich *Taube* monoplanes and Lohner and Albatros B.1 biplanes, the latter designed by Ernst Heinkel and manufactured in Austria under licence.

None of the aircraft in service when the war began were officially intended for fighting. It was simply left to the pilot of a scout or the observer of a two-seater when on reconnaissance or bombing missions to take a pistol or rifle with him if he wished in order to have a pot-shot at any enemy aircraft he might meet. Even that was not very

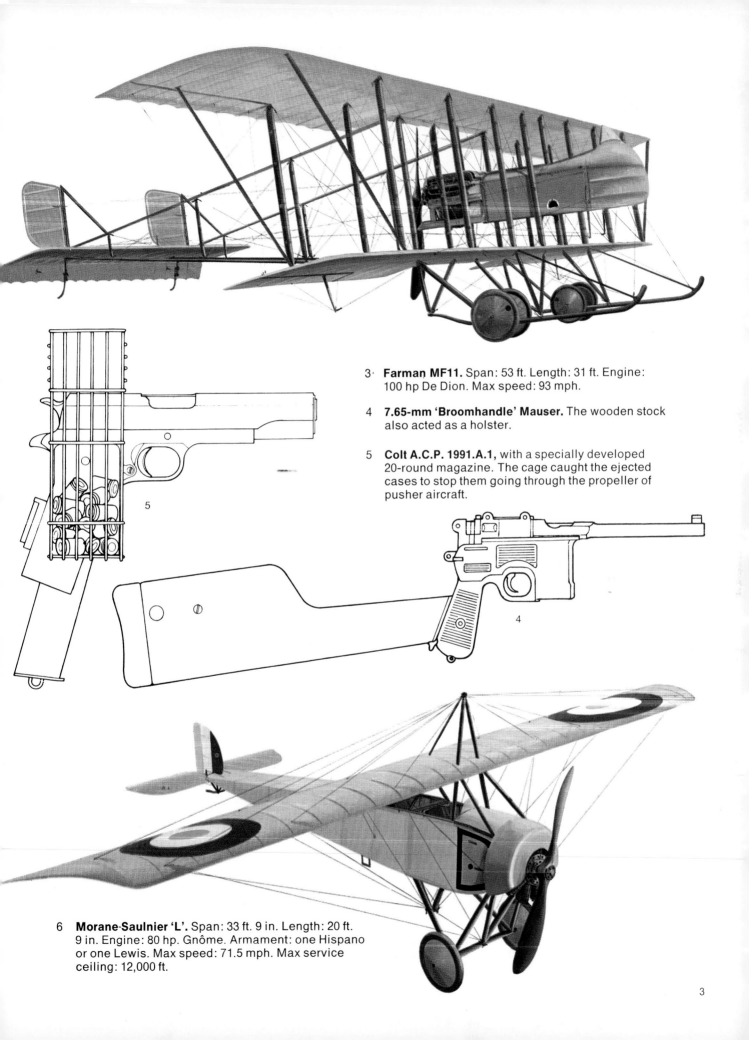

3 **Farman MF11.** Span: 53 ft. Length: 31 ft. Engine: 100 hp De Dion. Max speed: 93 mph.

4 **7.65-mm 'Broomhandle' Mauser.** The wooden stock also acted as a holster.

5 **Colt A.C.P. 1991.A.1,** with a specially developed 20-round magazine. The cage caught the ejected cases to stop them going through the propeller of pusher aircraft.

6 **Morane-Saulnier 'L'.** Span: 33 ft. 9 in. Length: 20 ft. 9 in. Engine: 80 hp. Gnôme. Armament: one Hispano or one Lewis. Max speed: 71.5 mph. Max service ceiling: 12,000 ft.

likely in the uncrowded skies of those early days and besides which there was an unspoken code amongst aviators that it was ungentlemanly to resort to such tactics. They had enough difficulty keeping their frail machines in the air, apart from the danger of being fired at by troops on the ground. At a time when the maximum speed of most aircraft was only around 65 mph, this could be reduced much further when flying against the wind, presenting an even easier target. German anti-aircraft guns on mobile mountings were particularly effective. And it was not only enemy guns that the pilots on both sides had to fear. It was not easy for untrained observers to distinguish between various types of aircraft, many of which were basically of French design anyway, and the infantry were inclined to shoot at anything that flew. Identification markings were an obvious necessity, but the British in fact entered the war with no national markings at all. The French had in 1912 adopted the tricolour roundel with a red circle outermost for their aircraft and the Germans chose the black Iron Cross of the old Teutonic Knights. It was left to the

7 **The principle of the Garros Wedge.**

8 **The principle of the Fokker interrupter gear.**

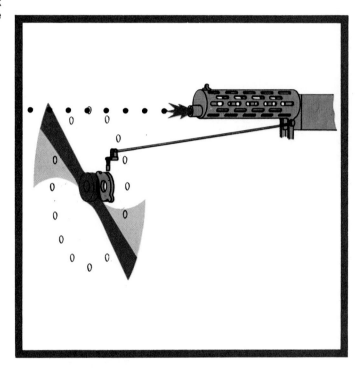

9 - 13 **Fokker E-III.** Span: 32 ft. 8 in. Length: 23 ft. 6½ in. Engine: 110 hp Oberursel. Armament: two Spandau. Max speed: 87.5 mph. Max service ceiling: 12,000 ft.

RFC pilots themselves to paint Union Jacks in prominent positions on their machines, usually in the form of a shield, but even this was not entirely effective as the St. George Cross could be confused at a distance with the German Cross. In December 1914 the RFC officially adopted the French roundel but with blue on the outside and red in the centre.

Parallel with advances made by aircraft designers was the development of the aero-engine industry, in which France and Germany were the leaders. At the start of the war Britain did not possess an aero-engine of her own; all the engines in British aircraft were French, either imported or manufactured under licence. France had developed one type of water-cooled engine, the Canton-Unne (Salmson) radial, and also several air-cooled engines including two types based on the rotary principle which had been invented by the Sequin brothers and first introduced in 1910 as the 70 hp Gnôme (15), installed in the Blériot XI (2) among others. In this design, which

was to revolutionize aircraft performance, the crankcase and radially disposed cylinders, usually seven or nine, revolved round a stationary crankshaft, taking the airscrew with them. Its lightness and compactness, giving a power-to-weight ratio superior to other types, made it possible for the French to concentrate on building light, fast aircraft.

The Germans on the other hand preferred the heavier water-cooled stationary engines with in-line cylinders developed by such companies as Mercedes (103), Benz and Austro-Daimler from their experiences in motor-racing. Excellent though these were and often more reliable than the frail rotaries, they required stronger and larger airframes to carry them. This was in line with German military requirements for aircraft of long range and high ceiling for reconnaissance purposes. But it was the rotary engine that powered the fast Allied scouts and made possible the first single-seat fighters. Its torque and gyroscopic effect made such aircraft difficult to control

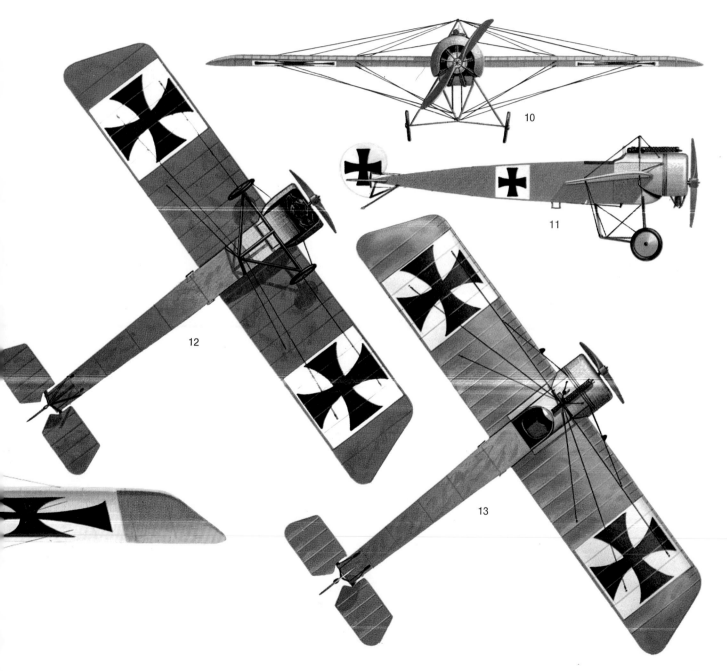

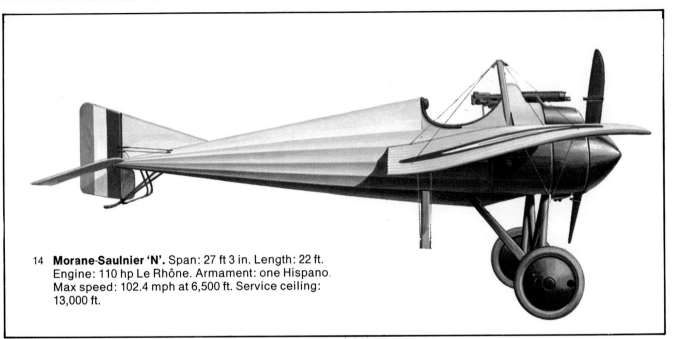

14 **Morane-Saulnier 'N'.** Span: 27 ft 3 in. Length: 22 ft.
Engine: 110 hp Le Rhône. Armament: one Hispano.
Max speed: 102.4 mph at 6,500 ft. Service ceiling:
13,000 ft.

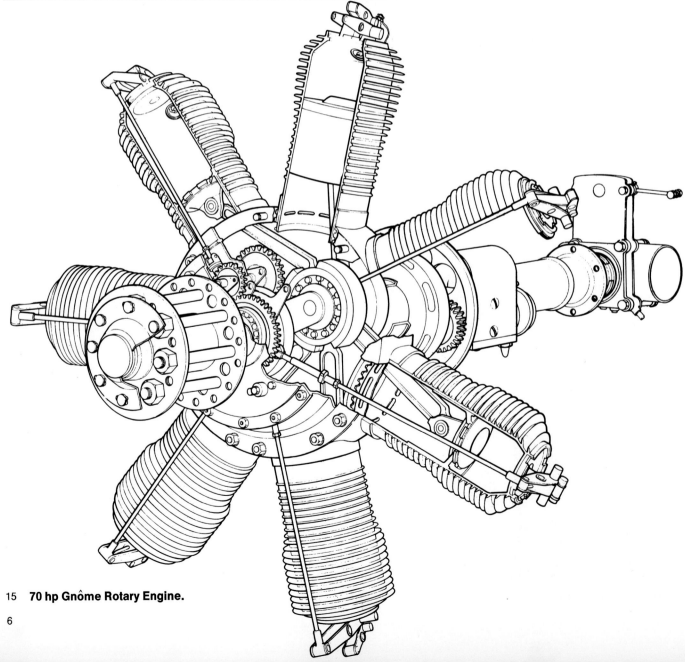

15 **70 hp Gnôme Rotary Engine.**

but when flown by skilled pilots gave them a manoeuvrability that could not at first be matched by conventional stationary engines. One problem with the Gnôme was that the atmospheric inlet valves in the crown of each piston caused performance to fall off at altitude or in hot weather. This was partly overcome with the development of the *Monosoupape* (single-valve) Gnôme in which one valve functioned for both induction and exhaust. But the better of the two rotary engines available by the outbreak of war was the Le Rhône, in which both inlet and exhaust valves were operated mechanically. The Le Rhône was copied by the Germans as the Oberursel rotary which eventually powered their first fighter, the Fokker monoplane.

As aircraft flew more or less freely across the trenches, providing information that was vital at times to the armies of both sides, it gradually dawned on the ground commanders that just as it was important to obtain intelligence of enemy troop movements, it was equally important to deny the other side of similar knowledge. Another factor was the increasing use of aircraft for bombing both troops on the ground and strategic targets such as airship sheds and railways. The French, who possessed the only true bomber force when the war began, led the way in this use of aircraft and during the first months were able to raid targets in Germany virtually without hindrance. The British followed suit soon afterwards, particularly the airplanes of the RNAS from their base first at Antwerp and then Dunkirk against the Zeppelin sheds at Dusseldorf and elsewhere. The four RFC squadrons which had arrived in France by mid-August and established a base at Mauberge near the headquarters of the British Commander-in-Chief, General Sir John French, were employed primarily for scouting. The Germans made the mistake of

using Zeppelins for low-level bombing to begin with and it was only after they had discovered how vulnerable these were to fire both from the ground and the air, losing four in August including one claimed by a French airman, that they turned more to the use of aircraft. It soon became apparent to both sides that aircraft would have to be employed against those of the enemy, to prevent reconnaissance as well as bombing. There were no fighters as such to undertake the task but it was certain that the aviators' code could not survive for long under such conditions.

First use of Machine-guns

Some individual pilots had already come to this conclusion before it was officially accepted. Among the RFC airplanes which had landed in France was a Henri Farman of No. 5 Squadron to which its pilot, Second Lieutenant L. A. Strange, had mounted a Lewis machine-gun in the front cockpit. On August 22nd, with Lieutenant L. da C. Penn-Gaskell as observer, he took off from Mauberge to chase an enemy aircraft. But laden with the extra weight the Farman could not climb higher than 3,500 feet and the enemy escaped. Three days later an Avro 504 biplane piloted by Lieutenant C. W. Wilson with Lieutenant Rabagliatti in the front cockpit was ordered on a similar mission, to head off a *Taube* monoplane approaching the British lines. Rabagliatti took a rifle with him and after guiding Wilson to fly into position ahead and below the

16 **Bristol M1C.** Span: 30 ft. 9 in. Length: 20 ft 5 in. Engine: 110 hp Le Rhône. Armament: one Lewis. Max speed: 130 mph at ground level. Service ceiling: 20,000 ft.

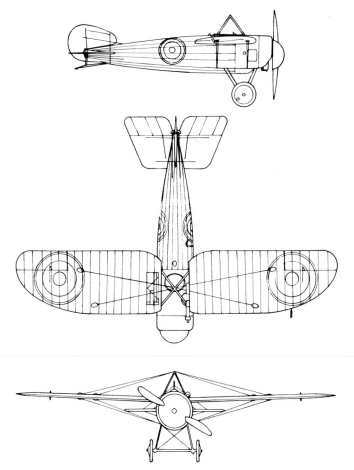

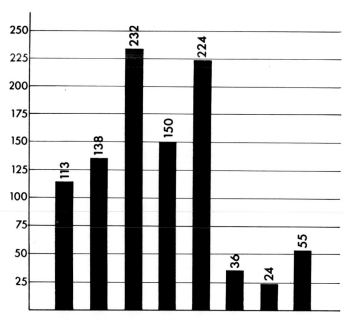

17 **First-line strength 1914.**

enemy, fired a number of shots. Thoroughly alarmed the German pilot landed his airplane near Le Quesnoy, where it was captured intact before he had time to set fire to it. This was the first victory credited in the official history of the Royal Air force and it set a new pattern of operations.

During the following weeks further aircraft were brought down in this manner and as friction developed between the Allied and German pilots, a variety of weapons were called into use. In addition to pistols and rifles, sporting shotguns loaded with chain shot were taken up by pilots and their observers, as well as grenades and steel darts called *flechettes* with the intention of dropping these on enemy aircraft flying below. Another idea was to trail grappling hooks on cables through the air in the hope of entangling them in the propellers of enemy aircraft, and even bricks and rocks were thrown on occasion by frustrated pilots. The Germans were the most fortunate in having the Mauser automatic rifle with a high rate of fire.

As Strange and others had foreseen, the ideal weapon for fighting in the air was the machine-gun. The problem was that none of the airplanes then in service had been designed to carry such a gun, and its weight alone was often enough to detract from performance. Experiments had been made by individual designers and pilots before the war, both in Germany and France in 1910 and in Britain in 1911 when Major Brooke-Popham fitted a machine-gun to a Blériot monoplane, only to be told promptly to remove it. As ever, the military authorities could see little value in aircraft, other than for reconnaissance, and certainly no point in arming them. The United States came closest to it in 1912 when a Wright B biplane was armed with a new type of air-cooled machine-gun which had just been invented by Colonel Isaac Newton Lewis and given official firing trials. But not only was the US Army disinterested in aviation, one reason for the fact that no airplane of American design fought in France during the First World War, but it also decided it did not want the Lewis gun, preferring to retain the standard Bénet-Mercie (Hotchkiss) gun. Colonel Lewis went to Europe and in 1913 set up a company at Liege, Belgium, where he found a ready market for his weapons. They were lighter than contemporary machine-guns and fed by detachable forty-seven round drums instead of the usual ammunition belts, thus protecting the cartridges from dirt as well as being easier to handle. A .303 calibre Lewis gun (22) was tested and accepted by the Royal Flying Corps that same year and later became the standard weapon for the first British fighters.

Although the fastest airplanes were tractor types, there was at that time no means of mounting a machine-gun in front of the pilot where he could take direct aim without also shooting off the blades of the revolving airscrew. Pusher types on the other hand, with the engine and propeller behind, had no such limitation and offered a wide field of fire to the gunner in the front cockpit. Among experiments carried out in France before the war, a 37-mm cannon was fired from a Voisin pusher biplane and this led to the first air combat involving an airplane armed with a machine-gun (1). On the morning of October 5th, 1914, Sergeant Joseph Frantz with his mechanic/gunner Corporal Louis Quenault had flown their Voisin 3 pusher biplane across the German lines to bomb enemy troop concentrations behind Fort Brimont. The Voisin, like eleven others of No. 24 Squadron, had recently been armed with an 8-mm Hotchkiss machine-gun (20) at the suggestion of Gabriel Voisin who had designed a special tubular mounting for that purpose above the pilot's head, so that the gunner behind him could stand up to shoot.

Quenault thus had an excellent and unrestricted field of fire forwards, upwards and sideways, and although he was blind to the rear this mattered little against the German two-seater reconnaissance airplanes which were mostly unarmed and could not shoot forwards anyway since they were tractor types. As Frantz flew back towards the French line at a height of about 7,000 feet, he suddenly spotted a German Aviatik biplane below him, about 800 yards to the east. The observer sitting in the front seat carried an automatic rifle but could only fire to the sides and rear.

Using the advantage of his greater height Frantz put the Voisin into a banking dive, hoping to head the Aviatik back across the French line. He did not want to land in German-held territory if his fuel ran out. As soon as the German pilot saw the Voisin he went into a hard bank which took him in just the direction Frantz had intended. Then followed a series of banks and dives as each aircraft manoeuvred for position. Every time the German tried to escape Frantz dived to cut him off until eventually, they were over the French line. By this time they had come down to about 600 feet and hundreds of troops on the ground were facing upwards, intent on watching the fight. The gunners in both aircraft took whatever opportunities occurred to fire at their fleeting targets. Quenault doubted the reliability of his gun with its awkward strip-feed system that had to be changed after twenty-five rounds and was firing single shots only. He had a great advantage in being able to fire forwards but after forty-seven shots, the Hotchkiss jammed as he had feared. It was while he frantically began trying to clear it that the Aviatik suddenly flipped over and spun out of control with smoke pouring from its engine, crashing with a loud explosion at the edge of a small wood. Quenault's last shot before the gun jammed had killed the pilot. The occupants of the Aviatik, Wilhelm Schlichting and Fritz von Zangen, became the first of a long list of airmen to die in air combat. They were buried with full military honours while decorations and a place in the history of aviation went to the victors of the first dogfight.

During the winter of 1914-15, although fewer sorties were flown because of bad weather that also restricted the war on the ground, the number of air combats increased as more aircraft were armed. The Lewis air-cooled machine-gun was the best available because of its lightness and simplicity, but the British were in short supply of these weapons. The French airplanes were hampered by the heavy Hotchkiss 8-mm which hindered flight performance and was in any case difficult to operate in the air. Most of them continued to carry cavalry carbines until a change to the Lewis gun was ordered in mid-1915. The Germans at this time did not possess a suitable machine-gun at all for aerial use. In fact, the rifle was not abandoned by either side immediately, even after machine-guns had come into general use. The fast Morane Parasol two-seaters were highly effective when the observer carrying a carbine was also a good marksman. And as late as July 25th 1915, during the course of a single evening patrol, Captain Lanoe G. Hawker in a Bristol Scout armed only with a single-shot Martini carbine mounted on the starboard side of the fuselage and firing obliquely forward to avoid the propeller arc shot down two German two-seaters and forced down another one, all of them armed with machine-guns. He was awarded the first Victoria Cross earned in air combat.

The period up to the end of 1914 was very much a time of experiment, when pilots more or less devised their own tactics as well as ways of aiming their aircraft. It was due to innovators like Strange that machine-guns were fitted

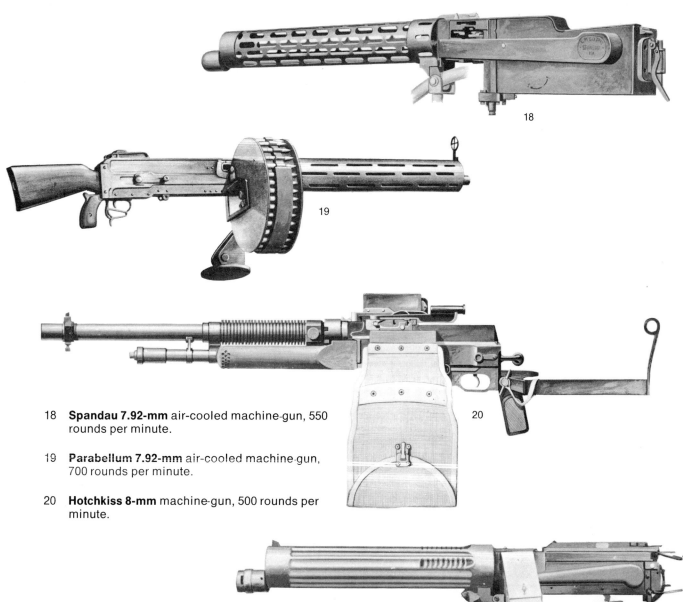

18 **Spandau 7.92-mm** air-cooled machine-gun, 550 rounds per minute.

19 **Parabellum 7.92-mm** air-cooled machine-gun, 700 rounds per minute.

20 **Hotchkiss 8-mm** machine-gun, 500 rounds per minute.

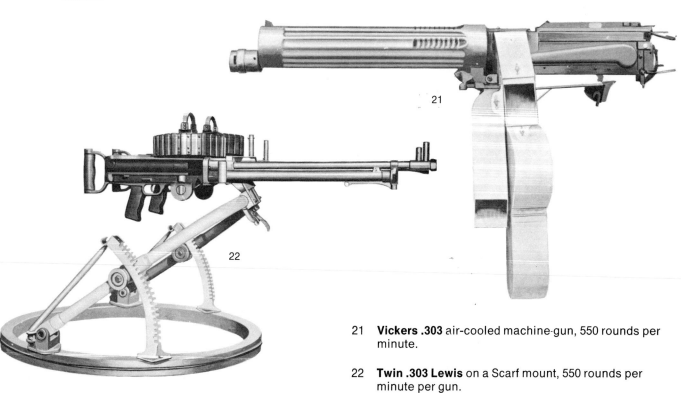

21 **Vickers .303** air-cooled machine-gun, 550 rounds per minute.

22 **Twin .303 Lewis** on a Scarf mount, 550 rounds per minute per gun.

for the first time to the faster single-seat tractor types like the Moranes and Sopwith Tabloid, Bristol and Martinsyde Scouts. One idea was to mount the gun at an angle on the side of the fuselage so as to avoid hitting the propeller, as in the case of Hawker's carbine. This meant that the aircraft had to approach an enemy in a crab-like manner in order to get a suitable target, but many early victories were achieved in this way. The idea was less successful in two-seaters were the observer sat in front, his usual position in the early airplanes, because his field of fire was often obstructed by wings, struts and wires. For this reason, quite early on, the places of pilot and observer on French and German airplanes were changed so that the observer sat behind with more freedom for firing. But inexplicably this was not done on the standard Farnborough-designed B.E. types such as the B.E.2c, with disastrous results later on. Another method on single-seaters was to mount a machine-gun above the centre section of the top wing so that it could be fired forwards above the propeller arc by means of pulling a cable attached to the trigger. This enable the pilot to use his aircraft as a means of aiming at a target, since the gun was aligned with a sight mounting in front of the cockpit, and continued in general use until the Allies introduced synchronised firing in 1916. Many Allied airplanes employed wing-mounted guns, including the Nieuport 10 which came into service at the end of 1914 armed with a modified Hotchkiss .303 from which the cumbersome water jacket had been removed to permit air cooling. This was later changed to a Lewis gun on the Nieuport 11 'Baby'. The main problem with this kind of mounting was that the pilot had to stand up to change the ammunition drums, but a sliding rail system was soon invented by Sergeant Foster of No. 11 Squadron RFC which enabled the gun to be pulled down into the cockpit for reloading.

But in the early days of aerial fighting it was the slow and cumbersome pusher type that held the upper hand as the only machine which could mount a machine-gun in the nose. This was the case with Britain's first combat aircraft specifically designed to carry a machine-gun, the F.B.5 'Gunbus' (24) produced in 1914 as a result of an experimental design by Vickers. It was similar in general layout to French equivalents such as the Farmans but with a much greater field of fire since the machine-gun was fixed to a spigot-mounting above the nose. Originally it was to have been armed with a Maxim or Vickers gun but this was changed to the Lewis gun when it proved to be the superior weapon. When the War Office continued to show little interest in any sort of aircraft other than those which were to be used for reconnaissance, Vickers took the decision to build fifty at their own expense, convinced that they would be needed when the inevitable war broke out. These were bought by the War Office in July 1914 and the first of them arrived in France early the following year. The F.B.5 was used to form the first-ever homogeneous fighter squadron, the RFC's No. 11 Squadron. Although its 100 hp *Monosoupape* Gnôme engine gave it a top speed of only 70 mph and a service ceiling of only 9,000 feet, the F.B.5 was a considerable success and proved a vital asset when the Fokker monoplane fighters appeared. The Germans, unlike the British and French, had no pusher aircraft on which forward-firing guns could be mounted. Prototypes had in fact been built in Germany before the war, notably the Schwade single-seater in 1913 and August Euler's experimental 'airship destroyer' in 1914 ,armed with one fixed and one movable machine-gun. But these were not developed as the military authorities preferred the more efficient tractor types for reconnaissance.

As the competition for air space increased, the Allies had things very much their own way. The German aircraft were mostly unarmed and in any case their pilots were under orders to concentrate on reconnaissance and avoid combat wherever possible. But even this was becoming more difficult as the British and French stepped up their offensive patrols. One or two armed single-seat scouts, flown by picked pilots, were attached to each RFC and RNAS squadron while the French were the first to see the value of specialised fighting units operating as a group. Towards the end of 1914 they formed a number of *escadrilles de chasse* and attached one to each of their armies for the purpose of hunting enemy aircraft. The outdated A-class monoplanes and B-class two-seater biplanes of the Germans stood little chance against such Allied aircraft as the Moranes and the pusher types which, although they had not yet developed into true fighters, were armed for fighting. By the end of October 1914 Germany had lost fifty-two pilots and over ninety airplanes, although a number of these losses was due to accidents owing to mechanical failure.

The balance was partly redressed by the development in November of the 7.92-mm Parabellum machine-gun (19), a light modified Maxim with the ammunition belt carried in a circular drum which at least gave Germany a suitable gun for air combat. It became a standard fitting on all the C-class two-seater biplanes such as the Albatross, Aviatik and Rumpler which began to come into service early in 1915. More powerful Mark III engines of up to 180 hp, double the 1914 specifications and mostly water-cooled with overhead valves and six in-line cylinders, gave these aircraft a greatly improved performance in terms of speed, ceiling and rate of climb that was now a vital factor in aerial fighting. The LFG Roland C.2 (28) was fastest of all the German aircraft at that time with a top speed of 103 mph. But they were still armed mainly for defence. The Parabellum was fitted on a ring-mounting in the rear cockpit so that the observer could fire at aircraft attacking from behind. It was not until the development of gun synchronising gear, which enabled bullets to be shot between the blades of a revolving propeller, that the Germans turned the tables on the Allies later in 1915 when it was first installed in the Fokker monoplane.

Gun synchronising Gear

There was nothing new about this 'secret weapon'. A Russian designer, Lieutenant Poplavko, had developed an interrupter gear in 1913 which was later fitted to the Sikorsky S-16. In that same year Franz Schneider, chief designer of the German L.V.G. company, who a year before had devised a method of shooting through the airscrew shaft of a tractor airplane, patented a similar idea. It was actually fitted to one of his company's experimental two-seater monoplanes, the E.6, which flew operationally until it crashed in December 1914. But the military authorities were not interested and that was also the fate of the Edwards brothers in England whose plans for synchronising gear, put forward early in 1914, were pigeon-holed by the War Office. In France meanwhile, Raymond Saulnier was working on the same problem in collaboration with the Morane brothers. By June 1914 he had devised a system which mechanically linked the trigger of a machine-gun to a cam on the engine shaft, thus enabling its fire to be synchronised to avoid the propeller

23 **Nieuport II.** Span: 24 ft. 9 in. Length: 18 ft 8 in.
Engine: 80 hp Le Rhône. Armament: one Lewis. Max
speed: 97 mph. Service ceiling: 18,000 ft.

24 **FB5 (Vickers).** Span: 36 ft. 6 in. Length: 27 ft. 2 in.
Engine: 100 hp Gnôme Mono. Armament: one Lewis.
Max speed: 70 mph at 5,000 ft. Service ceiling:
9,000 ft.

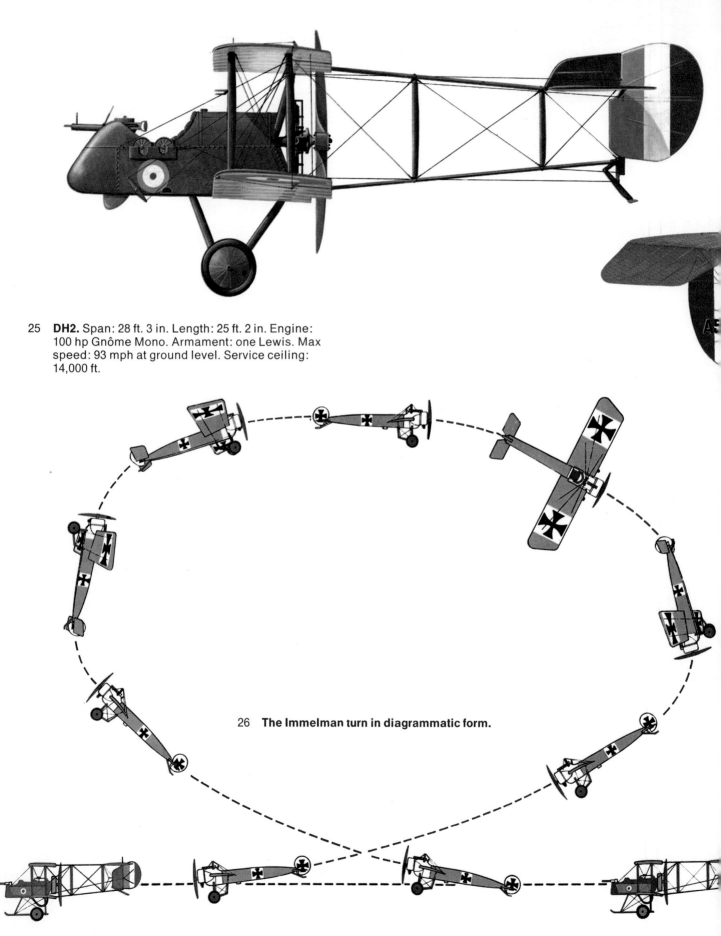

25　**DH2.** Span: 28 ft. 3 in. Length: 25 ft. 2 in. Engine: 100 hp Gnôme Mono. Armament: one Lewis. Max speed: 93 mph at ground level. Service ceiling: 14,000 ft.

26　**The Immelman turn in diagrammatic form.**

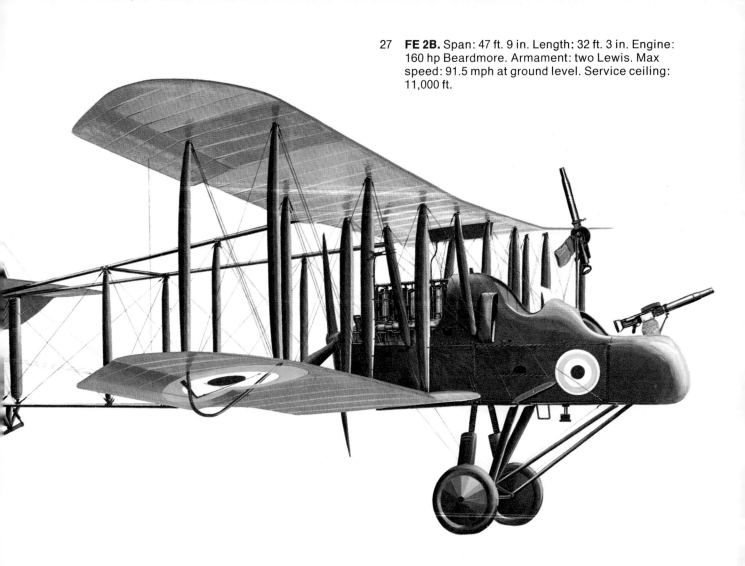

27 **FE 2B.** Span: 47 ft. 9 in. Length: 32 ft. 3 in. Engine: 160 hp Beardmore. Armament: two Lewis. Max speed: 91.5 mph at ground level. Service ceiling: 11,000 ft.

blades. Firing trials were held but the Hotchkiss gun he had borrowed from the army was not really suitable and the ammunition was unreliable, tending to 'hang fire' and thus endangering the blades. Not to be daunted, Saulnier discarded the interrupter idea and instead solved the problem by fixing steel plates to the airscrew that would deflect any bullets hitting the blades. But the French War Department was no more interested than its opposite numbers in Britain and Germany and this idea was also ignored.

The racy-looking Morane-Saulnier monoplanes had been among the best of the pre-war machines with speeds of up to 100 mph when most others were limited to 60-70 mph. Powered by Gnôme or Le Rhône rotary engines which gave them excellent manoeuvrability they quickly established an ascendancy when introduced shortly after the outbreak of war. It was with a Morane Parasol Type L that Flt Sub Lieutenant R. A. J. Warneford of the RNAS brought down the first Zeppelin to be destroyed in air combat, the L.Z.37 on June 7th 1915, for which achievement he won the Victoria Cross. Various types of the two-seater Parasol with its wing mounted above the fuselage and the single-seat mid-wing Type N were formed into three of the best-known of all French *escadrilles* at that time, MS 3 under *Commandant* Brocard, MS 23 under *Commandant* de Vergnette, and MS 12 under *Commandant* Tricornot de Rose who was one of the first to devise tactics for air combat. MS 23 included such notable aviators as Adolphe

Pegoud, the first pilot ever to loop-the-loop, Armand Pinsard who was to become the eighth highest scoring French ace with twenty-seven victories to his credit, and Roland Garros, the first man to fly across the Mediterranean and winner of many pre-war races. Garros had heard of Saulnier's experiments and in March 1915 he arranged to have the propeller of his L-type Parasol fitted with steel wedge-shaped deflector plates (7) so that a Hotchkiss machine-gun could be mounted above the fuselage immediately in front of the cockpit. Many of the bullets were kicked aside when the gun was fired but enough got past to be highly effective. For the first time a fast and manoeuvrable tractor monoplane, of the type of design most suited to air combat, was armed so that the pilot could use the aircraft itself for aiming directly at a target.

Success came at once. On April 1st Garros met four German Albatros two-seaters flying over the French lines at 10,000 feet. The Germans, intent on observing the trenches below, saw no reason to fear the approaching Morane. They knew that while biplanes could carry machine-guns monoplanes certainly did not, especially with only one occupant and at such an altitude. Then the incredible happened. As the French airplane headed straight at them, a spluttering flame appeared directly behind the propeller and bullets sprayed all around them. Before they could recover from their astonishment one of the German aircraft was spinning wildly to the ground in flames. The remainder turned and fled for home with news

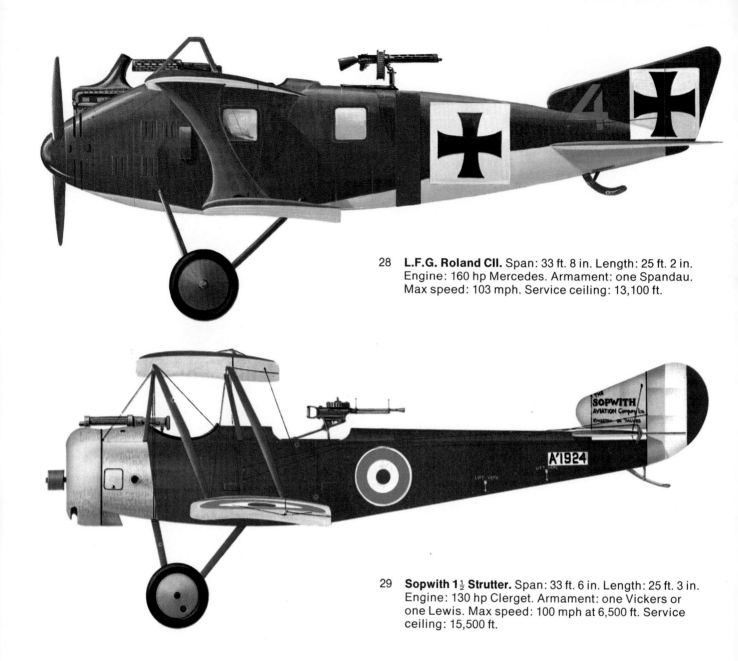

28 **L.F.G. Roland CII.** Span: 33 ft. 8 in. Length: 25 ft. 2 in. Engine: 160 hp Mercedes. Armament: one Spandau. Max speed: 103 mph. Service ceiling: 13,100 ft.

29 **Sopwith 1½ Strutter.** Span: 33 ft. 6 in. Length: 25 ft. 3 in. Engine: 130 hp Clerget. Armament: one Vickers or one Lewis. Max speed: 100 mph at 6,500 ft. Service ceiling: 15,500 ft.

of the mystery airplane that could fire bullets between the blades of a revolving propeller.

During the two weeks that followed, Garros shot down five more German aircraft. German pilots were in a state of near panic while their generals, at first disbelieving what they heard, hastily set up armament committees to develop a similar weapon. But they were saved the trouble. On April 18th, in spite of warnings not to fly over enemy-held territory, Garros was forced because of engine failure to land behind the German lines. Before he could set fire to the Morane it was captured by the Germans and he himself taken prisoner. The secret was revealed.

It so happened that the Dutch aircraft designer and pilot Anthony Fokker who was in Germany building airplanes for the German Signal Corps (before the war he had not been able to find any other European countries interested in his designs), was just completing military trials with a new single-seat monoplane, an *Eindekker,* which was to

go into service as the Fokker E.1. This was similar in many respects to the mid-wing Morane-Saulnier, an airplane Fokker had acquired and studied at first hand. It was powered by an 80 hp Oberursel rotary engine partially enclosed in an aluminium cowling and had a top speed of some 80 mph. Later models had the 100 hp Oberursel. Fokker was shown the deflector plates which had been fitted to Garros's Morane and ordered to copy the idea on his own monoplane. He went one better and within a few days had designed and installed a proper synchronising mechanism (8), consisting of a simple linkage of cams and push-rods between the oil-pump drive of the engine and the trigger of a Parabellum machine-gun, timed so that the gun fired once during every revolution of the propeller, the bullets passing clean between the blades. Fokker claimed credit for the idea himself but it was probably based on Schneider's original patent, of which his engineers must have been aware.

30 **Sopwith Pup.** Span: 26 ft. 6 in. Length: 19 ft. 4 in. Engine: 100 hp Gnôme Mono. Armament: one Vickers. Max speed: 110 mph ground level. Service ceiling: 18,500 ft.

By this time the German Air Service was becoming more aggressive and better organised as a result of the appointment of Major Hermann von der Leith-Thomsen as *Feldflugchef* with Major Siegert as his second in command and they immediately saw in Fokker's new weapon an answer to the air superiority established by the Allies. The first Fokker E.1 was given to Oswald Boelcke, an experienced pilot who had already been involved in four fights with an armed Albatros C.1 and by his skill in keeping his observer's gun within range had been instrumental in destroying a French Morane, claimed as Germany's first air victory. By July, eleven front-line pilots were flying the improved version of the Fokker with a higher-powered engine, the E.2. They included, as well as Boelcke, some of those who were to become the most famous German 'aces' such as Max Immelmann and Ernst Udet. Immelmann was the first to score. On August 1st, nine RFC two-seaters raided the aerodrome at Douai where both Boelck and Immelmann were based with Squadron (*Flieger-abteilung*) 62. The two men took off in their Fokkers and attacked the British raiders. Boelcke's gun jammed on his first pass and he was forced to break off the action. Immelmann meanwhile chased a straggler and wounded its pilot, Lieutenant Reid, in the arm, forcing him to land in German-held territory where he and his airplane were captured. So began what was widely publicised as the 'Fokker Scourge' which lasted for about six months and reached its peak in the winter of 1915-16.

The Fokker 'Scourge'

Operating in small groups attached to reconnaissance squadrons all along the Front, for even now their main function was defensive rather than offensive, the Fokkers achieved immediate success against the slow pusher types of the Allies which were defenceless to the rear and even more so against the B.E.2c biplanes of the RFC which not only were unable to fire backwards since the observer was placed in front but now revealed a great weakness in their lack of manoeuvrability unless in practised hands. The RFC was now being rapidly expanded but this meant that many of the new pilots arriving in France were inexperienced and under-trained. They suffered heavy casualties as the number of air combats increased – whereas only forty-six were recorded by the RFC throughout the whole of July, the same number occurred in a single day in December. An agitated British Parliament and Press referred to these unfortunate recruits as 'Fokker fodder' while the Germans suddenly discovered the morale-boosting value of 'ace' fighter pilots. Boelcke and Immelmann, operating first as a pair and then in different parts of the Front, were in friendly rivalry as their scores increased. In January 1916, when each had eight confirmed victories, they were the first aviators to be awarded Germany's highest decoration, the

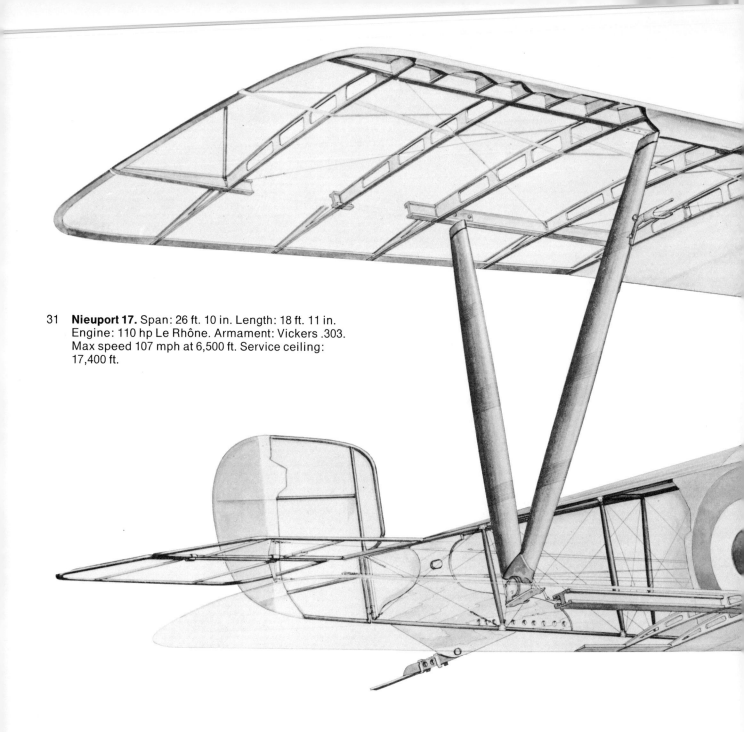

31 **Nieuport 17.** Span: 26 ft. 10 in. Length: 18 ft. 11 in. Engine: 110 hp Le Rhône. Armament: Vickers .303. Max speed 107 mph at 6,500 ft. Service ceiling: 17,400 ft.

Order *Pour le Merite,* and so instituted the ace system. This figure was used as a yardstick for the award until later in the year when so many airplanes were being shot down that it was doubled to sixteen.

The Fokker monoplane, of which the E.3 (10-14) was the major production type, was not an outstanding aircraft but its great asset was its gun. It was the only airplane at that time with synchronised firing and its belt-feed gave 500 continuous rounds while the Allied pilots had to change the drums on their Lewis guns every forty-seven shots and only had room to carry four extra drums. This was enough to tip the balance of air power in Germany's favour almost overnight. Also, the introduction of the Fokker came at a time when the German pilots, after a long period of docility, were beginning to fight back anyway, using their armed C-class biplanes with the observer in the back much more aggressively than before. New tactics were devised

during this period which were to govern air combat for the next fifty years. The best possible position was to have one's own guns at the closest range of the enemy but at a point where he was unable to fire back which, with forward-firing guns, meant behind and slightly above him. Where the enemy had guns firing aft, the best position was behind and slightly below his tail. Height was important for one could then take advantage of natural cover such as sun and clouds and gain extra speed by diving on an opponent. Tightness of turn was a vital factor, both offensively to get on an enemy's tail and defensively to keep out of an opponent's gunsight. With these tactics in mind, the main combat manoeuvres were seen to be the steep turn, dive and zoom climb, the main requirements for a fighter being a high ratio of thrust to weight and low wing loading for manoeuvrability. How these were provided by various designers over the years is the story of the development of the fighter airplane. Immelmann,

32 F.E.8. Span: 31 ft. 6 in. Length: 23 ft. 8 in. Engine: 100 hp Gnôme Mono. Armament: one Lewis. Max speed: 94 mph ground level. Service ceiling: 14,500 ft.

who became known as the 'Eagle of Lille', was particularly inventive. The Fokkers were of course themselves vulnerable from behind but it was found that by pulling up as if to loop and then doing a half-roll and dive to right the aircraft, a pilot could either escape in the opposite direction or, alternatively, he could half-roll and dive on the tail of his opponent, using the extra speed that his dive gave him. Although he was not the first pilot to employ this tactic and the French pilot Adolphe Pegoud had many times performed the loop before the war, it was Immelmann who perfected its use in air combat. It is still known as the 'Immelmann turn' (26).

The point came when a drastic change of policy was forced on the RFC. In January 1916 – "until the Royal Flying Corps are in possession of a machine as good as or better than the German Fokker," in the words of the official order – a switch was made to flying in close formation. Every reconnaissance aircraft had to be accompanied by at least three other machines and reconnaissance was to be abandoned if any became detached. In fact, the need for formation flying had already been seen by the French in the summer of 1915 when *Capitaine* Happe of *Escadrille* MF 29 taught his Maurice Farman bomber pilots to fly in 'V' formation while he took a roving commission to drive off any attackers. But even this did not end the massacre as groups of up to six Fokkers at a time patrolled the skies to attack the RFC formations. For the Germans, themselves taking a lesson from the French, had grouped their single-seaters into small fighting units instead of distributing them thinly among all their squadrons.

The Fokkers reached their zenith in February 1916 with the final E.4, powered by a two-row 160 hp Oberursel (developed from French experiments in placing two Le Rhône radials together in order to double the horsepower) and armed with two heavier but more reliable 7.92-mm Maxim machine-guns (18), known as Spandaus from their place of manufacture at Spandau. Immelmann's E.4 even carried three guns. In that same month the escort detailed

to accompany one B.E.2c on a reconnaissance mission totalled no less than twelve aircraft. By this time the Germans had also introduced other single-seat fighters; the first of the Pfalz monoplanes, again closely resembling the Morane-Saulnier design, the Halberstadt D.1 biplane, and the Siemens-Schukert monoplane whose 110 hp Siemens-Halske geared rotary engine revolved in the opposite direction to its airscrew, thus reducing the torque effect common to all rotaries.

The *Eindekkers* did not have things all their own way. Both Boelcke and Immelmann, amongst many other pilots, experienced the unpleasant situation of shooting off their own propellers when the synchronising gear malfunctioned. This may have been the cause of Immelmann's death on June 18th 1916,when, his score standing at fifteen Allied aircraft shot down, he crashed during a fight with an F.E. 2b of the RFC's No. 25 Squadron, flown by Lieutenant G. R. McCubbin and Corporal Waller. The British claimed it as a victory, insisting that bullets from the F.E.2b caused the structural failure. Immelmann's death marked the symbolic end of the 'Fokker Scourge' although it had been apparent for some months that the Allied fighters could by now more than hold their own. During its short reign the Fokker monoplane had revolutionized air combat and considering its great achievements it is both surprising and even more to its credit that no more than 425 were built. Nevertheless, in spite of the outcry it aroused, the Allied work of reconnaissance and bombing never entirely ceased. Nearly all the aircraft lost fell into German-held territory while on missions against the enemy, for the simple reason that the German fighter pilots were under strict orders not to fly over the Allied lines in case they should be forced to land and thus reveal their 'secret weapon'. In fact, two weeks before this did happen on April 8th 1916 and an example of the German synchronising gear eventually fell into Allied hands, the first British aircraft fitted with interrupter gear, a Bristol Scout, had already been delivered to the RFC in France.

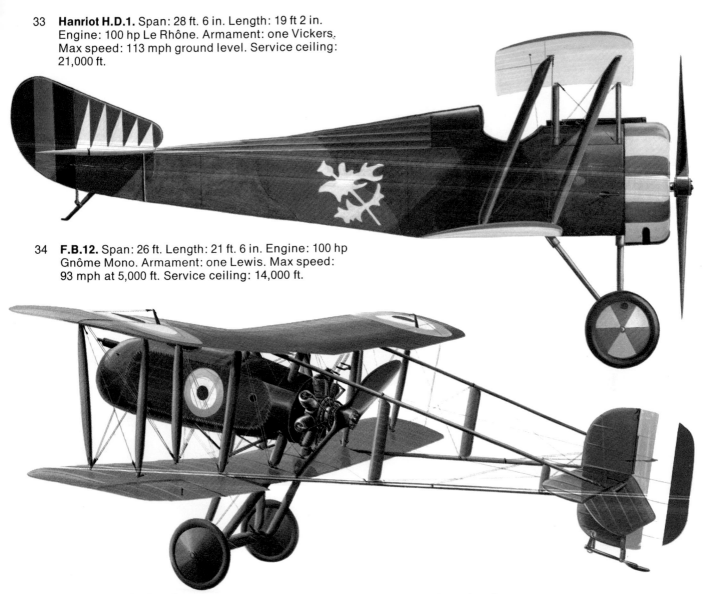

33 **Hanriot H.D.1.** Span: 28 ft. 6 in. Length: 19 ft 2 in. Engine: 100 hp Le Rhône. Armament: one Vickers. Max speed: 113 mph ground level. Service ceiling: 21,000 ft.

34 **F.B.12.** Span: 26 ft. Length: 21 ft. 6 in. Engine: 100 hp Gnôme Mono. Armament: one Lewis. Max speed: 93 mph at 5,000 ft. Service ceiling: 14,000 ft.

The Allies fight back

But answers to the *Eindekker* existed before that, which later in 1916 enabled the Allies to regain mastery of the air. The Nieuport 11 'Baby' (23), armed with a stripped Lewis gun above the top wing, was introduced into the British and French air services in the summer of 1915 and quickly became very popular because of its manoeuvrability and fast rate of climb. Its speed of 97 mph was ten miles an hour faster and its ceiling of 15,000 feet was 1,500 feet higher than even the Fokker E.4 (although it must be remembered that the performances of individual aircraft varied considerably and such figures only give a general indication of what particular types could achieve). It was with the Nieuport 'Baby' that the French and British fighter aces Georges Guynemer and Albert Ball achieved their early successes. The Vickers Gunbus was still capable of holding its own against the *Eindekkers* while two new pushers airplanes were coming into service with the RFC which were to represent the limit of that type of design for fighters before tractor airplanes displaced them entirely. These were the F.E.2b two-seater (27), originally designed as a Farman Experimental airplane by the Royal Aircraft Factory before the war, and the D.H.2 single-seat scout (25), designed by Geoffrey de Havilland for the Air-

craft Manufacturing Company.

The first squadrons equipped with these pusher fighters went to France early in 1916 and were quickly found to be superior to the Fokkers in speed, manoeuvrability and rate of climb. The F.E.2b was powered by a 160 hp Beardmore engine and carried two Lewis machine-guns, one mounted in front of the observer's cockpit and a second fitted on a telescopic mounting so that it could be fired backwards over the top wing. The D.H.2 was powered by a 100 hp Gnôme *Monosoupape* (25) or a 110 hp Le Rhône rotary engine which gave it a maximum ground speed of 93 mph. It was a sturdy aircraft but sensitive on the controls, tending to spin with little warning. A number of pilots were killed in this way until the phenomenon of spinning was understood. When its characteristics became known however, it established itself as a first-class fighter, able to carry out combat maneouvres with military precision, although with its open cockpit in front it was very cold to fly at altitude. The prototype was fitted with moveable mountings for a Lewis gun but production models had a fixed gun when it was realised that the best chance of success lay in aiming the aircraft as a whole at a target. The first squadron to be equipped with D.H.2s, No. 24 Squadron commanded by Major L. G. Hawker, VC, which went to France in February 1916, was also the first single-seat fighter squadron ever to be formed.

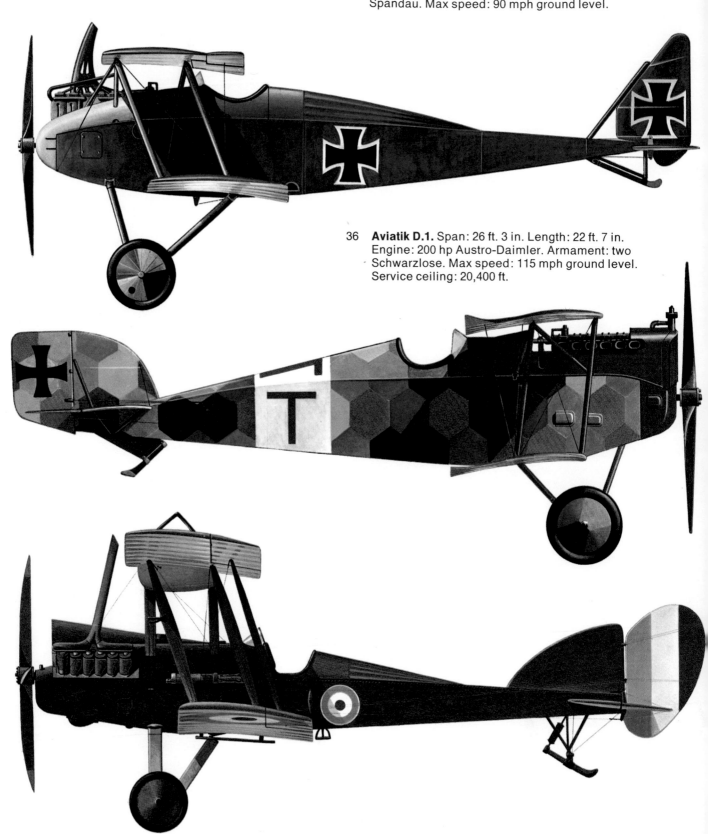

35 Halberstadt D.II. Span 28 ft. 11 in. Length 23 ft. 11 in. Engine: 120 hp Mercedes. Armament: one or two Spandau. Max speed: 90 mph ground level.

36 Aviatik D.1. Span: 26 ft. 3 in. Length: 22 ft. 7 in. Engine: 200 hp Austro-Daimler. Armament: two Schwarzlose. Max speed: 115 mph ground level. Service ceiling: 20,400 ft.

37 B.E.12. Span: 37 ft. Length: 27 ft. 3 in. Engine: 150 hp R.A.F. 4A. Armament: two Lewis or one Lewis and one Vickers. Max speed: 102 mph ground level. Service ceiling: 12,500 ft.

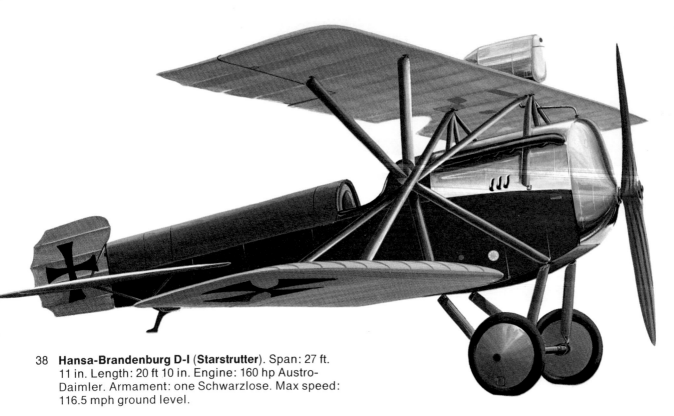

38 **Hansa-Brandenburg D-I (Starstrutter).** Span: 27 ft.
11 in. Length: 20 ft 10 in. Engine: 160 hp Austro-
Daimler. Armament: one Schwarzlose. Max speed:
116.5 mph ground level.

Italy meanwhile had entered the war on May 24th 1915 in a high state of readiness as far as her air forces were concerned, due to intensive training, but with aircraft which by then were out-dated. These were all French types and included four squadrons of Nieuport monoplanes, two of Maurice Farman pusher biplanes, built by the Italian firm of Nieuport-Macchi, and six squadrons of Blériots, some 150 airplanes in all. The main types opposing them on the Austro-Hungarian side were little better, mostly unarmed observation biplanes such as the Lohner, the Albatros B.I built by the Phoenix company of Vienna, and the Austrian Aviatik B models, built under licence from German designs. Operations were severely limited because of the hazards of flying over the Alps, where an engine failure almost certainly meant a fatal crash, and until better aircraft were available both sides confined their efforts to recon-

naissance and artillery spotting, together with a little bombing. In 1916 Nieuport-Macchi began manufacturing Nieuport 10 and 11 two-seater biplanes and also the Hanriot HD.1 single-seat fighter (33), armed with a single Vickers synchronised gun, which was very popular with pilots for its strength and manoeuvrability and became the standard Italian fighter. The Hanriot was also built in France for the Italian and Belgian air forces but was little used by French squadrons. Later machines carried two guns but it was found that these considerably reduced the aircraft's ceiling. The single-seat scout was not neglected on the Austrian side and Fokker biplanes were purchased from Germany and also built under licence. More successful, however, was the Hansa-Brandenburg D.1 'Star-strutter' (38), designed by Ernst Heinkel for the Austrian-owned company. The machine was built by

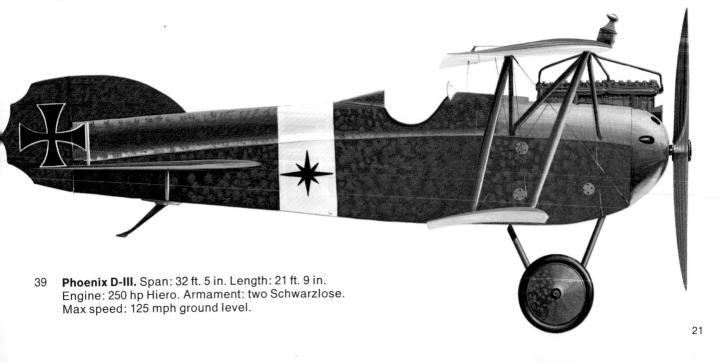

39 **Phoenix D-III.** Span: 32 ft. 5 in. Length: 21 ft. 9 in.
Engine: 250 hp Hiero. Armament: two Schwarzlose.
Max speed: 125 mph ground level.

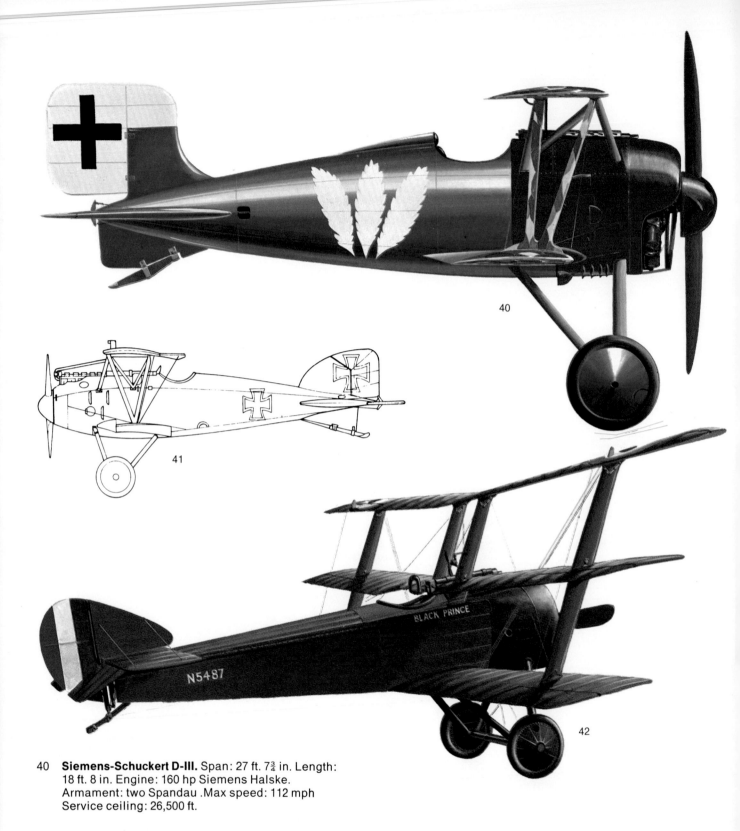

40 **Siemens-Schuckert D-III.** Span: 27 ft. 7¾ in. Length: 18 ft. 8 in. Engine: 160 hp Siemens Halske. Armament: two Spandau .Max speed: 112 mph Service ceiling: 26,500 ft.

41 **Albatros D-III.** Span: 29 ft. 7 in. Length: 24 ft. Engine: 160 hp Mercedes. Armament: two Spandau. Max speed: 109 mph at 3,280 ft. Service ceiling: 18,000 ft.

42 **Sopwith Triplane.** Span: 26 ft. 6 in. Length: 19 ft. 4 in. Engine: 130 hp Clerget. Armament: one or two Vickers. Max speed: 117 mph at 5,000 ft. Service ceiling: 20,500 ft.

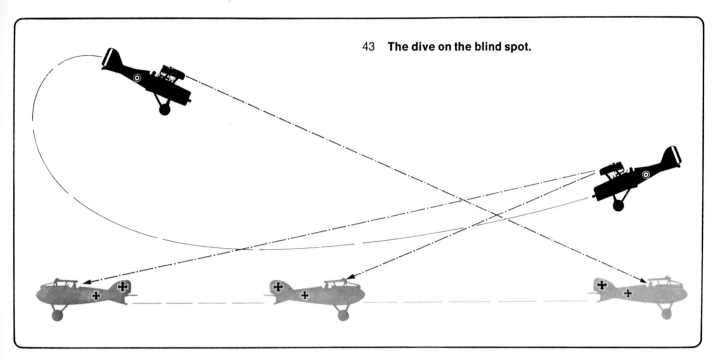

43 **The dive on the blind spot.**

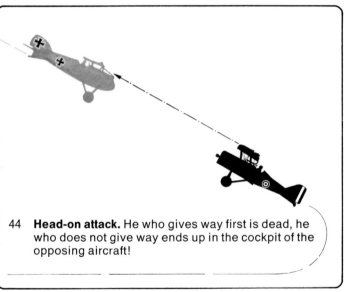

44 **Head-on attack.** He who gives way first is dead, he who does not give way ends up in the cockpit of the opposing aircraft!

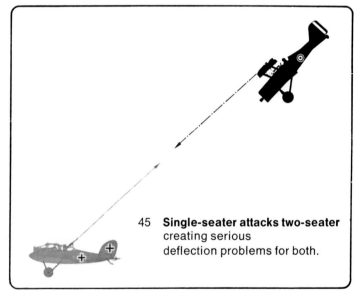

45 **Single-seater attacks two-seater** creating serious deflection problems for both.

46 **The attack from the sun.** 'Watch for the Hun in the sun'. A W.W.1 proverb unheeded by many.

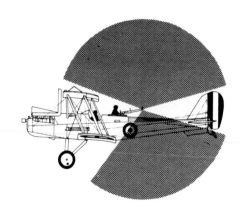

47 **Arcs of fire** available to a two-seater. For above 360° and to either side below.

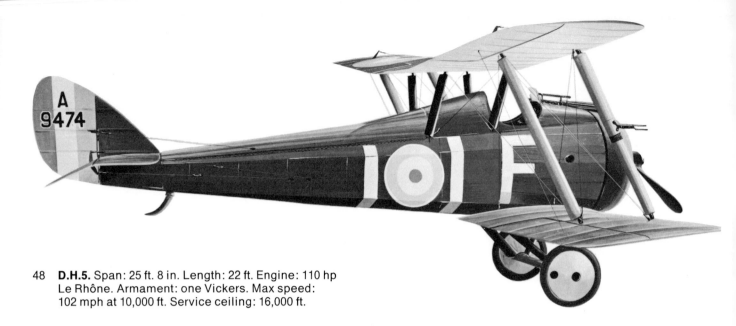

48 **D.H.5.** Span: 25 ft. 8 in. Length: 22 ft. Engine: 110 hp
Le Rhône. Armament: one Vickers. Max speed:
102 mph at 10,000 ft. Service ceiling: 16,000 ft.

Phoenix, with a 160 hp Austro-Daimler engine, and by
Ufag with the 185 hp version. A stripped Schwarzlose
machine-gun, enclosed in a light casing, was mounted on
the top wing to fire above the propeller.

Aerial warfare during 1915 was very much a personal
affair. Pilots on either side would drop messages to one
another or land close to an enemy they had forced down
to take him prisoner personally or collect souvenirs from
his aircraft. There was an element of 'sport' and 'good
hunting' about it all. The shooting down of a reconnaissance airplane was not considered to be as great an
accomplishment as scoring over a single-seat scout.
Challenges were issued, and sometimes accepted, for
individual combats. Fighter pilots often hated to see an
enemy go down for it usually meant his death – sometimes
a terrible death by burning for none of the pilots at this time
carried parachutes, although they were issued to balloon
observers. The official reason was that parachutes were
not reliable and that a suitable type did not exist for carrying in airplanes, but closer to the truth was the cynical and
mistaken suggestion that the possession of a parachute
would discourage a pilot from taking aggressive action.
Many who were wounded in the air or whose aircraft were
disabled could have escaped had they been able to bail
out. Luck played a large part in air fighting and none knew
this better than the pilots themselves. An airplane could be
riddled with bullets and still get away while another would
be downed by a single shot.

Tactics (43–45) were just as personal. Some pilots preferred to dive down out of the sun on their adversaries (46),
others would creep up from behind, while a more dangerous technique was to approach an enemy head-on, pre-
tend to climb, then at the last minute dive underneath and
rake its underside with machine-gun fire. Albert Ball, the
first British pilot to achieve fame as an 'ace' who scored
forty-four victories and was awarded the Victoria Cross
before he was killed, would deliberately allow a German to
get on his tail, then, at the instant his sixth sense told him
the enemy was about to open fire, he would make a short
dive and come up underneath before the German could
grasp what was happening. In the case of aircraft mounting
fixed forward-firing guns, such as the *Eindekkers,* the
pusher types, and the biplane scouts with guns attached to
their top wings, it was found that by 'wobbling' the controls a

deadly cone of fire could be produced instead of a single
stream of bullets. These individual methods and many
variations of them were employed throughout the war,
particularly by the elite 'aces' who were usually able to
insist on fighting their highly individualistic battles the way
they wanted. But meanwhile, organised air fighting was
also being developed as fighter squadrons were formed
for the specific purpose of intercepting enemy reconnaissance aircraft as well as escorting their own. The Front was
too wide of course and there were too few airplanes to
carry out such patrols continually, but they came to play a
vital role during any particular offensive. The first time that
organised air fighting took place on a big scale was during
the massive attack launched by the Germans against the
fortress of Verdun at the end of February 1916.

The Battle of Verdun

With their opening artillery barrage, the Germans specifically aimed at destroying as many of the French airfields as
possible. Then the *Eindekkers,* grouped together in force,
flew barrage patrols against the slow Farmans and Voisin
pushers which the French were using for reconnaissance.
The intention was to drive the French air force from the sky
and thus give their own reconnaissance airplanes free
reign while single-seat fighter detachments, *Kampfein-
sitzerkommando,* gave close support to the attacking
infantry, another new form of air warfare. The sturdy
Halberstadt D.1 single-seat biplane, armed with a synchronised Spandau gun on the starboard side of the engine, was developed specially for trench-strafing, as were
the later Hannover two-seater C-types. The Germans were
only too successful at the start of the offensive and it became an absolute necessity for the French to regain air
superiority to prevent the enemy from discovering just how
vulnerable the Verdun defences really were. For instance,
all the supplies were being brought in convoy along only
one road which, if bombed, would have had disastrous
consequences. New air units were hurriedly brought in,
including six Nieuport fighter squadrons, each comprising
twelve aircraft, which were regrouped under *Commandant*

Tricornot de Rose, air chief of the Second Army and already famous for his earlier exploits with the Morane squadrons.

Among the new arrivals were the five squadrons of *Capitaine* Brocard's *Groupe de Combat XII*, known as the 'Storks'. Each unit had as its badge a different kind of stork, a bird common in northern France. They were to become the most celebrated of the French combat groups, moving to whichever part of the Front they were most needed, and it was with the Storks that most of the French aces achieved their success. The French ace system was in fact instituted at Verdun by *Commandant* de Rose, following the German practice as a way of fostering an offensive spirit, and it was here that such flamboyant figures as Charles Nungesser and Jean Navarre first caught the public imagination. A score of ten was the usually accepted figure to denote an ace, although this was lowered to five after the United States entered the war in order that their pilots, naturally with less time available, could achieve similar status. The British frowned on the institution and although their best fighting pilots such as Mannock, McCudden and Bishop were aces in every sense of the word with scores equal to those of the French and German, the ace system was never officially recognised in Britain. Unlike the *Pour le Merite,* which was automatically awarded to German pilots once they achieved a certain score, the Victoria Cross as always was awarded only for outstanding acts of bravery and not for the number of victories scored, although the sixteen VCs won by flying personnel during the war included five of the leading aces. Major Edward Mannock, for instance, Britain's top scorer with seventy-three victories, did not live to receive the Victoria Cross, which was only awarded posthumously after the war.

As with the French and Germans, confirmation rules were very strict and required independent witnesses either in the air or on the ground before a victory could be credited to a pilot. Since the Allies were usually on the offensive and most of the air battles were fought over German-held territory, it was easier for the German pilots to make successful claims as the wreckage of the airplanes they brought down could actually be seen and identified. Richthofen made a habit whenever possible of collecting souvenirs from his victims' machines. Allied pilots on the other hand often saw the aircraft they had shot up crash in flames but were unable to claim them if they fell behind enemy lines and were not witnessed. The Germans were unlikely to report such crashes, one reason why the figures for losses on both sides are not always reliable.

The grim battle for Verdun lasted from February to June. Flying formations of three to six at a time the Storks gradually broke up the German barrage patrols and prevented their reconnaissance aircraft from discovering much vital information. When it was necessary for the French to make a breakthrough for reconnaissance, the squadrons were massed together to provide an escort, fighting off the *Eindekkers.* Included among these squadrons was the famous *Escadrille Lafayette,* composed entirely of American pilots who had been flying with the French since the very start of the war such as Gervais Raoul Lufbery and David Putnam whose victories totalled seventeen and twelve respectively before both were killed in 1918. The citadel of Verdun held out, although at a tremendous cost to the French Army. The French air force also suffered heavily, losing nearly one hundred aircraft against the Germans' thirty. *Commandant* de Rose was killed. Jean Navarrre, the first fighter pilot to score two victories in one day, was so severely wounded in a dogfight that he never flew operationally again. His score remained

at twelve. Georges Guynemer, who was to become the second highest scoring French ace with fifty-four victories, was also wounded.

Among the Nieuport fighters at Verdun, making its first appearance half-way through the battle, was the new Type 17 (31) typical of the Nieuport designs but the best of them all and one of the outstanding aircraft of its time. Popular though the 'Baby' still was, it had a structural weakness to which all vee-strutters were prone. With only a single spar holding the lower wing, this tended to twist and break under stress, causing the wings to collapse. The Type 17 was both stronger and larger, fifteen square metres against the 'Baby's' thirteen. Its standard engine was the 110 hp Le Rhône although the 130 hp Clerget was also fitted, giving it a maximum speed of 107 mph, a ceiling of over 17,000 feet, and a rate of climb of nine minutes to 10,000 feet. Some machines had transparent celluloid 'skylights' in their centre sections. Armament at first consisted of a Lewis gun on the top wing but this was later replaced or augmented by a mechanically synchronised Vickers gun fixed in front of the pilot. Le Prieur rockets, attached to the interplane struts, were sometimes carried for attacks on enemy balloons. Together with the British D.H.2 and F.E.2b pushers, it finally vanquished the Fokker *Eindekkers* from the skies. It was constructed in Italy by Nieuport-Macchi and also supplied to the RFC which was desperately short of aircraft in the summer of 1916 with only twenty-seven squadrons and 421 airplanes operational. Major-General Hugh Montague Trenchard was now in command of the RFC, with its headquarters permanently based at St. Omer, and it was he more than anyone who was responsible for the formation of fighting squadrons with a new offensive spirit after the hammering which the British pilots had received from the Fokkers.

Boelcke was only too well aware of the superiority of the Nieuport 17, especially after an encounter with one at the end of April when, after being out-manoeuvred at every turn and his Fokker E.4 riddled with bullets, he only escaped by stalling into a spin in the pretence that he was crashing out of control. He recommended to the military authorities that they should develop biplane fighters and also urged the formation of special combat units to take the offensive. The German High Command, and in particular General Ludendorff, was impressed with his reasoning and new groups known as *Jagdstaffeln* (pursuit squadrons) began to be formed in May. Boelcke, who was by now a national hero with eighteen victories to his credit, was put in command of *Jasta 2.* But before he could lead it in action he was sent on a tour of the Russian Front to inspire morale there. He left just when he was most needed on the Western Front. The Battle of the Somme was about to begin,

In the spring of 1916, after inexplicable delays, the first Allied aircraft fitted with synchronising gear arrived. Various systems were devised, such as the French Alkan and the Scarff-Dibovski developed by the Admiralty for use with Lewis guns on RNAS airplanes. The RFC however favoured a synchronising gear designed by Vickers and at the same time decided to adopt the .303 Vickers machine-gun (21), a light modified version of the Maxim, as standard armament on forward-firing airplanes instead of the Lewis gun. The latter was retained as the standard weapon for observers in two-seaters, using a mounting invented by Warrant Officer F. W. Scarff in which the observer sat encircled by a ring carrying a moveable arm to which the gun was attached. This became standard equipment on all Allied two-seaters and was used worldwide for many years after the war. Since the forward-firing guns were now fixed, mounted on the fuselage to shoot through the propellers, there was no objection to the Vickers on grounds that it was too cumbersome, and it had the advantage of being belt-fed so that frequent changes of ammunition drum were not required. The Vickers system was first fitted to a number of Bristol Scout biplanes, and then more generally to the Sopwith 1½-Strutter (29) which began to enter service with the RFC in May. This airplane, whose centre-section W-shaped struts gave rise to its name, had been ordered originally by the RNAS as a two-seater bomber but equipped with a forward-firing gun as well as the observer's rear gun in order to fight its way past defending fighters. The RFC, short of airplanes for the impending Somme campaign, appealed to the RNAS for help. Large numbers of 1½-Strutters were handed over to them and were used to equip the first operational squadron fitted with synchronising gear, No. 70 Squadron. Although designed as a bomber and too stable to be ideal for fighting, its two guns made it extremely effective and it was also significant as the pioneer of an entirely new class of two-seat fighters. German fighters, approaching from a direction where they expected to be shielded from the observer's gun, met instead a deadly and unexpected hail of fire from the synchronised gun. Another airplane originally developed by Sopwith Aviation for the RNAS but also adopted by the RFC was a small single-seat fighting scout known, in spite of official discouragement, as the Pup (30). Powered only by the 80 hp Le Rhône rotary engine it was so light, with a wing span of merely 26 feet 6 inches, that it had a top speed of 111.5 mph and performed particularly well at high altitudes. It was so manoeuvrable (McCudden wrote that it "could turn twice to an Albatros' once") and pleasant to fly that many pilots claimed it was the finest machine built during the First World War. It could keep circling during combat at 15,000 feet without losing height, a feat no contemporary German airplane could match. Its success in the kind of fighter-versus-fighter dogfights that were developing underlined the fact that many other qualities apart from speed were required in a good fighter such as rate of climb, ability to hold height and execute turns, in addition to the type of armament carried.

Engine power increases

The main difference between most Allied and German fighters at this time was in their engines. In the search for higher power the engine designers, now including such British companies as Rolls-Royce and Beardmore, were greatly helped by the increasing availability of light alloys, providing both strength and lightness. Steel for instance gradually replaced cast-iron for the manufacture of pistons. The rotary engine was still the main propulsion unit for most Allied fighters and reconnaissance aircraft and its power had continued to increase with the 130 hp Clerget and eventually the 150 hp B.R.1 designed by W. O. Bentley, although cooling problems prevented any advance in the two-row types developed by Gnôme and Oberursel. In Germany experiments were carried out by Siemens-Halske with a contra-rotating bi-rotary but in general the Germans concentrated on building more powerful stationary in-line water-cooled engines such as the 150 hp Benz and 160 hp Mercedes, most of them with six cylinders although a straight-eight was developed by Mercedes. These were the engines that gave many German aircraft designs a distinctive long-nosed look. The valves of the more advanced were operated by overhead camshafts instead of the pushrod-and-rocker system while rotational speeds had risen to the point where reduction-gearing was required between the crankshaft and propeller. The Allies were also trying out many types of in-line and Vee engines, both water-cooled and air-cooled. Henry Royce, rejecting design drawings bought by the British government from France, had instead built his own outstanding V-12 water-cooled Rolls-Royce Eagle engine in 1915, later developed also into the Falcon series. The 225 hp version of the Eagle was installed in the F.E.2d pusher in place of the 120 hp or 160 hp six-cylinder Beardmores which powered the F.E.2b.

A line-up of Sopwith Camels at Izel Les Hameau, No. 23 Squadron, RAF. *Imperial War Museum*

49 **S.E.5A.** Span: 26 ft. 7 in. Length: 20 ft. 11 in. Engine:
200 hp Hispano or Wolseley Viper. Armament:
one Vicker or one Lewis. Max speed: 137.8 mph at
ground level. Service ceiling: 22,000 ft.

50 **Sopwith Camel.** Span: 28 ft. Length: 18 ft. 9 in.
Engine: 130 hp Clerget. Armament: two Vickers. Max
speed: 115 mph at 6,500 ft. Service ceiling: 19,000 ft.

But the biggest advance was undoubtedly the 140 hp
water-cooled Hispano-Suiza Vee-8, designed by Marc
Birkit for the largely French company that was already
famous in motoring. An aluminium cylinder block with
steel sleeves gave it a first-rate power to weight ratio,
weighing only 442 pounds against contemporary 160 hp
sixes like the Beardmore and Mercedes which weighed
upwards of 600 pounds. Later versions of the Hispano-
Suiza gave 150 hp and 200 hp geared. The first airplane to
use this engine was the outstanding Spad S.7, designed by
M. Bechereau for the Société pour Aviation et ses Dérivés,

the company taken over by Louis Blériot from the former
Déperdussin firm. It was developed from the Spad A.2
which first made its appearance in mid-1915, a tractor
biplane but with the observer sitting in front of the propeller in a pulpit-like nacelle which gave him a wide
field of fire but also the likelihood of being crushed to
death by the engine in even a minor crash. This was one
of the solutions devised to overcome the Allied lack of
synchronised guns at that time. The Spad S.7 single-seat
biplane came into service in the summer of 1916, fitted
with a synchronised Vickers machine-gun in front of the

52

53

51 55 **Bristol Fighter.** Span: 39 ft. 3 in. Length: 25 ft. 10 in. Engine: 275 hp R.R. Falcoln III. Armament: one Vickers or one or two Lewis. Max speed: 121.5 mph at 5,000 ft. Service ceiling: 20,000 ft.

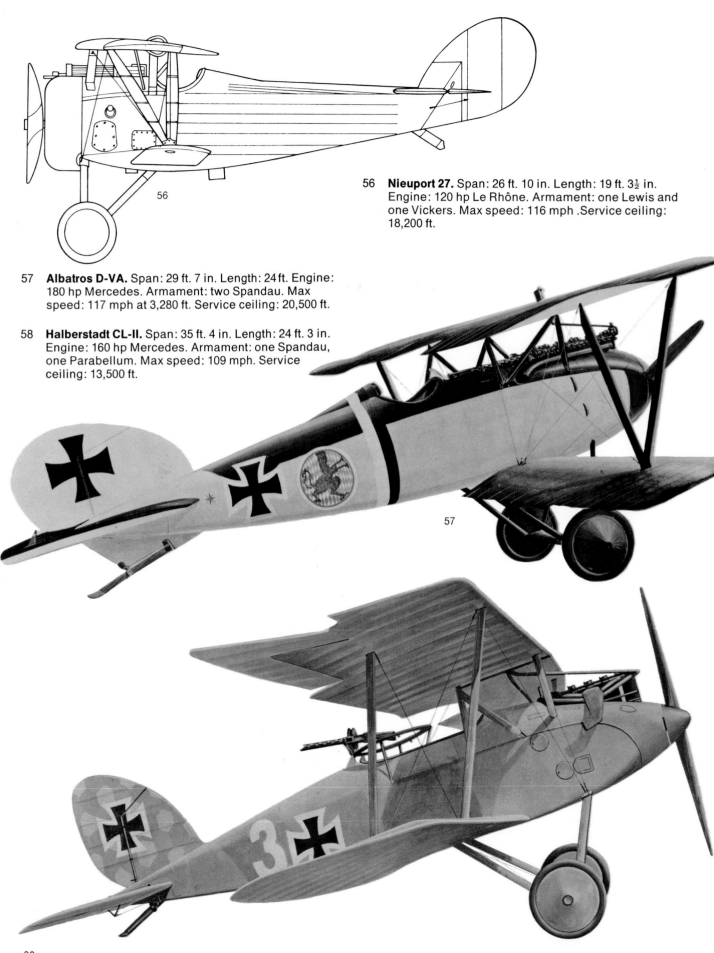

56 Nieuport 27. Span: 26 ft. 10 in. Length: 19 ft. 3½ in. Engine: 120 hp Le Rhône. Armament: one Lewis and one Vickers. Max speed: 116 mph .Service ceiling: 18,200 ft.

57 Albatros D-VA. Span: 29 ft. 7 in. Length: 24 ft. Engine: 180 hp Mercedes. Armament: two Spandau. Max speed: 117 mph at 3,280 ft. Service ceiling: 20,500 ft.

58 Halberstadt CL-II. Span: 35 ft. 4 in. Length: 24 ft. 3 in. Engine: 160 hp Mercedes. Armament: one Spandau, one Parabellum. Max speed: 109 mph. Service ceiling: 13,500 ft.

59 **Hannover CL-III.** Span: 38 ft. 4 in. Length: 24 ft. 9 in. Engine: 160 hp Mercedes. Armament: one Spandau, one Parabellum. Max speed: 103 mph at 2,000 ft. Service ceiling: 24,600 ft.

pilot, and became renowned for its great strength and speed, about 120 mph. It was the airplane flown by the leading French ace of the war, Réné Paul Fonck (75 victories), as well as Guynemer and other famous pilots of the Stork Group, and entirely replaced the rotary engine Nieuports and Moranes in the *Escadrilles de Chasse.* It was purchased for the FRC and also built in England.

The conventional airframe construction of the period, as represented in the Spad S.7, was of wire-braced wooden box-girders covered with fabric. But here, as in the case of engine design, experiments were being made with new materials. Plywood was being used increasingly by the British and French as a means of reinforcement, such as the top decking around the cockpits of the Sopwith 1½-Strutter, or as a means of fabricating a semi-monocoque fuselage as in the German Albatros D.1 and L.F.G. Roland C.2. Fokker had used wire-braced frames of welded steel tubing for the fuselage of his aircraft and two early experiments were made with all-metal designs. The Junkers J.1 (77), completed in 1915, was the world's first all-metal airplane, consisting of ribbed metal sheeting with internal tubular bracing. It was later developed as the J.2 single-seat fighter monoplane but was not brought into service. On the Allied side the Bristol company had produced a number of excellent single-seat monoplane fighters to the designs of Captain F. Barnwell, one of which, the M.R.1, was aluminium-clad over steel tubing. But the War Office was prejudiced against monoplane designs, based on the pre-war belief that they were structurally weaker than biplanes, a fallacy that had been strengthened by three fatal monoplane crashes in 1912. None of the Bristol mono-planes were used on the Western Front during the war, in spite of the fact that the M.1C (16) was one of the most highly developed airplanes of that time. A few saw operational service in the Middle East.

Great progress was made in aircraft design during 1916. It was the year in which the single-seat fighter came of age and saw the introduction of some of the famous types of the war. But it should be remembered that there was always a time-lag, sometimes a considerable one, between the appearance of a prototype airplane and its gradual introduction into service. Squadrons were mainly equipped with older types of aircraft still in production. For instance, at the end of 1915 when the 'Fokker Scourge' was at its height, the Germans only had eighty-six of these machines in front-line service. By February 1916, over a year after the Nieuports had made their first appearance,

only 210 had reached the Front and these were mostly two-seaters. The new fighters were naturally given to the best pilots to fly but as they eagerly sought to increase their scores to achieve 'ace' status, the bulk of recon-naissance and artillery spotting was still being carried out by pilots in what by then were obsolete aircraft. The B.E.2c, of which well over a thousand were built, was still flying in 1917. Courageous though the aces undoubtedly were, many of their successes were against old airplanes which in comparison were sitting ducks.

The Battle of the Somme, which opened on July 1st 1916, showed beyond any doubt the extent to which the Allies had regained supremacy of the air. The RFC concentrated 185 aircraft for the campaign and the French about 200. Of the British machines, sixty-six were fighters, mostly

60 **Maxim 1-pdr.** Anti-aircraft gun.

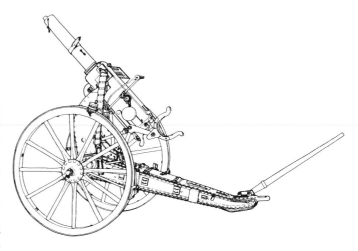

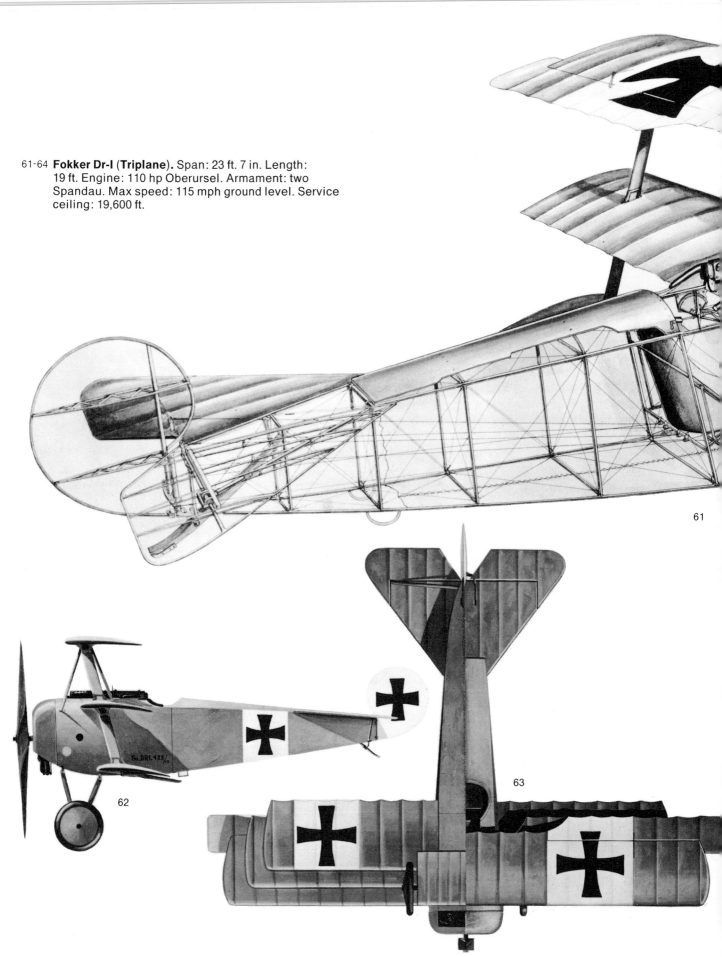

61-64 **Fokker Dr-I** (**Triplane**). Span: 23 ft. 7 in. Length: 19 ft. Engine: 110 hp Oberursel. Armament: two Spandau. Max speed: 115 mph ground level. Service ceiling: 19,600 ft.

61

62

63

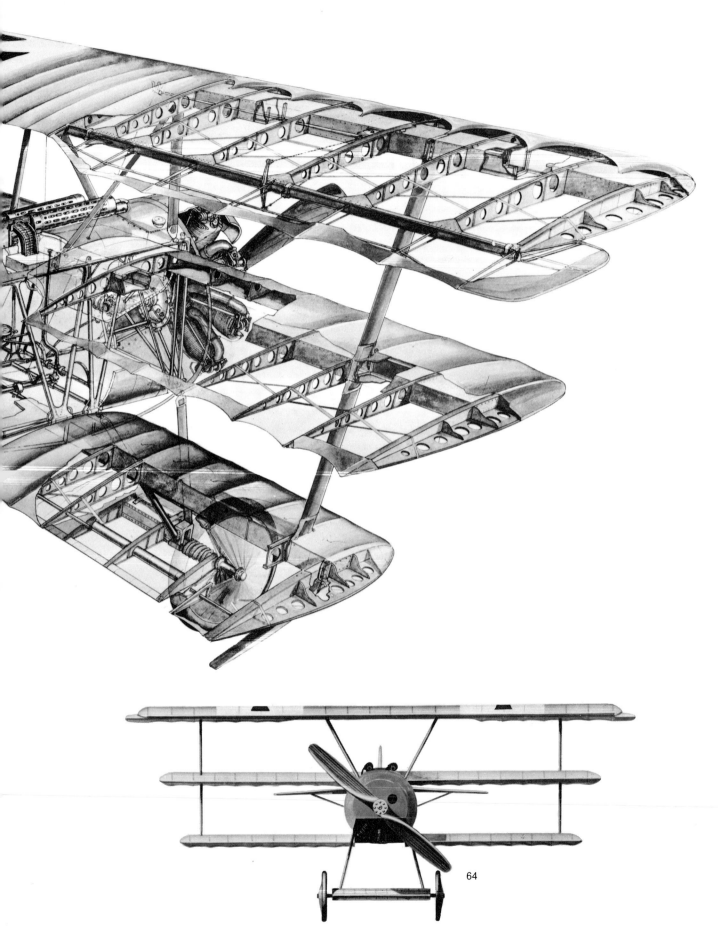

64

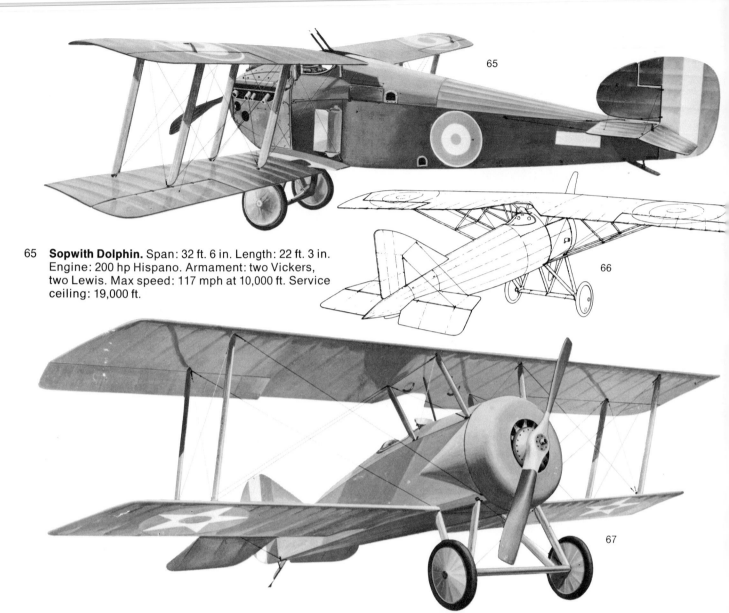

65 Sopwith Dolphin. Span: 32 ft. 6 in. Length: 22 ft. 3 in.
Engine: 200 hp Hispano. Armament: two Vickers,
two Lewis. Max speed: 117 mph at 10,000 ft. Service
ceiling: 19,000 ft.

66 Morane-Saulnier AI. Span: 27 ft. 10 in. Length:
18 ft. 6 in. Engine: 160 hp Gnome Mono. Armament:
one or two Vickers. Max speed: 129 mph at 6,500 ft.
Service ceiling: 23,000 ft.

67 Thomas Morse Scout 4B. Span: 27 ft. Length:
20 ft. 3 in. Engine: 100 hp Gnôme Mono. Armament:
two Marlin. Max speed: 95 mph ground level. Service
ceiling: 15,000 ft.

D.H.2 pushers with one squadron of Moranes and a few
Nieuport Scouts and Sopwith 1½-Strutters. The French
had seventy-two single-seat Nieuports formed into six
escadrilles based at Cachy. Of the 129 German machines
in service at that part of the Front only nineteen were
fighters and these, mostly Fokker E.3s with a few Fokker
and Pfalz E.4s and the new Halberstadt D.2s (35) had
already proved themselves to be inferior to the better
Allied fighters, even apart from the overwhelming difference in numbers. On the first day of the battle Major
L. W. B. Rees, the Commanding Officer of No. 32 Squadron,
set the pattern by a single-handed attack with his D.H.2 on
a formation of ten German two-seaters, forcing down two
and dispersing the rest. During the next few weeks the
German fighters were swept from the sky and Allied aircraft, although suffering considerable losses themselves
from anti-aircraft fire, were able to fly virtually unhindered
behind the German lines. In July and August the Germans
lost over fifty airplanes. Albert Ball, flying a Nieuport
Scout, accounted for seven of these, all Roland C.2s

which were basically reconnaissance biplanes but sometimes used as two-seater fighters with forward and back-
ward firing guns. They were in many ways the best of the
German aircraft then available but they were blind from
below, a weakness Ball exploited by flying underneath
and pulling back his Lewis gun to fire almost vertically. In
one encounter he attacked seven Rolands and shot one
down, then, still avoiding fire from the enemy machines,
attacked another five and shot two down. He was later
given a roving commission with the RFC's No. 60 Squadron
and by the end of September had thirty confirmed victories
and nineteen possible to his credit. His final score when he
was killed on May 7th 1917, as Flight Commander of No.
56 Squadron and having been awarded the Victoria Cross,
the DSO and two BARS, the MC and Legion of Honour,
was forty-four. On the French side Georges Guynemer was
the outstanding fighter pilot, shooting down nine enemy
aircraft during the first two weeks of the campaign and
having scored twenty-three by November.

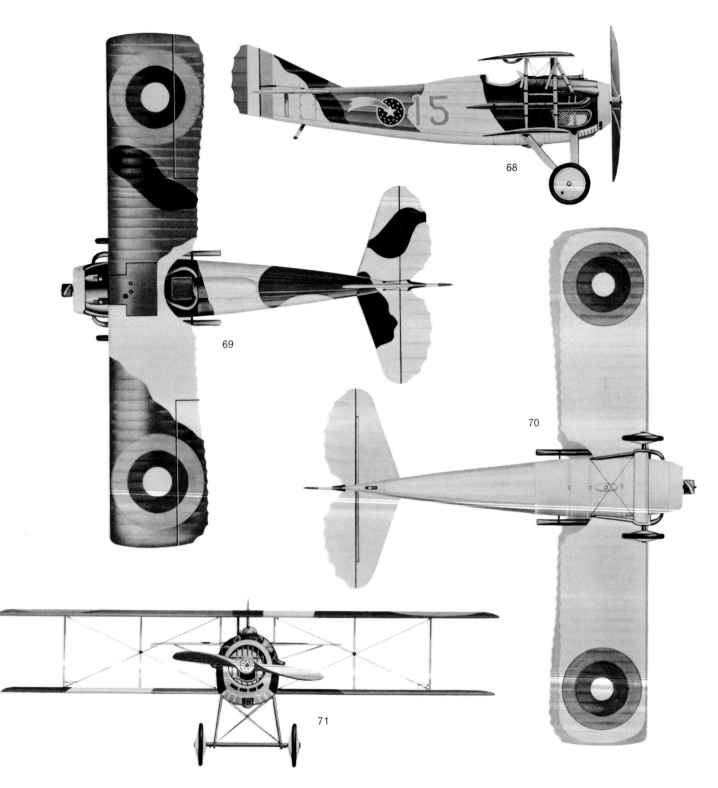

68

69

70

71

Apart from the exploits of individual fighter pilots flying alone, the opening of the campaign saw the first use by the RFC of formation flying employed offensively and not simply for defence, which had been its original purpose during the hey-day of the *Eindekkers*. On July 20th four D.H.2s of No. 24 Squadron attacked a formation of eleven enemy machines and shot down three of them. No. 24 was one of four specialised squadrons that had been formed of fast single-seat fighters and where possible they comprised aircraft of the same type. Apart from the commando groups temporarily formed for the Verdun offensive, this concept had not been applied in the German air services.

But the rout which they suffered at the start of the battle led the Germans to re-think their policy. The plans suggested by Boelcke were brought forward and all German fighting aircraft at the Front were grouped into *Jasta* units. In September, seven of these units were formed, comprising fourteen aircraft each, and Boelcke was brought back from his eastern tour to take command of the one originally assigned to him, *Jasta* 2, and to develop it as a model on which to base the others. He was allowed to choose his own men from among those pilots he considered most promising. Two he brought back from the Russian front were Leutnants Manfred Freiherr von

Richthofen and Erwin Bohme.

The new *Jasta* units were equipped with the D-class armed single-seat fighter biplanes on which German designers had been working as a result of the success achieved by the Nieuport biplane. As Boelcke had pointed out, although the *Eindekkers* could match the Nieuport in speed they did not have the same rate of climb or ability to turn quickly, two factors which had become vital in air combat. He considered a biplane design might be the answer and in desperation a decision was made to copy the French Nieuport, resulting in the famous vee-strut Albatros D.3 (41). Meanwhile, Fokker had already developed a biplane fighter, the D.2 with the 100 hp Oberursel rotary and the basically similar D.1 with the 120 hp Mercedes stationary engine, but neither were very successful. An improvement was made with the D.3 and D.4, fitted respectively with the two-row Oberursel rotary and the 160 hp Mercedes, but the four types were only supplied in small numbers, primarily for escort duty. More successful were the Halberstadt biplanes with their chimney exhaust pipes and car-type radiators, mounting a Spandau gun on the starboard side of the engine which was either a 120 hp Mercedes, 120 hp Argus, or 150 hp Benz. Another attractive aircraft in this series was the L.F.G. Roland D.1, nicknamed the 'Shark' when it went into limited production towards the end of 1916. Developed from the C.2, its 160 hp Mercedes engine was enclosed in a fishlike nose and there was no gap between the wings and the plywood fuselage. This improved the streamlining but also obscured the pilot's view and on the D.2 and D.3 models, powered by the 180 hp Argus, the top wing was raised first on a narrow pylon and then on struts. D-type Rolands were also built by Pfalz until their own designs were ready for production in 1917.

But the outstanding fighter of this period was the Albatros, with the characteristic 'fishtail' tail unit common to all the designs of that company. The D.1 which came into service in August 1916 was powered either by the 160 hp Mercedes or the 150 hp Benz and its semi-monocque structure of plywood was strong enough for it to carry two synchronised Spandau guns. Although not as fast as the

68-72 **Spad XIII.** Span: 26 ft. 11 in. Length: 20 ft. 8 in. Engine:200 hp Hispano. Armament: two Vickers. Max speed: 130 mph at 6,500 ft. Service ceiling: 22,300 ft.

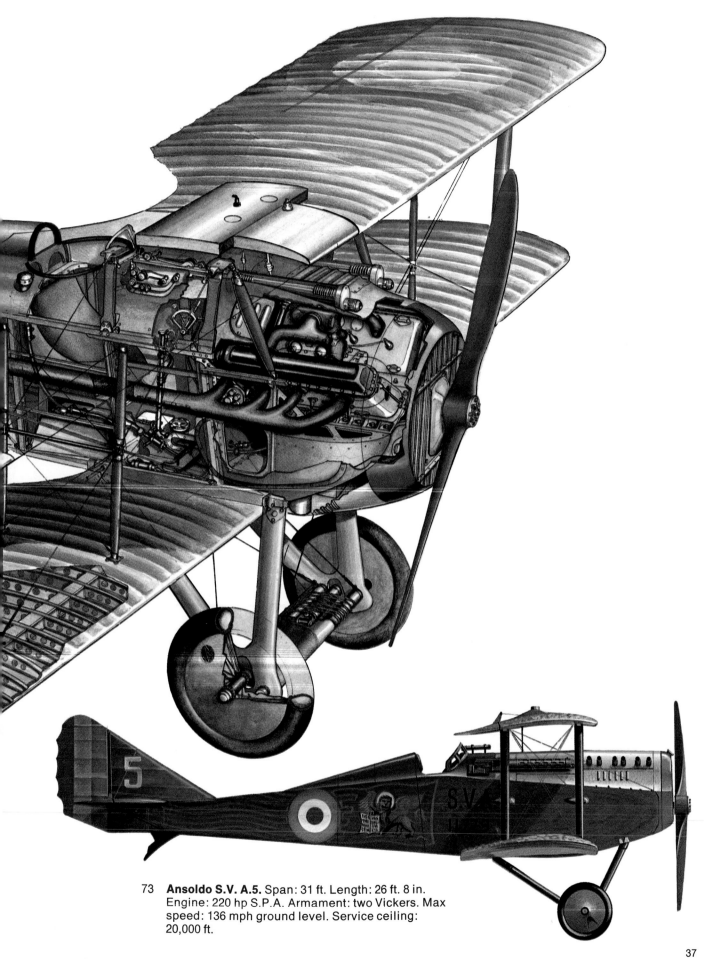

73 **Ansoldo S.V. A.5.** Span: 31 ft. Length: 26 ft. 8 in.
Engine: 220 hp S.P.A. Armament: two Vickers. Max
speed: 136 mph ground level. Service ceiling:
20,000 ft.

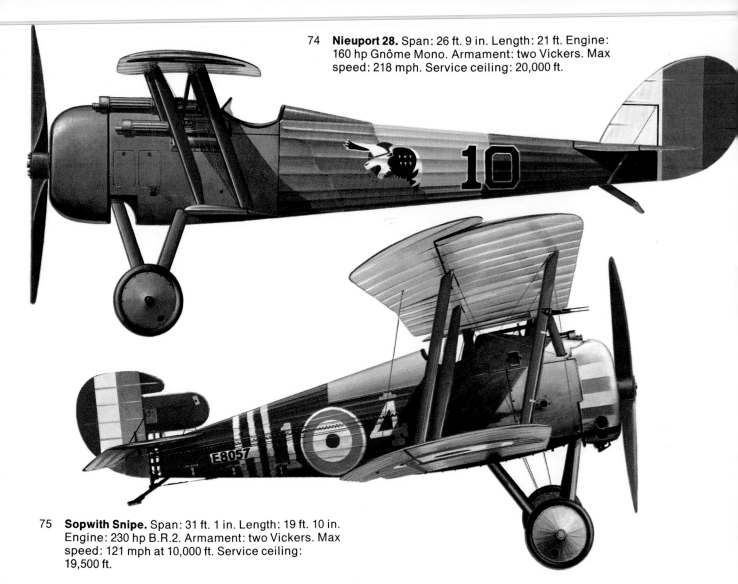

74 **Nieuport 28.** Span: 26 ft. 9 in. Length: 21 ft. Engine: 160 hp Gnôme Mono. Armament: two Vickers. Max speed: 218 mph. Service ceiling: 20,000 ft.

75 **Sopwith Snipe.** Span: 31 ft. 1 in. Length: 19 ft. 10 in. Engine: 230 hp B.R.2. Armament: two Vickers. Max speed: 121 mph at 10,000 ft. Service ceiling: 19,500 ft.

Spad S.7 or as manoeuvrable as the Nieuport, its more powerful engine gave it a better rate of climb and it had much greater fire-power. The D.2 version provided a lower top wing to give the pilot a better view forward and upwards while the D.3 when it came out in January 1917, adopting the Nieuport vee-strut sesquiplane layout, improved the downward view. It was powered by a high compression 260 hp Mercedes which gave an even better performance. A number were built for Austrian use with 185 hp Austro-Daimler engines. One structural weakness it inherited from the Nieuport was the single spar of the lower wing which could cause the wings to be wrenched off by violent manoeuvring. Richthofen himself nearly crashed when a dangerous crack appeared in the lower wing during a fight with an F.E.2b.

Another Albatros which came out at this time was the W.4 single-seat fighter seaplane, bearing a resemblance to the D.1 only larger, which was used by the German Naval Air Service at seaplane bases on the coast of Flanders. This was later replaced by the Hansa-Brandenburg W.12 two-seater seaplane which was just as fast but could also defend itself to the rear by means of the observer's flexible Parabellum gun. It proved a great problem to the Dunkirk-based Royal Naval Air Service in their general work of co-operating with the Fleet and bombing airship and submarine bases. The RNAS itself developed seaplanes for anti-submarine and anti-airship patrols, such as the Sopwith Schneider and Baby, and as early as 1916 a

Bristol Scout had been launched experimentally from the top wing of a flying boat in order to increase its endurance for anti-airship operations. In August of the following year a Sopwith Pup made the first-ever successful landing on the deck of a ship moving at sea and a special naval version of the Pup, the Beardmore W.B.3, which had folding wings and undercarriage for easy storing, was the first in a long line of carrier-borne fighters that would be formed into a special fighting service of their own. But for the time being most of the combat work done by the RNAS fighter pilots was at the side of the RFC over the Western Front. It was the RNAS in fact which was responsible for the introduction of the four great Sopwith fighters of the war, the 1½-Strutter, Pup, Triplane and Camel.

The German *Jasta* units came as a great shock to the Allies. On September 17th, Boelcke, flying a Fokker D.3 which he had chosen as his personal airplane, took his best pupils, flying Albatros D.2s, on their first operation. They included Richthofen and Bohme. Boelcke led the attack on two formations of British aircraft, eight B.E.2cs on a bombing mission with an escort of six F.E.2bs. After several other German aircraft had joined in, all six F.E.2bs and two of the B.E.2cs were destroyed. Richthofen scored his first victory, against an F.E.2b. During September to November, *Jasta* 2 alone shot down seventy-six British aircraft for a loss of only seven of its own. The air situation was completely reversed as even the Nieuport 17 found itself outclassed. German losses in October fell from

German mobile anti-aircraft guns, mounted on lorries, were very effective in the early stages of the war. On the bank to the right, an officer operates the range-finder. *Imperial War Museum*

twenty-seven the previous month to twelve, while the Allies lost eighty-eight. Altogether, during the Battle of the Somme which lasted from July 1st to mid-November, the RFC lost 782 aircraft of which 190 fell behind enemy lines, many of them brought down in the later stages of the battle by the *Jasta* fighters. As if to epitomise the RFC's defeat, on November 23rd, Major L. G. Hawker VC, the veteran fighter pilot from the Bristol Scout days, was shot down after a gallant battle in his outclassed D.H.2 by Richthofen, flying an Albatros D.2. The greatest loss on the German side was not, ironically, in combat but through an unlucky accident. On October 28th, Oswald Boelcke, who had done so much through his personal and tactical leadership to build up a new spirit in the German Air Service, now a completely separate branch of the Army, was killed after his aircraft had collided with Bohme's while pursuing a British machine. His score then stood at forty. By Imperial decree *Jasta* 2 was renamed *Jasta Boelcke* and its command passed to a succession of some of Germany's best-known fighter pilots, including Bohme until he too was killed. At the end of the war, when seventy-seven *Jagdstaffeln* had been built up, the record of *Jasta Boelcke* showed the loss of four of its commanders and twenty-six pilots against 336 acknowledged victories.

For the second time in the war, during the winter of 1916-17, command of the air passed to Germany. The main reason was the deadly fire of the twin guns mounted on the D-class machines which gave 1,000 continuous rounds. Even such excellent fighters as the Spad and the Sopwith Pup, the latter acknowledged by Richthofen as dominating the skies in which it flew, were at a disadvantage against such a weapon although they continued to cause heavy casualties among the German two-seater reconnaissance craft. Most Allied airplanes were still armed with non-synchronised guns pointing over the propeller arc or fired by observers. Only a few single-seaters were armed with synchronised guns and these were none too reliable at first, tending to jam when a pilot throttled back to dive. One such aircraft, the Farnborough-designed B.E.12 (37) based on the B.E.2c two-seater, was a complete failure. The Martinsyde G.100 and G.102 Elephant was intended to be a long-range single-seat escort fighter but it was too big and awkward for fighting duties although it made a satisfactory bomber. The most effective British two-seater was still a pusher type, the F.E.2d. Although easily out-classed by the new German fighters it had the advantage of two guns, which could be fired by the pilot as well as the observer, and the crews learned to fly in defensive circles when attacked in order to protect the blind spot under their tails. Other aircraft like the Farnborough R.E.8, in spite of the fact that the observer was at last placed behind the pilot, were easy meat for the Germans. Nevertheless the R.E.8 was put into mass production like the B.E.2c and suffered heavy losses in 1917. It should of course be remembered that the primary function of aircraft

39

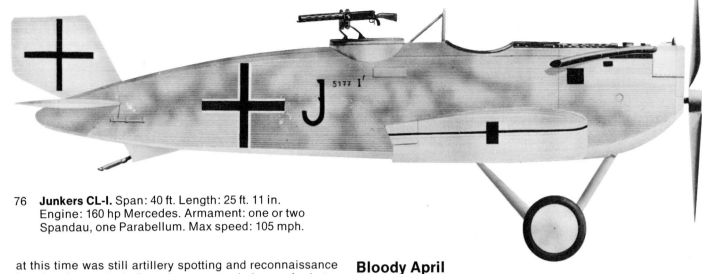

76 **Junkers CL-I.** Span: 40 ft. Length: 25 ft. 11 in.
Engine: 160 hp Mercedes. Armament: one or two
Spandau, one Parabellum. Max speed: 105 mph.

at this time was still artillery spotting and reconnaissance
for the Army, including the new technique of photo-
reconnaissance. In this the Allies were at a disadvantage
for it was they who were on the offensive and needed
knowledge of the enemy's troop concentrations while the
Germans were primarily on the defensive. Their main task
was to attack and shoot down the Allied reconnaissance
patrols which came over their lines and since large
numbers of aircraft were employed for this purpose, there
was no lack of targets. It was small wonder the Richthofen
and the other *Jasta* aces were able to build up their
scores so quickly. The situation was even more marked
in March 1917 when the Germans withdrew to the Hindenburg Line defences they had been building all winter.
They had the advantage of superior observation from high
ground which the Allies could only partly make up for by
reconnaissance from the air.

Bloody April

At the end of March the British High Command, spotting
what seemed to be a weakness in the German defences
where the Hindenburg Line ended at Arras, decided to
launch an offensive in that sector. The main RFC concentration of twenty-five squadrons, supported by RNAS
fighter units, was located near Arras, opposite the German
fighter station at Douai where Richthofen was now in
command of *Jasta* 11, equipped with the powerful new
Albatros D.3. It was one of thirty-seven *Jasta* units which
had been formed by then and all its aircraft, following
Richthofen's lead, were painted red. All the others however had some other distinguishing markings – Richthofen's
brother Lothar for instance had yellow ailerons and

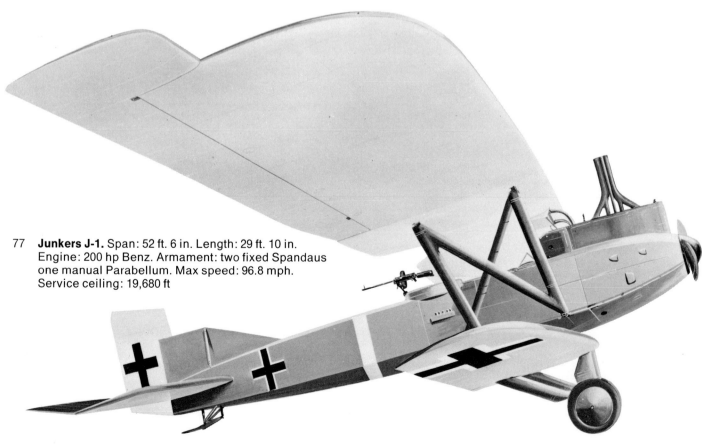

77 **Junkers J-1.** Span: 52 ft. 6 in. Length: 29 ft. 10 in.
Engine: 200 hp Benz. Armament: two fixed Spandaus
one manual Parabellum. Max speed: 96.8 mph.
Service ceiling: 19,680 ft

78 **Hansa-Brandenburg W.29.** Span: 44 ft. 4 in. Length: 30 ft. 8½ in. Engine: 185 hp Benz. Armament: two Spandau, one Parabellum. Max speed: 103 mph Service ceiling: 26,500 ft.

elevators – but Richthofen's remained the only all-red machine. Other units also adopted vivid colours, in contrast to the subdued khaki-green of the British aircraft, enlivened only by squadron markings. Some 754 British aircraft, including 385 single-seat fighters, opposed 264 German aircraft, of which 114 were single-seat fighters. The battle was due to start on April 9th but five days before that the RFC was in the air over the German lines, engaged on reconnaissance work and attempting to clear the skies of enemy aircraft. In those five days alone, seventy-five British airplanes were shot down. It was the start of what became known in the RFC as 'Bloody April' when, in the course of one month, 151 airplanes were shot down with a loss of 316 airmen killed in action, as against a loss of seventy German aircraft. Although outnumbered the German aircraft were greatly superior in performance and fire-power. It was a field day for the *Jasta* pilots, combining aggressive tactics and the team-work inspired by Boelcke and Immelmann. Both sides at this time decided that the best grouping consisted of two pairs in vee or diamond formation with a leader in front. *Jasta* 11 alone accounted for eighty-eight British aircraft, of which Richthofen shot down twenty-one, bringing his victories to a total of fifty-two. Nevertheless, in spite of these losses, the RFC and RNAS did some magnificent work. The trench-strafing of infantry targets, which was to become a permanent role of the fighter, was added to normal reconnaissance missions, artillery spotting, photography, bombing and escort duties. When the French joined the battle in mid-April with an offensive on the Aisne they brought with them an additional four *groupes* of 200 machines. But apart from the Spad S.7 flown to great effect by Guynemer and other aces, most of the aircraft were slow pushers like the Voisin and Farmans and flying operations were badly mismanaged by senior army officers who chose to ignore the recommendations of *Commandant* du Peuty in command of the fighter squadrons. Bad weather also affected their operations and when offensive patrols were made with five or six aircraft, the Germans avoided combat with them.

Although the Battle of Arras started so badly for the British, gradually coming into service with the RFC and RNAS during April were three fighters designed and developed towards the end of 1916 which were to prove more than a match for the Albatros. The first was one of those brilliant departures from the mainstream of conventional design which occur every now and again. It was the Sopwith Triplane, first supplied to the RNAS and used by No. 1 Naval Squadron when it went into action in

support of the hard-pressed RFC. Its narrow-cord wings gave the pilot a good all-round view and at the same time the combined area of the three mainplanes gave enough lift to out-climb and out-turn the Albatros. It was also 15 mph faster, power being provided by the 110 hp Clerget rotary engine, later replaced with the 130 hp Clerget. It was the first Allied fighter to mount two synchronised machine-guns although these were only fitted to six of them. The rest had just the one Vickers gun. Its appearance came as a great shock to the Germans, especially on one of their first encounters when two Triplanes flown by Flight Commander R. S. Dallas and Flight Sub Lieutenant T. G. Culling attacked a formation of fourteen German two-seaters, shot down three and sent the rest scattering. Frantic efforts were begun by the leading German and Austro-Hungarian aircraft manufacturers to design a similar type of machine, resulting eventually in a host of experimental triplanes and even quadruplanes. Only 150 Sopwith Triplanes were built for at the end of 1917 they were exchanged for Sopwith Camels. But before that, between May and July 1917, the all-Canadian 'Black Flight' of No. 10 Naval Squadron, led by Flight Sub Lieutenant Raymond Collishaw and equipped with triplanes, claimed no less than eighty-seven enemy aircraft of which Collishaw shot down sixteen during a period of twenty-seven days.

The other two fighters marked a departure from the usual rotary engine, just as the Spad had done in the case of the French. The Bristol F.2A two-seater was powered by the first of the Rolls-Royce V-12 Falcon engines, giving 190 hp. A synchronised Vickers gun was mounted under the cowling, fired through a hole in the radiator, and the observer was equipped with a Lewis gun on a Scarff ring. The cockpits were close together, making for easy communication, and the pilot sat with his eyes level with the top wing which gave him an excellent view. The 'Brisfits' as they came to be known also began their operational career in April but far less auspiciously than the Sopwith Triplane. On one of the first patrols, led by Captain William Leefe Robinson who had won the VC for shooting down a Zeppelin over London in September 1916, six F.2As were attacked by Richthofen and four other Albatros D.3s from Douai. Richthofen himself shot down two, his comrades accounted for another two, including Robinson's, and of the two which managed to reach home one was badly damaged. The mistake had been to use the Bristol Fighter as a reconnaissance two-seater, staying rigidly in formation and relying on the observer to defend against any attacking machines. When it was realised how fast and

The wreck of a British R.E.8 brought down behind German lines.
Imperial War Museum

manoeuvrable the Brisfit really was, pilots began using it aggressively like a single-seater, with the additional advantage of a 'sting in the tail'. These tactics were highly successful and Captain A. E. McKeever, the Canadian ace of No. 11 Squadron, scored most of his thirty victories in an F.2A. A later model, the F.2B (51-55) was fitted with the 220 hp Falcon 2 and various other engines such as the Hispano-Suiza and carried two Lewis guns for the observer. Over 3,000 were built by the end of 1918 and a modified version continued in service with the Royal Air Force until 1932.

The third of the new fighters was the S.E.5, rivalling the Camel as the most successful British single-seat fighter of the war. It was the best of the designs to come out of the Royal Aircraft Factory at Farnborough, powered by the same 150 hp water-cooled Hispano-Suiza engine that was installed in the Spad. It also incorporated the first major advance made by the British to improve their earlier unreliable gun synchronising gear. A new hydraulic system, in which the firing impulse was transmitted simply by oil pressure in a pipe sealed by plungers at either end, was invented in 1916 by George Constantinesco, a Roumanian mining engineer, and Major G. C. Colley of the Royal Artillery. Known as the CC gear it did away with the complicated linkage of mechanical types and had the great advantage that it could be fitted easily and rapidly to any type of engine. The first airplanes to be fitted with it were the D.H.5s of No. 55 Squadron which arrived in France in March 1917. The D.H.5 (48) was another new fighter, a single-seat tractor biplane designed by Geoffrey

de Havilland to replace the D.H.2 pusher, but it was not very successful in air combat. Its unusual staggered wings, the top wing being set back over two feet, gave the pilot an excellent view forwards and upwards but not rearward, from which direction most attacks could be expected. It was highly manoeuvrable but had a poor performance above 10,000 feet, tended to lose height rapidly in combat, and was difficult to land. It performed best at low altitudes and was eventually used extensively for ground-strafing. The S.E.5 was a much better fighter, although some teething problems were experienced with the CC gear which fired the Vickers gun fixed to the port side of the fuselage with its breach inside the cockpit. It also carried a Lewis gun on a Foster mounting on the top wing which could be fired forwards or upwards, of the type Albert Ball had adopted on his Nieuport Scout. The modified S.E.5a (49) was powered first by a geared 200 hp Hispano-Suiza and eventually by the Wolsey W.4a 200 hp Viper, based on the French engine. It was the airplane flown in the last eighteen months of the war by the leading British aces, Mannock (73 victories), Bishop (72) and McCudden (57). Over 5,200 S.E.5s and 5as were built and it was second only to the Camel in the numbers of British fighters constructed during the war.

Against the superior performance of the best Allied fighters, although every airplane had its disadvantages as well as advantages so that only the Sopwith Triplane could match the Albatros D.3 at heights above 16,000 feet while the new Albatros C.5 and C.7 two-seaters could outperform an S.E.5 at 10,000 feet, the Germans had the

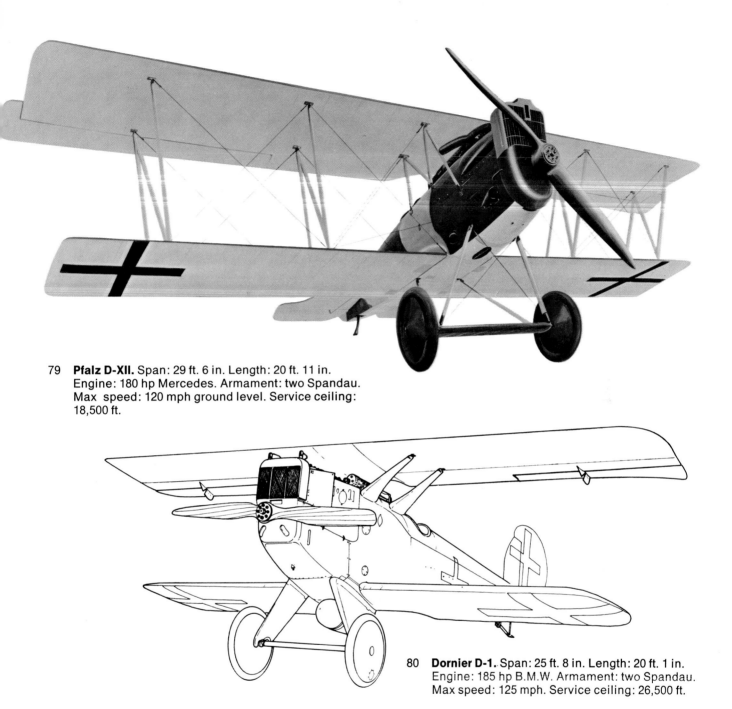

79 **Pfalz D-XII.** Span: 29 ft. 6 in. Length: 20 ft. 11 in.
Engine: 180 hp Mercedes. Armament: two Spandau.
Max speed: 120 mph ground level. Service ceiling:
18,500 ft.

80 **Dornier D-1.** Span: 25 ft. 8 in. Length: 20 ft. 1 in.
Engine: 185 hp B.M.W. Armament: two Spandau.
Max speed: 125 mph. Service ceiling: 26,500 ft.

benefit of many more targets to choose from as the Allies continued their work of observation with slower reconnaissance aircraft. Their rate of scoring was four or five times that of the RFC and on many occasions they simply avoided combat with Allied fighters, as when a force of Bristol Fighters and Sopwith Triplanes flying low over Douai failed to make Richthofen's *Jasta* 11 rise to the bait. This led to the adoption of a new policy by the German Air Service which took advantage of the more pressing reconnaissance needs of the Allies. Up until now it had been a time of the solitary hunter as the leading fighter pilots on both sides stalked the air for targets. But increasingly, the fighters began to hunt in packs. The first mass dogfights occurred towards the end of April when Richthofen led four *Jasta* units over the battle area and in one encounter with an offensive patrol of Triplanes, S.E.5s and F.E.2bs, six British aircraft were lost to five Germans. This concentration of German fighters enabled

the RFC machines attached to Army Corps to get on with their routine observation work with much less interference and their losses were never again as high as during 'bloody April'. But with the entry of the United States into the war that month it became Germany's policy to try to force a quick victory before the build-up of American manpower on the Western Front. In June it was decided to form four *Jasta* units, under Richthofen, into a self-contained *Jagdgeschwader* group that could be moved to whatever part of the Front where strategy required air supremacy at a particular time. Other groupings were made on a temporary basis for major offensives. The *Richthofen Jagdgeschwader* (J.G.1) was dubbed 'Richthofen's Circus' by the RFC as it toured up and down the Front as a mobile force of troubleshooters. Dogfights took place between scores of fighters as one side or another launched an attack on enemy reconnaissance or bombing aircraft and were themselves attacked by escorting

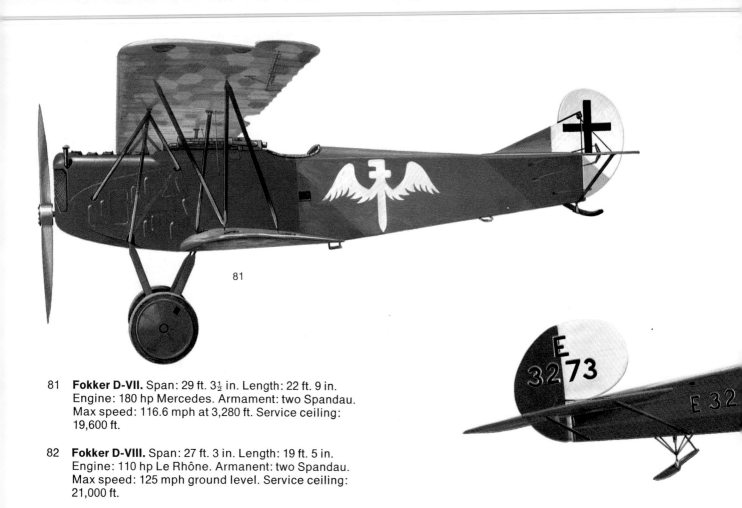

81

81 **Fokker D-VII.** Span: 29 ft. 3½ in. Length: 22 ft. 9 in. Engine: 180 hp Mercedes. Armament: two Spandau. Max speed: 116.6 mph at 3,280 ft. Service ceiling: 19,600 ft.

82 **Fokker D-VIII.** Span: 27 ft. 3 in. Length: 19 ft. 5 in. Engine: 110 hp Le Rhône. Armanent: two Spandau. Max speed: 125 mph ground level. Service ceiling: 21,000 ft.

fighters or others on offensive patrol. This as well as trench-strafing and other secondary tasks was to be the pattern of fighter operations for the rest of the war.

New fighters

The airplanes that were to take a major part in this final struggle were already coming into service or about to be introduced. As a result of attempts by German designers to find an answer to the Sopwith Triplane several designs of this kind were tried, such as the Pfalz Dr.1, but the only one that proved worthy of production was the Fokker Dr. 1

83

82

Triplane (61-64). It became renowned in the hands of some of the most expert German pilots, including the four leading aces, Richthofen (80 victories), Ernst Udet (62), Erich Loewenhardt (53) and Werner Voss (48), but was withdrawn in May 1918 and replaced by what was certainly the best German fighter of the war and possibly the finest of any, the Fokker D.7 (81) biplane. It was not particularly fast but had great manoeuvrability at high altitudes and was easy to fly. It had been the outright winner of a competition for single-seat fighters powered by the 160 hp

Mercedes engine and was notable for its cantilever wings which required no external bracing; the fact that N-struts were provided was more for the peace of mind of pilots who thought they should be there. Large numbers of this aircraft were ordered, built by Albatros as well as Fokker, and most of the *Jasta* units were equipped with them by the autumn of 1918. No less remarkable was the Fokker D.8 'parasol' type monoplane (82), the 'flying razor blade' as the British called it, powered by the 140 hp Oberursel rotary which again won a fighter contest in Germany and

83 **Avro 504 K (N/F).** Span: 36 ft. Length: 29 ft. 5 in. Engine: 110 hp Le Rhône. Armament: one Lewis. Max speed: 95 mph ground level. Service ceiling: 18,000 ft.

84 **Le Pere Lusac I.** Span: 41 ft 7 in. Length: 25 ft. 6 in. Engine: 400 hp Liberty R.A. Armament: two Hispano, two Lewis. Max speed: 132 mph at 2,000 ft. Service ceiling: 20,000 ft.

84

would have replaced the D.7 had the war lasted to the winter of 1918-19.

Much had been expected of the Albatros D.5 when it appeared in the summer of 1917 but it was found to be little better than its predecessor and the D.5a (57) version suffered badly from wing flutter. It was nevertheless ordered in large numbers and was still in operational use at the end of the war. A far better aircraft was the Pfalz D.12 biplane with two-bay interplane struts, introduced in 1918, but it was over-shadowed by the more manoeuvrable Fokker D.7 and only ordered in limited numbers. Other aircraft to see service before the end of the war were the L.F.G. Roland D.6b, the Simens-Schuckert D.3 (40) and D.4 with its eleven-cylinder contra-rotating rotary engine, the excellent Hannover and Halberstadt CL.2s (58) which were used primarily for trench-strafing, the first mass attack on British infantry taking place at the Battle of Cambrai in November 1917, and the Junkers CL.1 (76) which was a two-seater development of the D.1 all-metal fighter and also used for ground attack. Among the aircraft developed but not put into production was the Dornier D.1 (80) single-seat fighter of advanced design, built by a subsidiary of the Zeppelin company. No interplane struts were fitted and the fuselage and most of the cantilever wings were constructed of duralumin spars covered by a metal skin. Too many new ideas were incorporated for it to be considered safe, and in fact during a test by Wilhelm Reinhard, leader of the 'Richthofen Circus' after Richthofen's death on April 21st 1918, the wings broke at a height of 3,000 feet and Reinhard was fatally injured in the subsequent crash.

In mid-1917 the Italians began to produce their own fighter aircraft. First was the Ansaldo A.1 single-seat biplane, powered by the 220 hp SPA 6A engine. Its speed of 137.5 mph made it one of the fastest aircraft of that time but its heavy engine and short wing-span caused it to lack the manoeuvrability of the agile Hanriot HD.1. Only a limited number saw service from mid-1918 onwards. Much more successful was the Ansaldo S.V.A.5 (73), powered by the same engine, which early in 1918 was used for long-distance escort and strategic reconnaissance. Its even faster speed of 143.5 mph enabled it to shake off enemy fighters and it was also used in bombing raids. A third type, the Macchi M.5 single-seat fighter flying-boat was inspired by the success of the Austrian Hansa-Brandenburg seaplanes. Powered by the 160 hp Isotta-Fraschini V4B engine it had a speed of 118 mph and was used primarily for escorting bombers.

The first Austrian-built fighter had been the Austrian-Aviatik D.1 (36), known as the 'Berg Scout' and brought into service early in 1917. It was used until the end of the war, armed first with a single 8-mm belt-fed Schwarzlose gun mounted in front of the cockpit to fire forwards above the propeller arc and later by twin synchronised guns on either side of the engine. Towards the end of 1917, when it became apparent that the Hansa-Brandenburg D.1 single-seat fighter built by Phoenix could not accommodate the more powerful 200 hp Austro-Daimler engine, a new machine was designed which became the prototype Phoenix D.1. Production models had the 200 hp Hiero engine, increased to 230 hp in the D.3 type (39) which was introduced early in 1918. But in many ways the most successful Austrian designs were the Hansa-Brandenburg fighter flying-boats and seaplanes, culminating in an entirely new type of two-seater low-wing monoplane, the W.29 (78), designed by Heinkel at the end of 1917. It was heavily armed with twin synchronised Spandau guns and a Parabellum gun on a ring mounting for the observer and

with a speed of 110 mph, provided by the 195 hp Benz engine, was very effective with the German Naval Air Service against British flying-boats over the North Sea in the summer of 1918. A larger version was ordered in 1918, the W.33 with the 260 hp Mercedes engine.

Developments in France were primarily concerned with improving existing types of fighter. The Spad S.13 (68-72) was a larger and more powerful version of the S.7, with a speed of 130 mph provided by Hispano-Suiza engines of 200 to 235 hp. It replaced the S.7 during the summer and autumn of 1917 and became the standard French single-seat fighter. It was the first French machine to mount twin synchronised machine-guns and in one version, the S.12, a 37-mm Puteaux shell gun (*moteur-canon*), modified so that it could be loaded with one hand in flight, was mounted between the cylinder blocks of the engine to fire through the hollow airscrew shaft. A single Vickers machine-gun enabled the pilot to give a preliminary sighting burst. The shell gun was not widely used because of its excessive vibration and the degree of marksmanship demanded of a single-shot rate of fire but both Fonck and Guynemer shot down a number of enemy aircraft with it. Some 8,500 S.13s were constructed and it was also purchased by the United States, equipping sixteen pursuit squadrons of the American Expeditionary Force by the end of the war, and by Italy which had eleven squadrons equipped with this type. Several examples of an even later type, the S.17 which was produced in the autumn of 1918 with the 300 hp Hispano engine, were flown by the Stork Group. The Nieuport, still powered by the Le Rhône rotary engine, was improved with the better streamlined Types 24 and 27 (56). These were the last of the Nieuport vee-strutters and some pilots even preferred them to the Spad, including Charles Nungesser, the third highest-scoring French ace with forty-five victories. They were also flown by the British, American and Italian air forces. A new type produced early in 1918, the Nieuport 28 C-1 (74), marked a radical change from the usual sesquiplane design. It had the more orthodox two spars and staggered wings, the lower one carrying the ailerons. Power was provided by the 160 hp Gnôme-Rhône *Monosoupape* 9N rotary. Although limited numbers were flown by the French it was better known as the machine which equipped the first American fighter squadrons, for whom some 300 were purchased. Captain Edward Rickenbacker, the top American ace, scored a number of his twenty-six victories in the Nieuport 28 which, although it tended to shed fabric from its wings when dived too steeply and was later replaced by the stronger Spad S.13, was one of the most attractive-looking aircraft of the war. With the Nieuport-Delage 29, designed in 1918, an even greater change was made by installing the 300 hp Hispano-Suiza stationary engine in place of the rotary. It was manoeuvrable and very fast with a top speed of 147.5 mph but the Armistice was signed before it came into service. The only other new fighter used by the French during this period was the improved Morane-Saulnier A.1 single-seat parasol monoplane (66) with an incredible complexity of struts between wing and fuselage to provide the necessary strength for combat manoeuvres. It was delivered towards the end of 1917 but withdrawn from the Front in March 1918 and served as an advanced trainer for the French and American air forces.

After a slow start the British aircraft industry had made great progress during the war and produced some of the best fighters flying in the last eighteen months. The most famous of these was the Sopwith Camel (50), brought into service in July 1917 as a successor to the Pup and the first British airplane to carry twin Vickers machine-guns, their breeches being carried in a hump that gave the aircraft its name. The torque effect of its big rotary engine, either the 110 hp Le Rhône, 150 hp B.R.1, 130 hp Clerget or the 100 hp *Monosoupape* Gnôme, on a short and compact body made it probably the most manoeuvrable aircraft ever built and in the hands of an experienced pilot it could out-perform any of its contemporaries. It accounted for 1,294 enemy machines from the time of its intro-. duction to the end of the war, more victories in combat than any other single type. On the other hand it was difficult for a beginner to fly, tending to spin in a tight turn if not corrected in time, and the casualty rate of pilots training with Camels was very high. The standard Camel was the F.1. A number of these were used for night flying, specially modified when it was found the pilots became blinded by flashes from the guns; the pilot was seated further aft and instead of synchronised guns, twin Lewis guns on a Foster mounting were placed above the centre section of the top wing from where they could be pulled down for reloading. Night flying was instituted at the end of 1917 when the Germans, having been defeated in their daylight bombing raids on Britain by anti-aircraft guns and S.E.5 and Sopwith Pup fighters, turned to night bombing. The Camels were the first single-seat fighters to fly at night and two of them at the end of January 1918 scored the first victory in night combat between airplanes by shooting down a Gotha bomber. With the increasing variety of uses to which fighters were being employed, a

2F.1 version of the Camel with a shorter wing-span and detachable rear fuselage was specially designed for launching from ships. This technique had been pioneered by the United States before the war but was most widely developed by the Royal Navy. Altogether 5,490 Camels were built, the largest number of any British fighter.

Sopwith's next design, the 5F.1 Dolphin, was built around a stationary engine, the 200 hp geared Hispano-Suiza. Although it was very fast, up to 140 mph, and carried two Lewis guns on the centre section of the top wing in addition to its twin synchronised guns, it was not very successful in air combat and was used mostly for ground-attack duty. From late 1917 onwards this became an increasing activity of fighter units on both sides. Flying very low to strafe the trenches brought much harrassment to the already hard-pressed infantry but it was also dangerous work, causing casualty rates that were often as high as 30 per cent. Machines such as the Camels and Halberstadts were fitted with armour plating under their

An early production line – Sopwith TF.2 Salamanders under construction, showing their 230 hp Bentley Rotary engines and two fixed Vickers machine-guns, synchronised to fire between the propeller blades. Developed from the Sopwith Snipe for the specific purpose of ground-attack duties, the Salamander was fitted with 650 lbs of armour plating. It arrived too late however to see operational service before the war ended.
Flight International

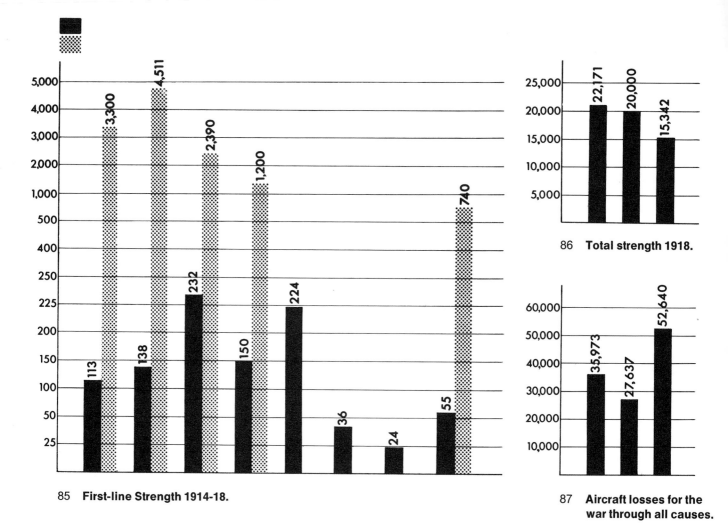

85   **First-line Strength 1914-18.**

86   **Total strength 1918.**

87   **Aircraft losses for the war through all causes.**

bellies to give additional protection to the pilot and engine and were sometimes armed with machine-guns fixed to fire downwards through the floor of the fuselage. It became obvious that armoured fighters would have to be specially designed for this purpose, one result being the Sopwith TF.2 (Trench Fighter) Salamander which was brought out in April 1918 at about the time when the Royal Air Force was formed, the world's first independent air force. The Salamander's standard armament was twin Vickers synchronised guns, carrying 2,000 rounds of ammunition, but on one experimental machine no less than eight machine-guns were fitted, directed downwards to fire through the cockpit floor. A decision was made to manufacture the Salamander in quantity in both Britain and France but the war ended before more than a handful had reached the Front. The Salamander was similar in many respects to the airplane that was generally recognised as the best all-round Allied fighter in use at the end of the war, the Sopwith 7F.1 Snipe (75). This had been specially designed to take the new 230 hp Bentley rotary engine, the B.R.2, and after extensive modifications to prototype machines it began entering service in the summer of 1918 with both the R.A.F. and Australian Flying Corps. It was not particularly fast but more than made up for this by its rate of climb, strength and maneouvrability. Another excellent single-seat fighter was the Martinsyde Buzzard, the F.3 with the 275 hp Falcon engine and the F.4 with the 300 hp Hispano-Suiza, which saw limited service towards the end of 1918 and was intended for use as a long-range escort. It was in fact faster than the Snipe but there was no place for it in the

R.A.F. after the Snipe was chosen as the standard post-war British fighter. The Martinsyde company closed down. The fastest of all the fighters built before the end of the war was the British Nieuport Nighthawk, designed by H. P. Folland to take the new 320 hp A.B.C. Dragonfly radial engine. Its top speed at ground-level was 151 mph and it also possessed great manoeuvrability. But the engine of which so much had been expected was found to be unreliable and although a few Nighthawks were produced before the 11,000-order programme was cancelled, the war ended before they were used operationally.

By the time the United States entered the war in April 1917, it was apparent that the country which had pioneered the airplane had fallen far behind Europe in military aviation. None of the fifty-odd aircraft operational with the Aviation Section of the U.S. Army were remotely suitable for air combat. It was decided that the U.S. would concentrate on building training airplanes and purchase combat types from the Allies, mainly France, which provided 4,881 machines together with 258 British and nineteen Italian. A massive programme was begun to expand the Aviation Section but the initial proposals were much too ambitious and in the event there were only forty-five American combat squadrons operational by the end of the war with a first-line strength of 740 airplanes, mostly Spads and Nieuports as far as fighters were concerned, compared with 4,511 French, 3,300 British, and 2,390 German. Nevertheless, from a state of complete unpreparedness, the Aviation Section was able to put a well-trained force into battle that was the equal in combat of any other;

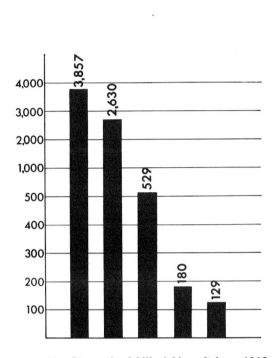

88   **Strength of Allied Aircraft June 1918.**

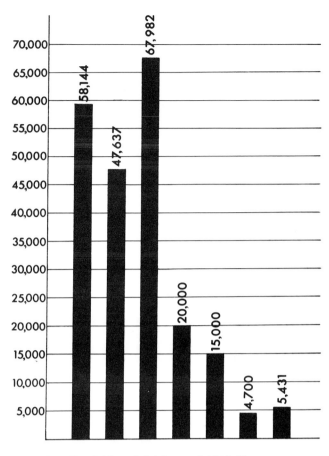

89   **Total Aircraft (airframes) 1914-18.**

American pilots accounted for 781 enemy aircraft destroyed against their own losses of 289, an impressive success ratio of nearly three to one.

In the field of design the U.S. was fortunate in having the excellent V-12 Liberty aero-engine (102), designed by the Packard Motor Car company in 1917, which at 400 hp was one of the biggest power units then available. This was installed in the prototype of a two-seater fighter biplane, the Le Pere Lusac 2 (84), completed by the company in mid-1918 to designs provided by *Capitaine* G. Le Pere, an aeronautical engineer on loan from the French government. It was heavily armed with twin Marlin synchronised machine-guns and twin Lewis guns on a Scarff ring for the observer. Its strength and manoeuvrability, combined with a fast speed of 132 mph, would have made it a formidable fighting machine had the war not ended while it was still undergoing service trials. The Liberty engine was also installed in the only Allied combat airplane to be built in quantity in America, the British D.H.4 day bomber which was the best of its kind to be produced in the war. Nearly 5,000 of these were built in the U.S., of which 1,440 had been shipped to France up to the time of the Armistice. Most of them were supplied by the Standard Aircraft Corporation which also built its own training aircraft such as the single-seat Standard E.1 biplane. A better machine of this kind was the rotary-engined Thomas-Morse Scout (67), built by the company founded by an Englishman who had emigrated to the U.S., which was also used as an advanced fighter trainer as well as being converted into a seaplane for use by the U.S. Navy.

Final victory

The fighter airplane had come a long way in the four years of its development which had seen experiments with an astonishing variety of types. With a few exceptions such as the triplanes and experimental all-metal mono-planes a standard single-seat type had evolved which was in service with all the major powers during the last year of the war. This was a tractor biplane with open cockpit, fixed undercarriage and synchronised forward-firing guns, and it was to remain the standard configuration until the mid-1930s with only gradual improvements in performance resulting from the development of more powerful engines and a switch from fabric-covered construction to plywood and finally to metal. In two-seat fighter design, pioneered by the Sopwith 1½-Strutter, followed by the Halberstadt CL.2, the first German aircraft of this type, and reaching its peak with the Bristol Fighter, the main problem for the designers was to provide the rear gunner with the least possible obstruction to his field of fire. This led to more variations in design than for the single-seater. In the Bristol for instance the top line of the fuselage was swept down and the fin and rudder placed partly below the fuselage to give the gunner a better view. The Hannover CL.2 had a biplane tail unit while the all-metal Junkers CL.1, best of the German two-seaters which came out in the last months of the war, had a single thick-sectioned cantilever wing so there was no top wing to obstruct the view and the tail unit was also of cantilever type, requiring

1

2

3

4

9

10

11

12

Aces of the First World War

British

1. Major Edward Mannock, VC, DSO & Bars, MC & Bar; Britain's top-scorer with 73 victories, mostly with S.E.5s; born Aldershot, May 24th, 1887, killed in action July 26th, 1918. *Imperial War Museum*

2. Lieutenant-Colonel William A. Bishop, VC, DSO & Bar, MC, DFC, *L. d'H, C. de G;* 72 victories; born Ontario, Canada, February 8th, 1894, died September 11th, 1956; awarded the Victoria Cross for a single-handed attack in a Nieuport 17 on a German aerodrome during which he shot down three enemy aircraft. *Imperial War Museum*

3. Lieutenant-Colonel Raymond Collishaw, DSO & Bar, DSC, DFC, *C. de G;* 60 victories of which 40 were scored in the Royal Naval Air Service where he was the leading naval ace; born British Columbia, Canada, November 22nd, 1893; also served with distinction in Second World War. *Imperial War Museum*

4. Major James T. B. McCudden, VC, DSO & Bar, MC & Bar, MM, *C. de G;* 57 victories; joined Royal Flying Corps as an air mechanic and was with first unit to arrive in France in 1914; died in an air accident July 9th, 1918. *Imperial War Museum*

5. Captain Anthony W. Beauchamp-Proctor, VC, DSO, MC & Bar, DFC; 54 victories; born in South Africa and joined RFC in 1917; died in an air accident June 21st, 1921. *Imperial War Museum*

6. Flight Sub Lieutenant R. A. J. Warneford, VC; received that award while serving with the RNAS for destroying the first Zeppelin in air combat, on June 7th, 1915. *Imperial War Museum*

7. Major Lanoe G. Hawker, VC, DSO; on July 25th, 1915 forced down three German two-seaters armed with machine-guns during a single evening patrol, although his Bristol Scout was only fitted with a single-shot carbine. *Imperial War Museum*

German

8. Rittmeister (Cavalry Captain) Manfred Freiherr von Richthofen, 'The Red Baron'; leading ace of the war with 80 victories, mostly with Albatros Ds and Fokker Triplanes; born 1892, killed in action April 21st 1918; awarded *Ordre Pour le Mérité* in January 1917; seen here in hospital at Courtrai after being wounded on July 6th, 1917. *Imperial War Museum*

6

7

8

14

15

9. Manfred Richthofen (centre) with pilots of his pursuit flight in *Jasta 11*; left to right – Vizefeldwebel Sebastian Festner (12 victories), Leutnant Karl Schaefer (30), Oberleutnant Lothar von Richthofen (40), and Oberleutnant Kurt Wolff (33). *Imperial War Museum*

10. Oberleutnant Ernst Udet in a Fokker D.VII biplane when he commanded No. 4 Fighter Flight of Richthofen's squadron; 62 victories; awarded *P. le M*. June, 1918; committed suicide November 17th, 1941. *Imperial War Museum*

11. Hauptmann Oswald Boelcke; 40 victories; born May 9th, 1891, killed in air collision October 28th, 1916; awarded *P. le M*. January, 1916; commanded *Jasta 2* which was later named after him and devised many combat tactics used not only in the First but also the Second World War. *Imperial War Museum*

12. Oberleutnant Max Immelmann, 'Eagle of Lille'; 41 victories, mostly with Fokker monoplane; born September 21st, 1890, killed in action June 18th, 1916; awarded *P. le M*. January 1916; seen here beside the wreckage of his seventh victim. *Imperial War Museum*

13. Left to right – Hauptmann Bruno Loerzer (41 victories); Anthony Fokker; Oberleutnant Hermann Goering (22 victories). Both Loerzer and Goering were awarded the *P. le M*. Goering commanded Richthofen's famous formation, *J.G.1*, from July 1918 to the end of the war. *Imperial War Museum*

French

14. Capitaine Georges Guynemer, *L. d'H, MM, C. de G;* second highest-scoring French ace after Fonck with 54 victories; born December 24th, 1894, killed in action September 11th, 1917. *Imperial War Museum*

15. Lieutenant Charles Nungesser, *L. d'H, MM, C. de G;* 45 victories; born March 15th, 1892, lost in flight May 8th, 1927. *Imperial War Museum*

American

16. Left to right – Lieutenant Douglas Campbell and Lieutenant Alan Winslow, who on April 14th, 1918 became the first American pilots to shoot down enemy aircraft. Each scored a victory within seconds of one another, although Campbell had the distinction of being first. He had six victories to his credit when he was wounded in June 1918, which ended his combat career. *Imperial War Museum*

90

94

The Heraldry of the Air

90 The famous hat in the ring—
    94th Aero Squadron
    (USA).

91 Insignia of Lt. Charles
    Nungesser (France).

92 The German 'Ordre pour
    le Merite' (The Blue Max).

93 Motif on Fokker D-VII flown
    by Georg von Hantelmann
    of Jasta 15/JGII (Germany).

94 The Escadrille Lafayette
    (USA).

95 70 Squadriglia Caccia
    (Italy).

96 The French Escadrille.

97 The Victoria Cross.

91

95

92

96

93

97

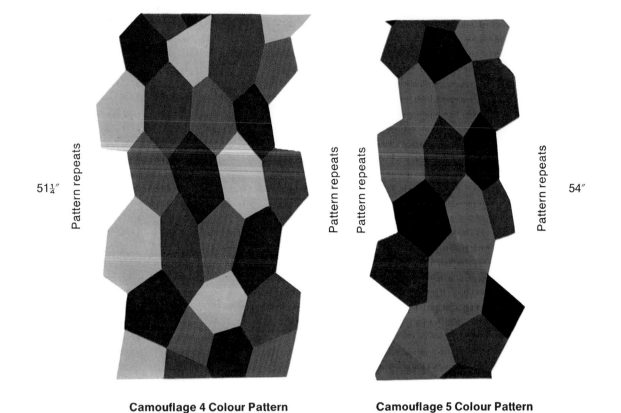

Camouflage 4 Colour Pattern

$51\frac{1}{4}''$ Pattern repeats

Camouflage 5 Colour Pattern

Pattern repeats   Pattern repeats   Pattern repeats $54''$

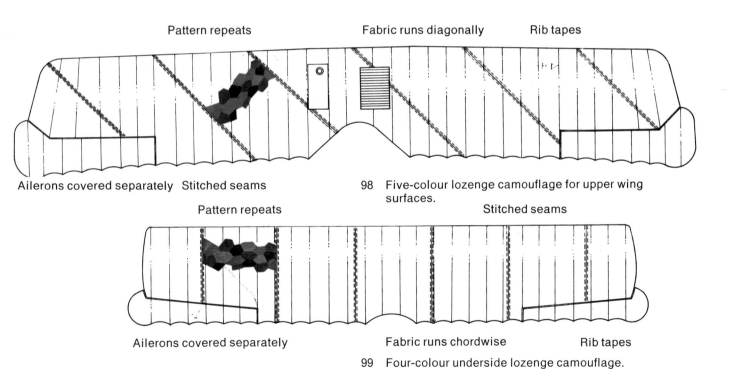

Pattern repeats   Fabric runs diagonally   Rib tapes

Ailerons covered separately   Stitched seams

98   Five-colour lozenge camouflage for upper wing surfaces.

Pattern repeats   Stitched seams

Ailerons covered separately   Fabric runs chordwise   Rib tapes

99   Four-colour underside lozenge camouflage.

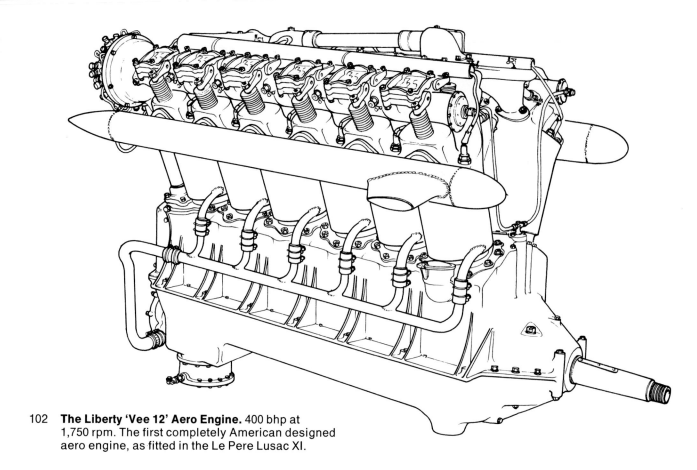

102 **The Liberty 'Vee 12' Aero Engine.** 400 bhp at 1,750 rpm. The first completely American designed aero engine, as fitted in the Le Pere Lusac XI.

103 **The Mercedes 'in line 6' Aero Engine.** 180 bhp at 1,400 rpm as fitted to such famous aircraft as the Fokker D-VII and the Albatross D-V series.

no external bracing. In the case of the Hansa-Brandenburg monoplane and biplane seaplanes on the other hand, the problem was resolved by having no upright fin at all. The rear fuselage was made very deep to compensate for this while the rudder was mounted below the top line of the fuselage.

The average single and two-seat fighter of 1918 was powered by an engine of around 220 hp giving it a top speed of about 130 mph and a ceiling of up to 20,000 feet. Although rotary and radial engines continued to power many Allied aircraft, the water-cooled stationary engine, always preferred by the Germans, had found increasing favour. It was relatively heavier but its long clean shape enabled the nose of an aircraft to be made of very good streamline form and the trend was for airframes to be designed around a selected engine. In fact the engines of many aircraft were more expensive than the airframe; thus the cost of a Sopwith Camel airframe was £874 compared with the £907 cost of the 130 hp Clerget to power it. The main difference was that the British and French tended to concentrate on the Vee-type configuration with eight or twelve cylinders, following the lines of the Hispano-Suiza, while the Germans did not develop a Vee at all but based their efforts on six in-line cylinder designs by Mercedes and others.

By 1918 all fighters were armed with at least two forward-firing synchronised machine-guns with greatly increased rates of fire. The Italian dual-mounted 9-mm Villa Perosa invented by Major Revelli and introduced in 1917 could fire 1,500 rounds a minute from each gun. A Siemens motor gun, in which a large number of Gatling-style barrels mounted on a rotor were driven round at high speed by the engine, was fitted experimentally to a German fighter and estimated to have a maximum firing

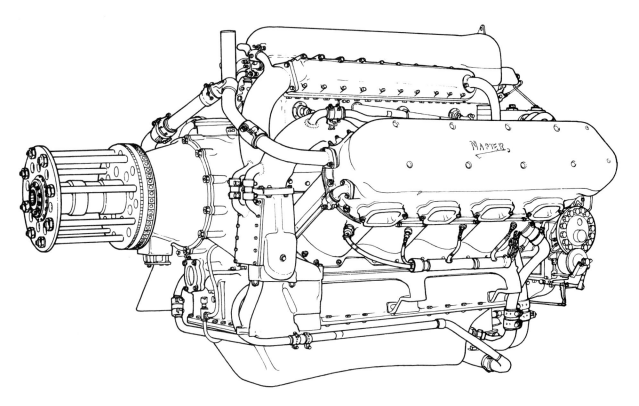

104 **The Napier 'Lion'** 12 cylinder, triple bank, aero engine, 450 bhp at 1,925 rpm. As being developed at the end of the 1914-18 war.

rate of 7,200 rounds a minute. The Germans also developed two 20-mm aircraft guns, the Becker and Skakatz, a few of which were installed in twin-engined airplanes. The United States produced the .30-inch Marlin gas-operated aircraft gun, a modification of the Colt-Browning, which replaced the Vickers gun on the American-built D.H.4s and was also used by a number of American fighter squadrons in service at the Front while also from the U.S. came the Davis-type recoilless gun which was fitted to some British bombers and flying boats. The gun's recoil was offset by the simultaneous discharge of a blank round in the opposite direction. The French employed the 37-mm Puteaux shell gun to a limited extent and in 1918 devised a short-barrelled cannon which fired a cartridge containing thirty-two spherical bullets through the airscrew hub. This would have been highly effective at short range but the war ended before it could be issued to squadrons. In Britain experiments were carried out with the 37-mm Hotchkiss single-shot gun and also with one-pounders; the Armstrong-Whitworth, C.O.W. (Coventry Ordnance Works) and Vickers pom-pom, the last of which was used in action for night attacks on ground targets by several F.E.2bs. The tracer bullet had already been developed in Britain before the war and was in general use on both sides while incendiary and explosive bullets were invented for attacks against air ships and balloons. In the last year of the war it was common to carry a mixture of ball ammunition in various sequences of tracer, armour-piercing and incendiary which were repeated to the end of the belt. Rockets were tried on a number of British and French fighters but became obsolete with the development of more effective incendiary ammunition.

The spring and summer of 1918 saw the greatest air battles of all as first the Germans launched their great offensive in

March and then, when that failed, the Allies counter-attacked in July and August using trench-strafing fighters to support infantry and tank assaults. It was not unusual for over one hundred aircraft to take part in the first really full-scale air battles of the war, with each side losing as many as thirty aircraft a day. But by now the Germans were greatly outnumbered, their first-line strength of about 2,390 aircraft facing some 10,000 of the Allies, vastly different from the situation at the beginning of the war when the Germans had nearly twice as many aircraft as the British and French put together. In total number of fighters the Allies possessed nearly ten times as many as the German Air Service. Even though the best of the German fighters were a match for any others, there were too few of them to affect the final outcome. They were fighting a losing battle in the air as were the German armies on the ground. For the first time in any war, air superiority had become a deciding factor. Reconnaissance played a vital part in the struggle, bombing less so although it had pointed the way to the future. Fighters themselves were used for many other duties such as ground attack but their primary function was clear, that of securing control of essential air spaces by destroying all enemy aircraft operating there, whatever type they might be and for whatever purpose they were being used. It was equally clear that in future wars, victory would be dependent on achieving such control. The means of doing so would lead to the development of many specialised fighter types, equipped for day and night flying, long-range bomber escort, fighter reconnaissance, using bombs as well as guns. They would be adapted to operate from the decks of naval craft, fitted with floats and skis, and launched from other aircraft. All these developments were conceived and first tried in one form or another during the course of the First World War.

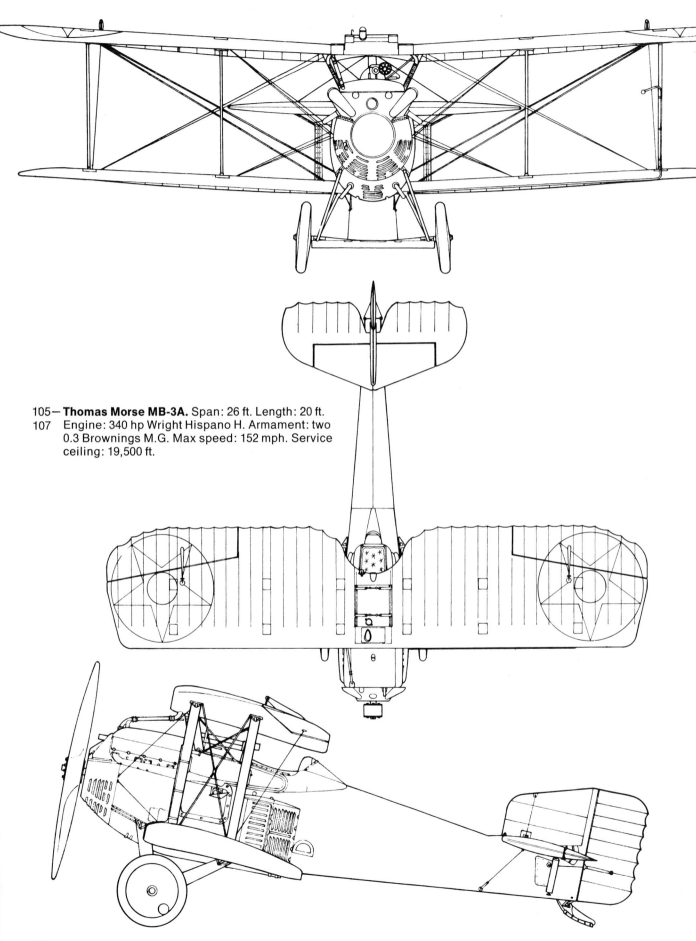

105— **Thomas Morse MB-3A.** Span: 26 ft. Length: 20 ft.
107 Engine: 340 hp Wright Hispano H. Armament: two
     0.3 Brownings M.G. Max speed: 152 mph. Service
     ceiling: 19,500 ft.

American Development

The United States got off to a very slow start in military aviation as a result of the niggardly sums of money allocated to development by the American government. When the First World War broke out in 1914 the U.S. Army had no more than twenty operational aircraft and a few dozen trained pilots. This situation had not greatly improved by the time the U.S. entered the war in 1917 and it was much to the credit of the American flying services that they achieved what they did from such an inauspicious beginning. No airplane of original American design took part in the fighting in France, although flying-boats designed by Glen Curtiss were used by Britain's Royal Naval Air Service for anti-submarine duties. During the period between the two world wars, however, America developed some notable fighter aircraft both for land and carrier-based operations that were to lead to even greater developments in the Second World War. In the early 1930s it was America which led the way in changing over to modern monoplane design for combat aircraft.

In 1918 the policy of using foreign designs to equip the U.S. Army Air Corps was reversed and a number of American companies were invited to submit designs for a single-seat fighter of better performance than the French Spad S.7s which were then in general use with American squadrons. One of these companies was the Thomas Morse Aircraft Corporation which was already producing a series of biplane scouts, used as advanced trainers as well as being converted into a seaplane for the U.S. Navy. The Thomas-Morse MB-3 (105–107) became the first American single-seat fighter to be taken into service. It strongly resembled the Spad with a 300 hp Wright 'H' engine based on the Hispano-Suiza and in the early 1920s was accepted as the standard pursuit single-seater for the Army Air Corps. But for the greater part of the 1920s and 1930s, the responsibility for American fighter design was largely in the hands of the Curtiss and Boeing companies.

The Curtiss company had already become involved in fighter production when it was chosen to build the British-designed S.E.5a, but in the event only one was completed. Meanwhile the Army Engineering Division had been working on its own designs, resulting in the appearance in January 1919 of a conventional biplane, the Orenco D, which was in fact the first single-seat fighter of U.S. design. Curtiss was given the contract to produce a limited number of these but they did not enter service as the decision had been made to take the MB-3 instead. It was not a very impressive start for Curtiss but its own version of the Orenco, powered by a 330 hp Wright-Hispano engine, was notable as being one of the first aircraft to fit an experimental exhaust-driven turbo-supercharger in place of the more common mechanically-driven superchargers. Curtiss then went on to build a number of small biplane fighters designed by the Naval Aircraft Factory for service on board America's first aircraft carrier, the USS *Langley*, commissioned in March 1922. Naval aviation had had its beginning as far back as November 1910 when an American pilot, Eugene Ely, took off in a Curtiss biplane from a wooden platform built over the fore-deck of the cruiser *Birmingham* while at anchor, and in January of the following year he also made the first landing on a ship, the USS *Pennsylvania*. But for many years after the introduction of aircraft carriers, ship-borne aircraft were inferior than those designed for land use because of the need for folding wings, arrester gear, and other special equipment which increased both weight and drag.

It was not until 1924 that a fighter of Curtiss's own design appeared. This was the PW-8 (108), first of the Curtiss single-seat fighters which resulted in the famous Hawk line, which with a top speed of 165 mph distinguished itself by making the first coast-to-coast flight across the United States within the hours of daylight. Designed around the 435 hp Curtiss D-12 water-cooled in-line engine, the PW-8 had a conventional welded steel-tube fuselage and wooden two-bay wings but was distinctive for its radiators which formed part of the wing surface. Armament consisted of one .30-inch and one .50-inch machine-gun under the engine cowl which became common on most American fighters of the period. One of the original test aircraft was modified to have a tunnel-type radiator fitted under the nose and tapered planform wings and this version in 1925 became the Curtiss P-1 Hawk (109), first of the new pursuit (P) category for fighters instituted by the Army Air Corps. The Hawk was also ordered by the U.S. Navy, only with an air-cooled radial engine instead which was better suited to carrier operations and with the designation F6C (112) since the Navy preferred the term fighter to pursuit and believed in giving credit to the manufacturer. Production models of the Curtiss Hawk, fitted with a variety of Wright, Curtiss and Pratt & Whitney engines, were widely used by the Army and Navy up until the mid-1930s. The last development in the series was the P-6, in which ethylene glycol was used instead of water in the cooling system and enabled the radiator for the new Curtiss Conqueror V-1570 engine to be made smaller. The final P-6E with a new metal fuselage, delivered in 1932, achieved 220 mph at 15,000 feet. It was the last biplane fighter procured by the Army Air Corps. A separate development for the U.S. Marine Corps, which in 1927 sought a two-seat fighter also capable of observation and light bombing roles, resulted in the Curtiss F8C which carried four .30-inch machine-guns, two in the lower wings and two in the rear cockpit. But it was as a dive-bomber, first of the famous Helldivers, that it became best known.

One of the most historic and certainly unusual Curtiss types produced in this period was the F9C Sparrowhawk (110), designed as a parasite fighter to be carried by the U.S. Navy's airships *Akron* and *Macon*. At a time when the argument between heavier or lighter-than-air craft was still largely unresolved, massive Zeppelin-type airships were still being built by Germany, Britain, France, the United States and Italy. During the First World War they had been superseded by aircraft for bombing missions over land, so vulnerable were they to fire from fighters and anti-aircraft guns, but they had done excellent work at sea on observation and anti-submarine patrols. In 1929 the U.S. Navy designed the *Akron* and *Macon*, both 785 feet long and powered by eight 580 hp Maybach engines, which were intended as the first of a marine fleet of airships to serve in a reconnaissance early-warning role. The need to defend airships from attack was already apparent and it was decided that they should carry small single-seat fighters which could be launched from a hangar in the mother ships and also taken back again by means of a power-operated trapeze which would hook on to a mounting above the fuselage. A number of aircraft were evaluated for this purpose in a design competition and the Curtiss F9C, powered by the Wright R-975 close-cowled radial engine and armed with two forward-firing guns, was eventually chosen. Eight of these fighters were built and in June 1932 began a series of hook-on tests with the *Akron* unit. Over one hundred successful contacts were made during the evaluation trials and the airplanes remained with *Akron* until she crashed ten months later. They were then transferred to the *Macon* and operated successfully for two years with-

108

108 **Curtiss PW-5.** Span: 32 ft. 6 in. Length: 22 ft. 6 in.
Engine: 420 hp Curtiss D–12. Armament: two 0.3
M.G. Max speed: 127 mph. Service ceiling: 21,700 ft.

109

111

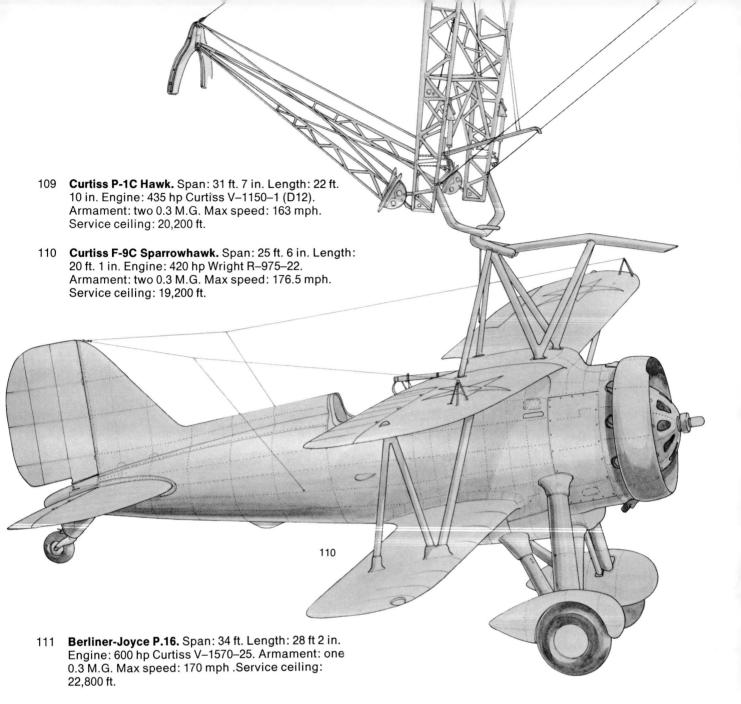

109 **Curtiss P-1C Hawk.** Span: 31 ft. 7 in. Length: 22 ft. 10 in. Engine: 435 hp Curtiss V–1150–1 (D12). Armament: two 0.3 M.G. Max speed: 163 mph. Service ceiling: 20,200 ft.

110 **Curtiss F-9C Sparrowhawk.** Span: 25 ft. 6 in. Length: 20 ft. 1 in. Engine: 420 hp Wright R–975–22. Armament: two 0.3 M.G. Max speed: 176.5 mph. Service ceiling: 19,200 ft.

111 **Berliner-Joyce P.16.** Span: 34 ft. Length: 28 ft 2 in. Engine: 600 hp Curtiss V–1570–25. Armament: one 0.3 M.G. Max speed: 170 mph .Service ceiling: 22,800 ft.

out serious accident until she too was lost in February 1935 with four of the F9Cs on board. This ended the experiment with parasite fighters, and indeed any further American development of rigid airships.

Continuing to develop a series of multi-purpose aircraft for use on board aircraft carriers, in 1932 Curtiss produced the F11C Goshawk, a single-seat fighter that could also carry small bombs under its wings. Most of the previous naval aircraft had been two-seaters since it was felt that the pilot should have a navigator with him, the problem being that their base might have moved a considerable distance by the time they came to find their way back to it. But this attitude gradually changed with the need for fast single-seat fighters that were comparable in performance to those operating on land. The Goshawk was a conventional biplane, developed from the F6C and the Army's P–6E Hawk, and the last version in 1934 was in fact the last of the Curtiss biplanes to serve with the U.S. Navy. One notable feature was its retractable undercarriage which made it easier to ditch in an emergency and lessened drag

in the air, thus increasing its top speed by 25 mph to 225 mph. The wheels retracted into the sides of the fuselage but in the case of the P–36 monoplane which Curtiss produced in 1935, also with a retractable undercarriage, the wheels retracted outwards to lie flush with the wings.

The decision to design a monoplane single-seat fighter was taken by the Curtiss-Wright Corporation when it was apparent that the Hawk biplane series could not be developed further. The prototype P–36 was a sturdy low-wing monoplane with an enclosed cockpit for the pilot and powered by the experimental 900 hp Wright R–1670 two-row radial engine. It was submitted for a design competition in May 1935 and various modifications were made over the next three years until it was eventually put into production in 1938. These developments, together with the Curtiss Hawk 75 export version for which the original name was revived, are dealt with in a later chapter.

Meanwhile the Boeing company had also been producing excellent military aircraft, starting with its first single-seat

112

113

114

112 **Curtiss P-6E Hawk.** Span: 31 ft. 6 in. Length: 23 ft. 2 in. Engine: 600 hp Curtiss V–1570–23. Armament: two 0.3 M.G. Max speed: 197 mph. Service ceiling: 24,700 ft.

113 **Boeing P-26A Peashooter.** Span: 27 ft. Length: 23 ft. 10 in. Engine: 600 hp Pratt & Whitney R–1340–27. Armament: two 0.3 *or* one 0.3 and one 0.5 M.G. Max speed: 234 mph. Service ceiling: 27,400 ft.

114 **Grumman F3F-1.** Span: 32 ft. Length: 23 ft. 3 in. Engine: 700 hp Pratt & Whitney R–1535–84. Armament: one .5 Browning, one .3 Browning. Max speed: 231 mph. Service ceiling: 28,500 ft.

115 **Boeing F-4B4.** Span: 30 ft. Length: 20 ft. 5 in. Engine: 550 hp Pratt & Whitney R1340–16. Armament: two .3 *or* one .3 and one .5 M.G. Max speed: 188 mph. Service ceiling: 26,900 ft.

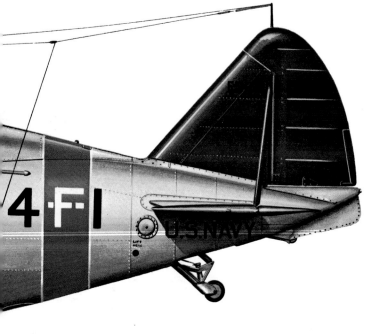

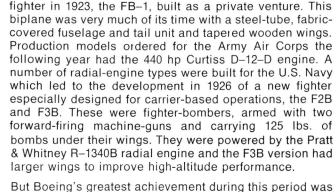

fighter in 1923, the FB–1, built as a private venture. This biplane was very much of its time with a steel-tube, fabric-covered fuselage and tail unit and tapered wooden wings. Production models ordered for the Army Air Corps the following year had the 440 hp Curtiss D–12–D engine. A number of radial-engine types were built for the U.S. Navy which led to the development in 1926 of a new fighter especially designed for carrier-based operations, the F2B and F3B. These were fighter-bombers, armed with two forward-firing machine-guns and carrying 125 lbs. of bombs under their wings. They were powered by the Pratt & Whitney R–1340B radial engine and the F3B version had larger wings to improve high-altitude performance.

But Boeing's greatest achievement during this period was the classic F4B (115) of which 586 were built between 1928 and 1933, a production record for a single type of U.S. military airplane that was not beaten until 1940. The F4B biplane was designed to meet the requirements of both the Army for land-based operations and the Navy for use on carriers and was successful in both roles. The basic type had wooden wings, aluminium-tube fuselage structure and open cockpit, behind which a feature on later versions was a very large headrest. The engine was a 400 hp Pratt & Whitney Wasp radial, surrounded by a drag-reducing cowl which made stubby aircraft of this type so distinctive. Later models were built with an all-metal fuselage and speeds were increased from 176 mph to 187 mph at 6,000 feet. The type was known as the Model 100 in the export market, to which Boeing in common with the other rapidly expanding American aircraft manufacturers were selling their products in increasing numbers.

Although Boeing was a major supplier of fighters and trainers during the inter-war period, it was for its famous bomber series that it would eventually become best known. The first of these appeared in 1931 as the B–9 and was one of the outstanding aircraft of its time. It was an all-metal twin-engined cantilever monoplane with a semi-retractable undercarriage and variable pitch propellers

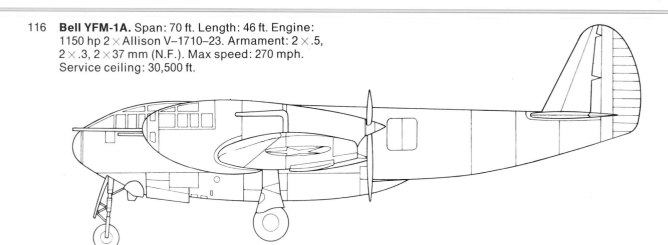

116 **Bell YFM-1A.** Span: 70 ft. Length: 46 ft. Engine: 1150 hp 2 × Allison V–1710–23. Armament: 2 × .5, 2 × .3, 2 × 37 mm (N.F.). Max speed: 270 mph. Service ceiling: 30,500 ft.

which in terms of maximum speed and climb put bomber performance in the same category as contemporary fighters. Some of these features were quickly adapted in the last of the Boeing fighters to enter service, the P–26 (113) which first flew in 1932 and was ordered by the Army Air Corps the following year as its first monoplane fighter and first all-metal production fighter. The low-set wing was externally braced by wires attached to the fuselage and fixed undercarriage, the vertical legs and wheels of which were covered with streamlined casings. Flaps were added to the trailing edge of the wings on later versions, becoming standard equipment on monoplane fighters of the late 1930s, and it was also one of the first airplanes to be fitted with a fuel-injection engine.

The first U.S. Navy fighter to have a retractable undercarriage was the Grumman FF–1 two-seater which came out early in 1931 and, powered by the 575 hp Wright R–1820E engine, had a top speed of 195 mph which was claimed to be more than any single-seater in service at that time. A single canopy enclosed the two tandem cockpits. This was the first of a long line of carrier-based combat aircraft built by Grumman for the U.S. Navy and its design features were incorporated in the F2F single-seat fighter which appeared the following year with the 625 hp two-row Pratt & Whitney Wasp Junior radial engine. As with all the Navy fighters small bombs were also carried in addition to the armament of two .30-inch machine-guns. A later version, the Grumman F3F (114), had a lengthened fuselage and increased wing span to improve manoeuvrability, but this also made it heavier and somewhat slower until the single-row Cyclone XR–1820–22 engine was fitted in 1937, giving a top speed of 264 mph at 15,000 feet.

As a result of the success of the Boeing P–26, in 1935 and 1936 the Army Air Corps held a series of design competitions for an all-metal low-wing monoplane fighter with enclosed cockpits and retractable undercarriage. An order was won for the Seversky P–35, designed by Alexander Kartveli, beginning a line which resulted in the famous Republic P–47 Thunderbolt of the Second World War. The prototype was a tandem two-seater, but at the speeds then being achieved by fighters of about 250 mph it was felt that the gunner would have difficulty in aiming his free-mounted gun and this led to the abandonment of the two-seater fighter in the United States. The Seversky P–35 was rebuilt as a single-seater and it was in this form that it was ordered, powered by a Twin Wasp engine that gave a top speed of 280 mph at 10,000 feet. Other countries did not have the same inhibition about two-seaters, however, retaining them for later and much faster fighters. The two-seater version of the P–35 was exported as well as the single-seater.

German development

The defeat of Germany in the First World War resulted in the surrender of 15,174 aircraft and 27,757 aero-engines to the Allies, most of what remained of the 47,637 airframes and 40,449 engines manufactured by German industry during the war. As in the case of the other aircraft-producing countries a great variety of types had been designed and tested. Some were very successful, such as the Fokker D.7 which was so highly regarded by the Allies that its surrender was specifically mentioned in the Armistice terms. Others were purely experimental and never reached beyond the prototype stage, such as the Fokker V.8 Quintuplane which had three wings in front and two half-way along the fuselage just behind the cockpit, in addition to the usual tail unit.

Although in terms of ceiling height and rate of climb the fighter made great advances during the war, the same could not be said of speed. Neither the Sopwith Snipe nor the Fokker D.7, the outstanding fighters of the last year of the war, were as fast as the experimental S.E.4 biplane built at Farnborough in 1914 which, with a top speed of 135 mph, was the fastest airplane in the world at that time. One reason for its speed was the attention paid to streamlining by the provision of a plywood-covered fuselage of circular section and single-strut interplane bracing, among other innovations to reduce drag. It had been obvious to many designers even before the war that a smooth and rounded monocoque type of fuselage, in which the skin itself bore all the main stresses, and monoplane wings which did away with wind-resisting braces and struts, would greatly assist such streamlining. The material that was best suited to meet these requirements was metal, as seen by Professor Hugo Junkers when he built the world's first all-metal airplane in 1915. This was the Junkers J.1, nicknamed the 'Tin Donkey', whose structure consisted of a ribbed metal sheeting with internal tubular bracing. Its great strength meant that the thick monoplane wings could be cantilevered with no external bracing. The authorities were sufficiently impressed to persuade Professor Junkers to co-operate with Anthony Fokker on military versions of the J.1, resulting in a series of one and two-seater prototypes with corrugated aluminium replacing the thin sheet iron of the original. The Junkers D.1 single-seat low-wing monoplane fighter which first appeared in October 1917 had remarkably modern lines. It was fast and manoeuvrable and, armed with twin forward-firing Spandau guns, it could have made a considerable contribution to the war. But at a time when vast numbers of aircraft were

117 Arado Ar 65. Span: 36 ft. 9 in. Length: 27 ft. 6 in. Engine: 750 hp B.M.W. V.1. Armament: two 7.9 mm M.G. 17. Max speed: 153 mph at 4,595 ft. Service ceiling: 24,935 ft.

118 Arado Ar 68. Span: 36 ft. 1 in. Length: 31 ft. 2 in. Engine: 680 hp Junkers Jumo 210 E9. Armament: 2 × 7.9 mm M.G. 17. Max speed: 190 ground level. Service ceiling: 26,575 ft.

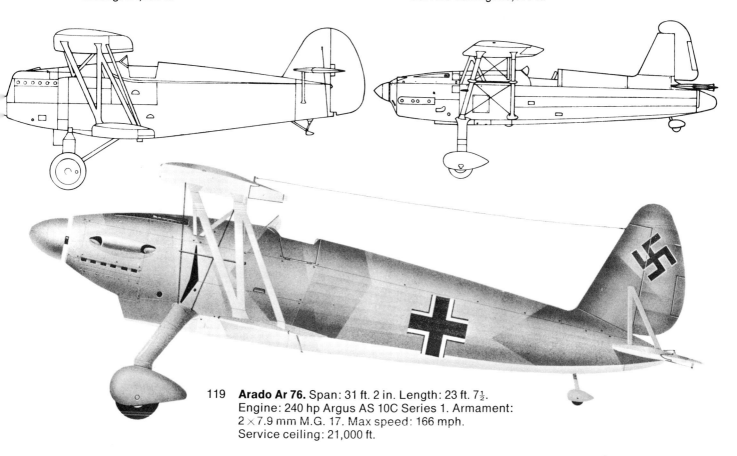

119 Arado Ar 76. Span: 31 ft. 2 in. Length: 23 ft. 7½. Engine: 240 hp Argus AS 10C Series 1. Armament: 2 × 7.9 mm M.G. 17. Max speed: 166 mph. Service ceiling: 21,000 ft.

required, simple wooden and fabric structures that could be built by non-aviation companies as well as aircraft manufacturers were the best means of achieving the required production, while inevitable difficulties were met with the new and more complex metal construction. Only forty-one D.1s had been delivered to the Front by the end of the war, although they were the forerunners of a whole generation of Junkers aircraft and had a considerable influence on later aircraft design.

Monocoque and semi-monocoque fuselages could of course be built of wood and many aircraft of the First World War were so constructed, including the Albatros fighters. But as far as monoplane designs were concerned there was some official prejudice against these, particularly in Britain, because of the number of pre-war accidents with such aircraft. For that reason the monoplane did not receive the attention it deserved from designers and air forces during the war although several types were produced such as the Morane-Saulnier parasol and mid-wing fighters, the Fokker and Pfalz *Eindekkers,* the Bristol M.1C, the Hansa-Brandenburg seaplane, the Fokker cantilever parasol D.8, and of course the all-metal Junkers one- and two-seaters. But because of its proved success in terms of manoeuvrability and rate of climb, many post-war designers were reluctant to depart from the biplane form. This was evident in the first fighter designs to emerge after the war and which in some instances lasted even up to the beginning of the Second World War.

The German Air Service came to an abrupt end in November 1918 and under the terms of the Armistice Germany was precluded from manufacturing any military aircraft. But the ban did not apply to the construction of sporting aircraft for flying clubs or civil aircraft to meet the requirements of small airlines which were then springing up in Germany as elsewhere. By the mid-1920s all the firms existed that would later produce military aircraft for the *Luftwaffe,* including Junkers, Heinkel, Dornier, Focke-Wulf and Messerschmitt. The German Army continued to take a close interest in aviation and managed to build up a secret reserve of trained pilots who were taught at flying schools and in Russia with whom a secret agreement was concluded for that purpose. By the time the clandestine *Luftwaffe* was formed in 1933, under the former First World War fighter ace Hermann Goering, it could call on a nucleus of fighter and reconnaissance pilots who were well-versed in military flying.

Under the guise of building civil aircraft, the German aviation industry had already begun experimenting with its first military aircraft since the war. Two standard single-seat fighters bearing civil registrations of course were chosen to equip the new German Air Force, the Arado Ar 68 (118) and the Heinkel He 51 (120), both biplanes of tubular steel and wooden construction. The Arado Ar 68 had an open cockpit, forward-staggered wings and 'N'-type interplane bracing struts that gave it, apart from the spats over the wheels of the fixed undercarriage, a distinctly First World War look. But there was nothing outdated about the new 610 hp Junkers Jumo 210 liquid-cooled inverted-Vee engine, Germany's most powerful aero-engine at that time which was also to power the first Messerschmitt Bf 109 (133). The production version of the

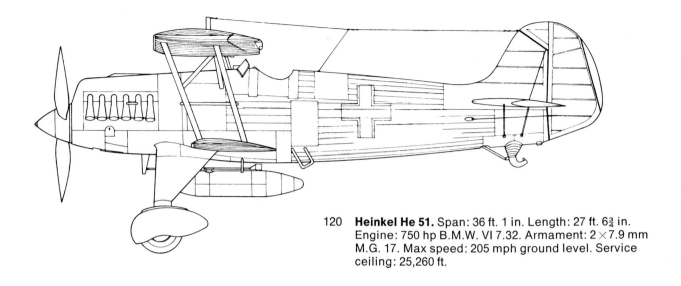

120 **Heinkel He 51.** Span: 36 ft. 1 in. Length: 27 ft. 6¾ in. Engine: 750 hp B.M.W. VI 7.32. Armament: 2×7.9 mm M.G. 17. Max speed: 205 mph ground level. Service ceiling: 25,260 ft.

Arado was equipped in 1935 with two 7.9-mm MG 15 machine-guns which were mounted in the upper engine decking. It was in that year that Hitler felt confident enough to reveal his previously secret air force to the world, consisting of over 1,800 aircraft of all types and 20,000 officers and men in squadrons which had been concealed as 'flying clubs' or 'police units'. A later version of the Ar 68 was powered by the 750 hp BMW VI in-line engine which gave a speed of 192 mph at 13,000 feet. But by the beginning of the Second World War it had been greatly outclassed by other German fighters and was used mainly for training.

The Heinkel He 51 was a better aircraft of the same type, sturdy and well-streamlined with unequal-span wings. It was based on a series of sporting biplanes built in the late 1920s by the Heinkel company and, powered by the 750 hp BMW engine, deliveries to the *Luftwaffe* began in 1933. In 1936 and 1937 a number served with the Condor Legion during the Spanish Civil War, without particular distinction as their performance was inferior to other fighter types involved in that conflict but their good low-level flying ability made them suitable for ground attack duties. A later version fitted with floats was supplied to the air arm of the German Navy.

As already described under American development, the 1930s saw a major revolution in the design of aircraft in which fast monoplanes with fully cantilevered wings, retractable undercarriages, all-metal stressed skin construction and enclosed cockpits took the place of fabric-covered fixed-undercarriage biplanes. Germany had been the leader of some of these innovations during the First World War and was still well-advanced in the field of electronics and engine-design which had such a great effect on fighter development between the wars. It was not surprising that the first fighters to equip the *Luftwaffe* were somewhat outdated but even while they were being delivered, the flight testing of a second generation of German combat aircraft had already begun, aircraft that were to prove themselves at least the equal of any in the world, including one of the greatest single-seat fighters in aviation history, the Messerschmitt Bf 109. These developments are described later.

British development

One of the major advances in the use of fighter aircraft towards the end of the First World War was their service with ships of the Royal Navy. Although an American pilot had been the first to take off from an anchored ship, the first to achieve this feat from a moving ship had been the remarkable C. R. Samson, later to command the Royal Naval Air Service in France, when in May 1912 he took off from a platform on HMS *Hibernia* during a review of the Fleet. From that time onwards, most of the advances in naval aviation were pioneered by the Royal Navy.

During the First World War the RNAS, apart from its bombing operations and those of its fighter squadrons attached to the RFC on the Western Front, had developed along two distinct lines in its work of reconnaissance for the Fleet and maritime patrols against submarines, Zeppelins and, later, bombers. Aircraft, mostly seaplanes and flying-boats, were flown from coastal bases in England and France while at the same time other aircraft also took part in ship-based operations, flown into the wind from flat-decked lighters towed by destroyers or from landing decks installed on battleships and cruisers. At first fighter seaplanes were used for this purpose, taking off on trolleys which fell away as the machines became airborne, but in 1916 it became possible for faster landplanes to take off from ships. The Sopwith Pup was the first to be used for such operations. Unless airplanes happened to be close to land they had to be ditched in the sea after each sortie, the pilot hoping that the special flotation bags provided would keep his aircraft afloat until he could be picked up. A great stride forward was made in August 1917 when Squadron Commander E. H. Dunning became the first man to make a landing on a moving ship, putting his Pup down on the deck of HMS *Furious*. He was drowned when his airplane crashed during further experiments but he showed the way to the true aircraft carrier which was gradually developed as superstructures were removed from existing ships to make way for bigger flight decks. Skid landing gear was normally fitted in place of wheels, with horn attachments to catch hold of wires stretched across the

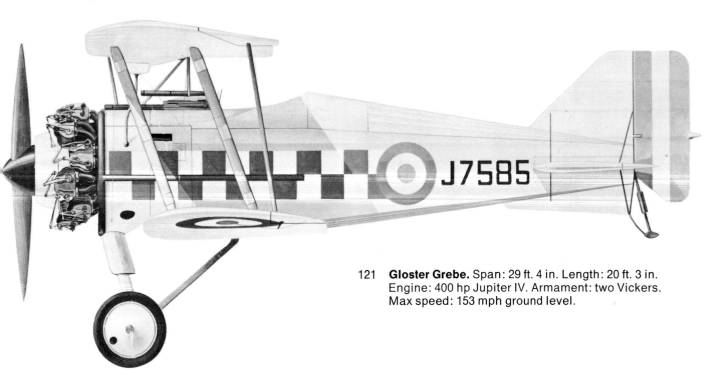

121 **Gloster Grebe.** Span: 29 ft. 4 in. Length: 20 ft. 3 in. Engine: 400 hp Jupiter IV. Armament: two Vickers. Max speed: 153 mph ground level.

deck and so arrest the landing speed. HMS *Argus* was the first ship to dispense completely with superstructure and in the early 1920s wheeled undercarriages replaced skids.

The possibility of landing on a ship as well as taking off enabled high-performance fighters like the Sopwith Camel to be used in carrier operations far beyond the range of shore-based aircraft. The last German airship of the war to be destroyed in air combat was shot down by a Camel on August 11th, 1918, flown from a lighter by Lieutenant S. D. Culley. This action against the Zeppelin L.53 was fought at 19,000 feet, a height at which combats were increasingly taking place requiring oxygen for the pilot as well as heat to prevent the lubricating oil in the guns from freezing. This meant more equipment had to be carried, to which after the war was added heavier armament and firing-gear, radio equipment, more instruments, and a parachute at long last. Fighters became larger and heavier, especially those carrier-borne which in addition required such special equipment as arrester gear, folding wings for below-deck stowage, flotation bags and a rubber dinghy for the pilot in case of ditching. Catapult gear was also necessary to assist the take-off of heavily-loaded aircraft. Speed was increased by the provision of more powerful engines, variable-pitch propellers, and closer attention to the need for streamlining, resulting in a trend towards cantilever monoplane wings, retractable undercarriages, enclosed cockpits and smooth metal coverings. While between the wars fighters became simpler externally, they were vastly more complicated inside.

But the major British fighter type of the 1920s and 1930s was still the single-seat biplane, as represented by the first standard carrier-borne fighter chosen to equip the Fleet Air Arm when it was formed in 1924, again establishing two separate air forces in Britain, although the RAF continued to exercise some degree of control until the Royal Navy took it over enirely in 1937. This was the Fairy Flycatcher (122), its equal-span single-bay wings fitted with flaps along the whole length of the trailing edges in order to shorten the take-off and landing runs and to steepen the glide path. The Flycatcher could thus operate from platforms mounted on the gun turrets of capital ships in addition to carriers as such, although it

was the last airplane to employ this technique. The fuselage was of composite wood and metal construction, covered with fabric, and had a distinctive upswept underside and low aspect ratio fin. The undercarriage could be interchanged with floats or wheels and floats combined and although the wings did not fold, the whole airframe could be rapidly dismantled into sections no longer than 13 feet 6 inches for ease of stowage. On one occasion six were landed and stowed below deck in just over four minutes. As with most British fighters of this period it was powered by the 400 hp air-cooled Armstrong Siddeley Jaguar IV radial engine and the armament, also more or less standard, consisted of two fixed forward-firing Vickers machine-guns, synchronised to fire between the propeller blades and providing very little more fire-power than the Camel of the First World War. The Flycatcher was an excellent aircraft of its type, rugged, highly manoeuvrable and easy to land with a top speed of 133 mph at 5,000 feet. It remained in service with the Fleet Air Arm until 1934. Launching operations on board the carriers *Furious*, *Courageous* and *Glorious* could be speeded by flying the aircraft straight out of the hangar deck and over the bows along a 60-foot tapered runway below the main deck, although they would drop alarmingly and almost touch the water before climbing.

The standard single-seat fighter in service with the RAF immediately after the war was the Sopwith Snipe, but this was replaced in 1924 by the Gloster Grebe (121), a single-bay biplane with a larger upper wing and the Jaguar IV engine. The fixed undercarriage and fuselage of braced box-girder structure covered with fabric were all conventional, but it was improved aerodynamically by the ailerons of the upper wings being hinged parallel with the tapered trailing-edge of the outer ends of the wing while the lower wing ailerons were hinged at right angles to the airflow. A number of experiments were made with the Grebe after it had entered service, including a successful launching from the airship R.33. A two-seat dual-control version was made for training. Another fighter which came into service at this time was the Armstrong Whitworth Siskin 111, a high-performance single-seat fighter with a sesquiplane wing arrangement, the lower wing being only

one-third the area of the upper wing which was the only one fitted with ailerons. It was built partly of metal, the first fighter of such construction to enter RAF service, although most of the covering was still fabric. An improved version, the Siskin 111A, was also the first fighter to have a super-charged engine, the 450 hp Armstrong Siddeley Jaguar IV which gave it a top speed of 186 mph at 15,000 feet.

After the drab khaki-green colour with which most British fighters were painted during the First World War, a feature of the RAF's post-war period was the dazzling collection of colour schemes provided in order to distinguish various squadrons. Pennants were even flown to mark the leader of a flight or squadron, the latter consisting of nine aircraft. This was the time of aerobatic flying displays, often by large formations, which became popular public spectacles at Hendon and elsewhere. And a new name was added to the list of aircraft manufacturers that was to become world-famous for its single-seat fighters, that of the H. G. Hawker Engineering Company which was formed in 1920 as a successor to the Sopwith firm. Its first aircraft of this type was the Hawker Woodcock (123), a single-bay biplane powered by the 420 hp Bristol Jupiter radial engine which with the Armstrong Siddeley Jaguar IV was the other most widely used British engine of the period. Metal covers were fitted over each cylinder head to reduce drag but otherwise the structure was of conventional wood and fabric. An unusually wide undercarriage simplified land-ing. The Woodcock remained operational with the RAF from 1925 to 1928. It was during this time that the Gloster Gamecock (124) also entered service, often described as the last fighter of wooden construction to serve with the RAF – until the de Havilland Mosquito of some years later – but certainly the last wooden biplane. Developed from the Grebe it incorporated many improvements, such as a rounded fuselage of better aerodynamic form and im-proved streamlining. Powered by the Bristol Jupiter engine it had outstanding manoeuvrability and during flight trials was dived at 275 mph. The upper wing was slightly larger than the lower and made in two halves like the Siskin, supported on inverted vee-struts at the centre and a pair

The first successful landing on a ship at sea, being made by Sqn Ldr E. H. Dunning in a Sopwith Pup on the deck of HMS *Furious,* August 2nd, 1917. *Imperial War Museum*

of interplane struts at each outer end.

Although fighter types were officially replaced by improved aircraft from time to time, such were the financial problems of the period and the niggardly attitude of both government and public towards military expenditure that some re-mained in service for much longer than intended. Thus the Sopwith Snipe, whose production had ceased in 1919, was still operational with some squadrons until 1926. The same applied to the Bristol Fighter two-seater which had first been introduced in 1917; production continued until 1926 when over 3,000 had been built and it remained in service with the RAF until 1932. Post-war versions were progres-sively improved, including the provision of a balanced rudder, more efficient wings, and the patented Handley Page wing slots which gave a high degree of lateral stability. In 1927 the Air Ministry decided to hold competi-tive trials for a single-seat day and night fighter to replace the Siskins and Gamecocks which were then in service. The contract was won by the all-metal framed, fabric-covered Bristol Bulldog biplane (126) which went into ser-vice in 1929 and remained the most widely used British fighter until 1936. The staggered single-bay wings of un-equal span had a marked dihedral and were joined at each end by a single pair of interplane struts. Power was pro-vided by the 490 hp Bristol Jupiter air-cooled radial engine and in a later improved version by the Bristol Mercury geared engine fitted with a cowling ring. A two-seat version was used for advanced training.

Without doubt the finest biplane fighter of the period was the Hawker Fury (125), adopted after competitive trials in 1931 as the RAF's standard interceptor. It was the first aircraft to enter squadron service with a speed of over 200 mph (207 mph at 14,000 feet to be exact), for which endurance was sacrificed, and in order to provide a high rate of climb, up to 20,000 feet in nine and a half minutes compared with the Bulldog's fifteen minutes, equipment

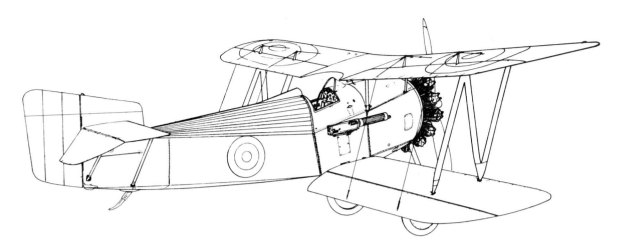

122 **Fairy Flycatcher.** Span: 29 ft. Length: 23 ft. Engine: 400 hp Armstrong Siddeley Jaguar III or IV. Armament: 2 × .303 Vickers. Max speed: 133½ mph at 5,000 ft. Service ceiling: 19,000 ft.

such as night-flying gear was dispensed with. The reasoning behind these requirements was that bombers were fast approaching fighters in speed and height and even outpacing them on occasion. Oswald Short was pioneering experimental aluminium-covered monocoque designs which resulted in a new generation of smooth-hulled flying-boats while the 156 mph Fairy Fox of 1926, powered by the 480 hp Curtiss D-12 liquid-cooled engine which had so impressed Sir Richard Fairy during a visit to the United States, raised the speed of RAF day bombers by nearly 40 per cent in one step. As most British cities were within close range of the sea it was seen even then that bombing raids could occur with very little warning and a high rate of climb was the essential requirement of a new

123 **Hawker Woodcock.** Span: 34 ft. 8 in. Length: 25 ft. 7 in. Engine: 358 hp Jaguar II. Armament: two Vickers. Max speed: 143 mph. Service ceiling: 20,550 ft.

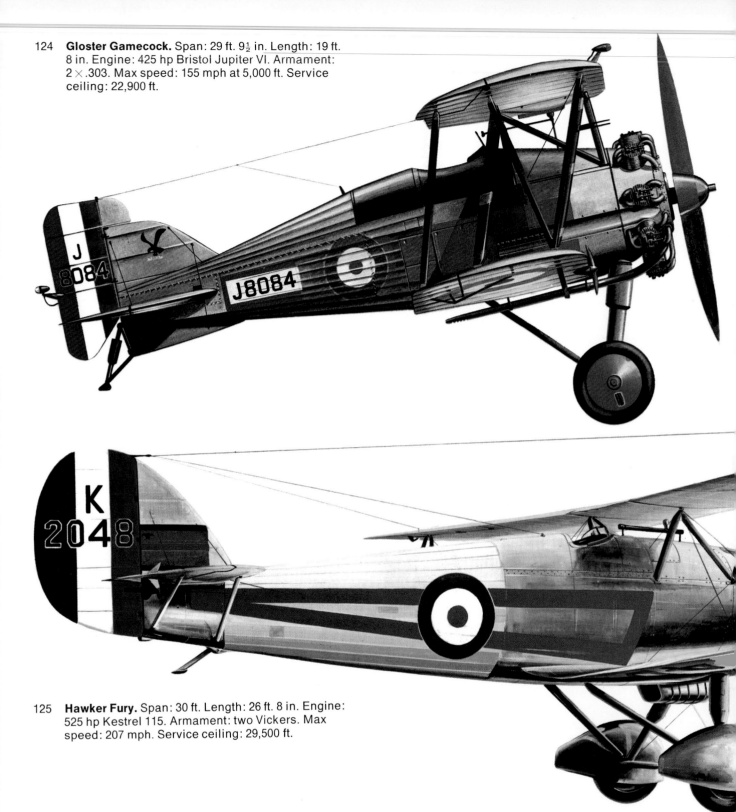

124 **Gloster Gamecock.** Span: 29 ft. 9½ in. Length: 19 ft. 8 in. Engine: 425 hp Bristol Jupiter VI. Armament: 2 × .303. Max speed: 155 mph at 5,000 ft. Service ceiling: 22,900 ft.

125 **Hawker Fury.** Span: 30 ft. Length: 26 ft. 8 in. Engine: 525 hp Kestrel 115. Armament: two Vickers. Max speed: 207 mph. Service ceiling: 29,500 ft.

class of interceptor fighter as represented by the Fury. It had unequal-span staggered wings, with ailerons fitted to the top wing only. The braced metal box-girder fuselage was mainly covered with fabric but the nose consisted of metal cowling panels which could be quickly detached. The standard engine was the 525 hp Rolls Royce Kestrel IIS, but Pratt & Whitney Hornet or Bristol Mercury radials were fitted to machines delivered to the Persian Air Force. A Mark II Fury was brought into service in 1937 as a stop-gap until the monoplane Hurricane became available. Closely resembling the Mark I except for the spatted

wheels now fitted, its 640 hp Kestrel VI engine increased the speed to 223 mph and improved the rate of climb by 30 per cent.

Meanwhile, a move had been made to re-introduce into the RAF a class not used since the Bristol Fighter of the First World War, that of the two-seat fighter. The prototype Hawker Demon (127) of 1930 was a conversion of the Hawker Hart bomber only with a higher powered 560 hp fully-supercharged Kestrel V(DR) engine and a redesigned rear cockpit fitted with a tilted gun-ring to improve the field of fire. It was of fabric-covered all-metal construction

126 **Bristol Bulldog.** Span: 33 ft. 11 in. Length: 25 ft. Engine: 490 hp Jupiter VII. Armament: two Vickers. Max speed: 174 mph.

with unequal-span single-bay staggered wings, supported at the outer ends by a pair of N-type interplane struts. When first issued for squadron service in 1931, armament consisted of two fixed Vickers machine-guns mounted on either side of the engine and synchronised to fire between the propeller blades and a Lewis machine-gun in the rear cockpit. At speeds of 180 mph the slipstream made it difficult for the rear gunner in his open cockpit to operate efficiently, for which reason the Americans later decided not to continue development of two-seat fighter types. The British answer to the problem however was a special hydraulically-operated lobster-back shield developed by Frazer Nash to protect the gunner from the rush of air. The metal sections folded over one another and opened automatically in the direction to which the gunner desired to fire. This power-driven gun turret was fitted to all later Demons, which then became known as Turret Demons, and eventually led to a new departure in fighter design in which the entire armament was placed in the turret, as represented in the Boulton Paul Defiant (149) which first flew in 1937. The idea was in fact a sophisticated throwback to the two-seat tractor airplane of the First World War in the day before synchronised forward-firing guns were

available and when only the observer in the rear cockpit could fire a machine-gun.

Soon after the Demon came into service, the Hawker company also produced a replacement for the long-serving Fairy Flycatchers of the Fleet Air Arm. This was the Hawker Nimrod (128), a single-seat carrier-borne version of the Fury interceptor. Although similar externally to the Fury the fuselage was strengthened to allow catapulting from ships other than carriers. To the usual additional equipment required by carrier-borne aircraft such as hoisting gear and arrester hooks was added a larger fuel tank and cockpit lighting and heating. Rolls Royce Kestrel engines were used, increasing in power from 480 hp and 525 hp in early versions to 650 hp in the slightly modified Nimrod Mark II.

The last open-cockpit single-seat fighter to serve with the RAF, for canopies were already being fitted to larger airplanes beginning with the Westland Wallace general-purpose two-seater in 1933, was the Gloster Gauntlet which entered service in 1935 and for two years remained Britain's fastest fighter. A top speed of 230 mph was largely due to the extreme care taken to streamline the fuselage, wings and fittings, partly made possible by a greater use of metal as in the case of the thin section fabric-covered wings. The forward part of the fuselage was covered with metal panels. A 645 hp Bristol Mercury air-cooled radial engine provided the power plant and the performance of some aircraft in this series was improved by the use of a three-blade fixed-pitch metal propeller in place of the standard two-blade wooden type. It was from the Gauntlet that the famous Gloster Gladiator was developed in 1934, entering service in 1937 as the RAF's last biplane and representing the ultimate peak of technical proficiency of this type.

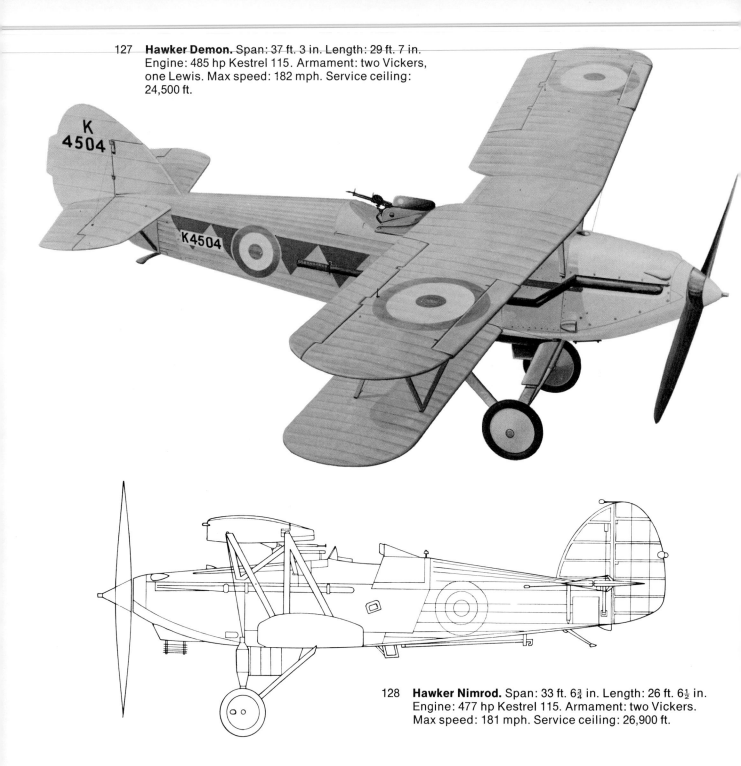

127 **Hawker Demon.** Span: 37 ft. 3 in. Length: 29 ft. 7 in.
Engine: 485 hp Kestrel 115. Armament: two Vickers,
one Lewis. Max speed: 182 mph. Service ceiling:
24,500 ft.

128 **Hawker Nimrod.** Span: 33 ft. 6¾ in. Length: 26 ft. 6½ in.
Engine: 477 hp Kestrel 115. Armament: two Vickers.
Max speed: 181 mph. Service ceiling: 26,900 ft.

Other nations

While the fighters brought into service in Britain between
the two world wars were exclusively biplanes, until a
dramatic step forward was taken with the Hurricane and
Spitfire of the late 1930s, other countries took a much
earlier lead in metal-constructed monoplanes. In the
United States the first development on these lines was
with bombers and it was France that led the way in the
design of single-wing fighters although biplanes continued
to form the basic equipment of many French fighter
squadrons until the early 1930s.

The main biplane types were Nieuport and Spad, both of
which carried on the series that had become so well-
known and respected in the First World War. The monocoque Nieuport 29 was too late to enter service in 1918 but
it became the standard post-war fighter in France with an
impressive performance in terms of climb and maximum
speed (146 mph). A considerably modified version, the
Nieuport-Delage (ND) 29 appeared in 1921 and was also
used by the air forces of other countries including Spain,
Sweden, Belgium, Italy and Japan. It was the last of the
Nieuport biplanes for the following Nieuport-Delage
designs were all sesquiplanes, developed in fact from a
parasol monoplane prototype. The ND 42 which was produced in 1924 had a 500 hp Hispano 12 Hb engine which

gave it a remarkably high speed for that time of 165 mph, capturing a number of world speed and distance records. Some light metal was used together with wood for the wings and monocoque fuselage structure but the ND 52 which followed in 1928 had an all-metal fuselage and radiators installed in the lower wing. It was one of the fighters which took part in the Spanish Civil War, fighting on both sides as it happened after several had been captured by the Nationalists. Later all-metal Nieuport-Delage types widely used by French fighter squadrons were the ND 62, ND 622 and ND 629.

Development of the Spad biplane continued at the same time and although it was not widely used in France, considerable numbers were built for other countries including Poland and Roumania. The first post-war design which appeared at the end of 1918 was the two-seater Spad XX, notable for its clean lines with only one interplane strut on each side. The Spad 61 which first flew in 1923 was a single-seater with a wooden monocoque fuselage and an even more streamlined design. The major production version in 1925 had a maximum speed of 174 mph and a ceiling of 29,000 feet. Last of the Spad biplanes was the 510, built to meet the requirements of the 1930 fighter programme and in fact the last biplane to serve with the French Air Force, comparable in some respects to the RAF's Gloster Gladiator. Steel and duralumin were used for the monocoque fuselage, to which were attached fabric-covered metal wings. Powered by the 690 hp Hispano V-12 engine it had a top speed of 236 mph and a ceiling of 34,000 feet. Armament consisted of four machine-guns, two in the wing and two in the engine cowling, but a few types were fitted with a Hispano *moteur canon,* re-introducing the device that had originally been installed in the Spad XII of the First World War but not used since then. It was in France that cannon armament was mainly developed in the 1930s, leading to the Hispano 20-mm gun which fired automatically instead of single shots and had much greater accuracy as a result of its long barrel. Guns of this type were later made in Britain where they were known as the British Hispano.

Two monoplane single-seat fighters came into service with the French Air Force in the mid-1920s when a move was made to replace the out-dated machines left over from the First World War. First was the Loire-Gourdou-Leseurre 32 parasol-type which, with the excellent 420 hp Jupiter engine had a remarkable rate of climb and in 1927, fitted with floats instead of wheels, took the world altitude record for seaplanes to 30,478 feet. The other was the Wibault 7 and 72 series, also a parasol monoplane and notable for its strong metal construction which included the use of aluminium instead of fabric for the outside covering. As well as the two synchronised Vickers machine-guns in the engine cowling two Darne machine-guns were mounted in the wing. A naval version was developed for carrier-operation and the Wibault 7 was also manufactured by Vickers in Britain. A number were built for Chile under the designation Vickers 121.

The early 1930s saw the appearance of the first Morane-Saulnier single-seat fighter since the war, the M-S 225 which was also a parasol monoplane with swept-back wings and constructed of duralumin with a fabric covering. It was compact and streamlined and became well-known for its performances by a French aerobatic squadron, the *Patrouille de Dijon*. A later Morane-Saulnier, the 406, was to become the most famous French fighter of the Second World War. Meanwhile, the last development of the parasol-wing monoplane came with the Dewoitine series which began in 1921 with the D.1. These were all of simple

light metal construction with fabric-covered wings and had an excellent performance – a D.1 in 1924 captured the world speed record at 144.84 mph – but they were mostly built for the air forces of other countries such as Switzerland and Yugoslavia. It was not until the D.37 of 1932 that orders were obtained from the French Air Force and the French Navy as a replacement for its carrier-borne Wibaults. These did not begin to enter service until 1934 as a result of delays in obtaining the Gnôme 14 Kds engines. The D.37 and its derivatives, armed either with two cannon in the wings or four machine-guns, was France's last parasol monoplane fighter for already Emile Dewoitine was developing a low-wing fighter to meet the requirements of the 1930 programme. The result was the all-metal Dewoitine D.500 series, the prototype of which first flew in 1932. Large orders were received for the D.500, D.501 and D.510 which began entering service from 1935 onwards with even more powerful Hispano-Suiza engines and by 1938 they comprised nearly two-thirds of the 359 fighter aircraft in the French Air Force. Many had been withdrawn however by the time the Second World War broke out. The D.501 attracted a great deal of notice abroad because of its Hispano 20-mm *moteur* canon mounted above the crankcase and firing through the propeller shaft, which became standard on the Dewoitines.

Several other nations began building fighters between the wars, although most air forces were equipped with machines either built under licence or bought from the major aircraft producing countries. In the Netherlands, to which Anthony Fokker had returned after Germany's defeat, his company continued to build fighters developed from the outstanding D.7 of 1918, both for the Dutch Air Force and also for sale abroad, particularly to the Soviet Union, Finland, Scandinavia and Italy. The last Fokker biplane was the D.17 for in 1936 a new type emerged, the D.21 low-wing cantilever monoplane (144) with a fixed 'spatted' undercarriage, powered by the 830 hp Bristol Mercury air-cooled radial engine and armed with four 7.9-mm FN-Browning machine-guns, two in the upper engine cowling and one in each wing. Sweden, in addition to purchasing a variety of fighters from other countries, developed one of her own as a result of a private venture in 1929, the Svenska J.6 Jaktfalk (132). This was a single-bay biplane with a fixed spatted undercarriage and although relatively few were built, it saw long service with the Swedish Air Force. Poland built the P.W. S.10, typical of the high-wing braced monoplanes of the period which saw service as a fighter and trainer with the Polish Air Force up to the Second World War and also took part in the Spanish Civil War, but it was the Polish all-metal gull-wing P.Z.L. series which became better known. These are described in more detail later. An even more remarkable design came from Italy where Fiat produced an excellent series of fighter biplanes between the wars which were the mainstay of the Italian Air Force. The first of these, the C.R.I., had an upper wing smaller than the lower, in complete contrast to other airplanes of unequal wing span in which the upper was always bigger than the lower. The more orthodox design was followed for the next fighter in the series, the C.R.20, leading to the classic C.R. 32 sesquiplane (146) of 1933 built of steel and light alloy with fabric covering and a markedly spatted under-carriage. It was a very agile airplane, conforming to the notion of Italian designers at this time to stress manoeuvra-bility rather than speed, and played a major part in the Spanish Civil War on Franco's side when used to form *La Cucaracha* squadron. A Fiat monoplane, the G.50 (145) also saw combat in that war.

The first Russian-designed single-seat fighter to be built

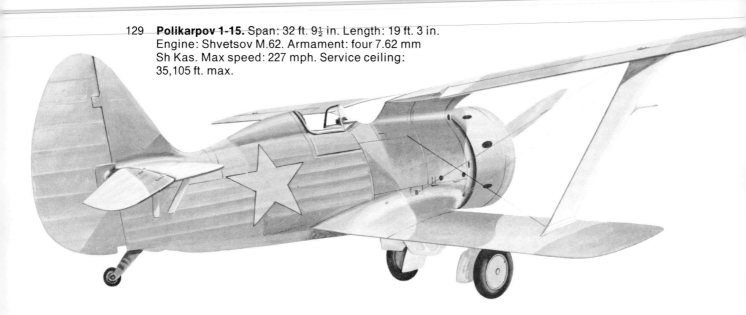

129 **Polikarpov 1-15.** Span: 32 ft. 9½ in. Length: 19 ft. 3 in. Engine: Shvetsov M.62. Armament: four 7.62 mm Sh Kas. Max speed: 227 mph. Service ceiling: 35,105 ft. max.

in large numbers was the Grigorovich I-2 biplane, first produced in 1925. It had a plywood-covered monocoque fuselage and was powered by a 400 hp M-5 water-cooled engine. Armament consisted of two synchronised 7.62-mm machine-guns. This was followed by the Polikarpov-Grigorovich I-5 biplane and the Polikarpov I-15 (129), a sesquiplane in which the top wing was gull-shaped to give the pilot an excellent view forward. A later development of this, the I-153, had the unusual feature of an undercarriage which retracted rearward to lie in wells in the bottom of the fuselage and lower wing roots. Another sesquiplane, the Tupolev I-4, was developed in 1928 as an all-metal single-seater, modified so that a pair could be carried one on each wing of a TB-1 bomber and air-launched should the bomber be attacked.

In the early 1930s the Russians developed a large-bore recoilless gun, similar to the Davis-type fitted experimentally on British aircraft in the First World War, and it

was decided to build a light fighter to carry two 75-mm APK cannon fitted underneath the wings. The result was the Grigorovich PI-1, a long-wing monoplane which first flew in 1934. Because of its unreliability and low rate of fire the APK cannon was not a success however and the PI-1 was discontinued in favour of the higher-performance Polikarpov I-16 (140) which was then in production. This low-wing monoplane with a smooth metal skin, retractable undercarriage and enclosed cockpit, powered by an air-cooled radial engine, was one of the best fighters in the world when it entered service in 1934. It had a maximum speed of 282 mph, a ceiling of some 30,000 feet, and two wing-mounted 7.62-mm ShKAS machine-guns that could fire 1,800 rounds a minute. These were later changed for two 20-mm cannon while two synchronised machine-guns were fitted above the engine. A version of the I-16 fought in the Spanish Civil War where it out-performed the early Messerschmitt Bf 109B of the Condor Legion. The Polikarpov I-17 produced in 1936 had an 860 hp water-cooled

130 **Potez T.O.E.** Span: 46 ft. 4¾ in. Length: 29 ft. 10¼ in. Engine: 450 hp Lorraine 12EB. Armament: one Vickers, two Lewis. Max speed: 136.7 mph. Service ceiling: 23,622 ft.

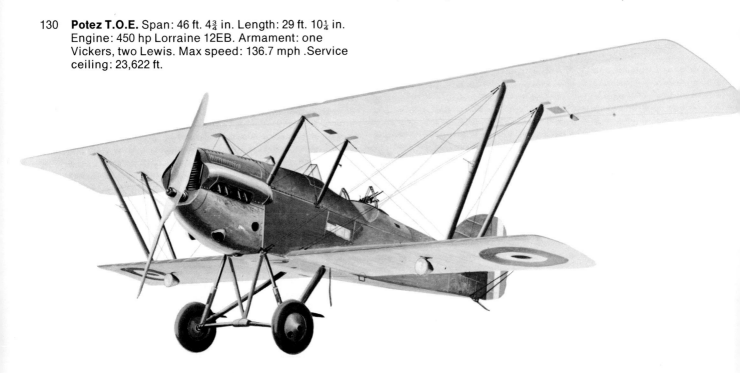

in-line engine which gave it a speed of 311 mph and was armed with four machine-guns in the wings and a cannon firing through the propeller shaft.

Taking a lead from the Americans, the Japanese concentrated their aircraft development in the 1920s and 1930s on the dive-bomber, used to such effect in the attack on Pearl Harbour. Fighters were at first bought from other countries, such as the Gloster Sparrowhawk from Britain, and it was not until 1923 that the first Japanese-built fighter came into service. This was the Mitsubishi 1MF1 biplane, designed in fact by a team of Sopwith engineers for use on board Japan's first aircraft-carrier, the *Hosho,* launched at the end of 1921. Mitsubishi's next fighter, the 15M single-seat Navy fighter (142) for land-based operations which first flew in 1935, was an original design and showed the considerable progress that had been made in Japanese aeronautics. It was a low-wing monoplane of all-metal construction with fixed undercarriage and enclosed cockpit, powered by a Japanese version of the Bristol Jupiter radial engine which gave it an impressive speed of 265 mph. The two other companies which provided the bulk of Japan's fighters during the inter-war period were Nakajima and Kawasaki. The Nakajima Type 91 single-seat parasol-wing monoplane which was in production from 1931 until 1934 was the first Japanese-designed fighter to replace the foreign machines then in service with the Japanese Army Air Force. It again used the Nakajima version of the nine-cylinder Bristol Jupiter radial and was armed with two synchronised 7.7-mm machine-guns. For the Navy in 1934 Nakajima produced the last of the naval biplane fighters, the A4NI, which saw combat during the Sino-Japanese war in 1937. Kawasaki in 1930 produced the first of a long line of fighters, the Type 92 biplane powered by its own licence-built version of the BMW VI water-cooled engine, which in many ways was better than the Nakajima monoplane and was ordered by both the Army and Air Force. This led to the Kawasaki Ki-10 (131) five years later, similar to the Type 92 only incorporating many improvements and a higher-powered 800 hp water-cooled Vee engine. This also saw combat in China and was the last biplane fighter to serve in the Japanese Army Air Force for Japanese designers were already working on a series of advanced all-metal low-wing monoplane fighters that would take the Western powers by surprise when Japan entered the Second World War, causing them to revise their previous opinion that the Japanese had merely copied their ideas and techniques.

Prelude to the Second World War

While the mid-1930s saw the continued use of biplanes in most of the air forces of the world, a new generation of monoplane fighters was already beginning to appear that would make the biplane forever obsolete and constitute the main fighter type by the beginning of the Second World War. The main ingredients were cantilever monoplane wings, retractable undercarriages, enclosed cockpits, smooth metal skins and variable-pitch propellers. More powerful engines of up to 1,000 hp gave speeds of around 350 mph. As the First World War had proved, altitude was of equal importance to speed and this was generally increased to 30,000 feet or more by the use of superchargers. The world altitude record in 1938, held by the Italians, was 56,000 feet, while in the following year Germany took the speed record to 469 mph. Combat range was a much greater factor in the wider-ranging war to come and this varied from around 400 to 1,000 miles with the use of extra fuel tanks which could be jettisoned. Armament was increasingly mounted in the wings, either machine-guns or cannon, so that synchronising gear was no longer required. The reflector type gunsight was adopted, which projected a pattern of rings and lines onto a glass reflector inside the cockpit by means of an electric light, and the introduction of radio telephones for the first time made it possible for pilots in the air to communicate verbally instead of giving hand signals as before. As airplanes became vastly more complicated, so did the art of flying them. Whereas at the start of the First World War pilots went into combat with as little as seventeen hours flying time, by 1939 at least 150 hours training was required.

131 **Kawasaki Ki-10.** Span: 31 ft. 3 in. Length: 23 ft. 7 in. Engine: 850 hp Kawasaki Ha–9–11a. Armament: two 7.7. mm. Max speed: 248.5 mph at 9,845 ft. Service ceiling: 32,810 ft.

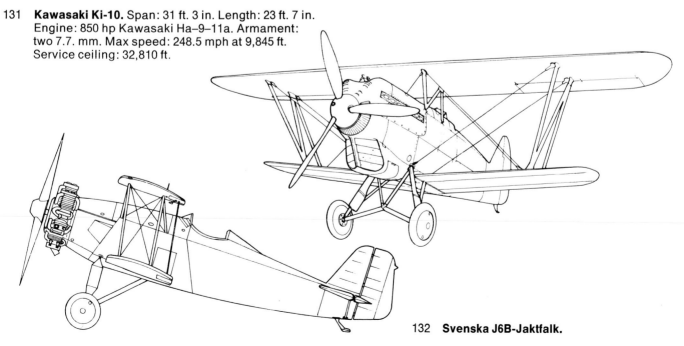

132 **Svenska J6B-Jaktfalk.**

As the nation arming for war it was not surprising that Germany took an early lead in fighter development. It is arguable whether the Messerschmitt Bf 109 (133) was the greatest single-seat fighter in aviation history but it was certainly produced in larger quantities than any other; an estimated 35,000 machines were built between 1936 and 1945, accounting for nearly two-thirds of Germany's total output of single-seat fighters. With many modifications the type remained in construction in various other countries until the mid-1960s, equipping the air forces of Spain, Czechoslovakia and half a dozen other nations. The first prototype Bf 109 VI was designed by Willy Messerschmitt in 1933 shortly after the Nazis had come to power and his company, Bayerische Flugzeugwerke AG, was given a government contract to produce a single-seat monoplane fighter. Although Messerschmitt had no previous experience in military aircraft he had built a number of very successful fast touring monoplanes and this enabled him to better the designs of Focke-Wulf and Heinkel in a design competition. It was intended that the airplane should be built around the most powerful German aero engine available at that time, the 610 hp Junkers Jumo 210A, but these were in short supply and the 109 prototype when it first flew in 1935 was powered by the 695 hp Rolls-Royce Kestrel V engine. The first production order was given a year later for the Bf 109 V4, powered by the Jumo engine and armed with two synchronised 7.9-mm MG 17 machine-guns above the engine cowling and a third firing through the hollow propeller shaft Numerous other models were built, mainly with more powerful versions of the Jumo engine and heavier armament. The B-1 and B-2 series were delivered to the Condor Legion in 1937 during the Spanish Civil War, some armed with an MG FF cannon firing through the propeller shaft. But it was the E-series (162) which was the most widely in use during the early battles of the Second World War. Known throughout the *Luftwaffe* as the 'Emil', production began towards the end of 1938, using the Daimler-Benz 1,100 hp DB 601A inverted-vee twelve-cylinder engine with direct fuel injection which considerably improved the performance to a top speed of 354 mph and an initial climb rate of 3,100 feet a minute. Armament varied somewhat but the most usual form was two synchronised machine-guns with 1,000 rounds of ammunition each and two 20-mm Oerlikon cannon in the wings, each containing sixty rounds. The only other fighter in front-line service with the *Luftwaffe* at the start of the Second World War was the Messerschmitt Bf 110 (152), a twin-engine two-seater conceived as a long-range escort

fighter and known in Germany as a *Zerstorer* (destroyer). Three prototypes first flew in 1936, matching the Hurricane for speed but lacking its maneouvrability. The main production series which began reaching *Luftwaffe* squadrons early in 1939 was the Bf 110C, powered like the Bf 109 by the excellent 1,100 hp Daimler-Benz engine with direct fuel injection. Armament consisted of two 20-mm cannon and four MG 17 machine-guns fixed in the nose, where there was naturally no need for synchronising gear since the engines were carried in the wings, and a free-mounted machine-gun at the rear.

Much of the knowledge of fighter tactics that had been gained in the First World War was either forgotten or neglected in training during the inter-war period. Fighter squadrons, especially those of Britain and Italy, spent much of their time on aerobatics and precision flying with the generally accepted tactical unit being three fighters in tight vee formation, although the two most important lessons of the early air battles were that simple dive and loop manoeuvres were far more successful than complicated aerobatics and the best combat formation was the well-spaced line abreast style. It was thought however that with the advent of fast monoplanes, high-speed manoeuvres would not be possible because of the 'g' effect on the pilots and that dog-fighting was a thing of the past. Tactical training was based on the fighters' role as a bomber interceptor with less consideration given officially to the possibility of combat between fighters themselves. The Germans tended towards the same mistaken views after the *Luftwaffe* was formed but they had an ideal opportunity to try out fighter tactics during the Spanish Civil War which began in 1936. Against the agreed policy of non-intervention by the major powers both Germany and Italy provided air forces to support General Franco while Russia supported the Republicans who also flew some American and French fighters. The German fighters and bombers were grouped into the tactical air force of the Condor Legion, with Manfred von Richthofen's cousin Wolfram as chief of staff and including the man who was to become Germany's greatest air fighter in the Second World War, Adolph Galland. Although the highly manoeuvrable Italian Fiat C.R.32 biplane (146) was able to hold its own and became the mainstay of Franco's fighter forces, the Heinkel 51 biplanes which were first sent to Spain were easily outclassed by the Polikarpov I-16, Russia's first low-wing single-seat monoplane fighter, and the American Curtiss Hawks. When the Messerschmitt 109Bs arrived in 1937 however, they proved superior to all

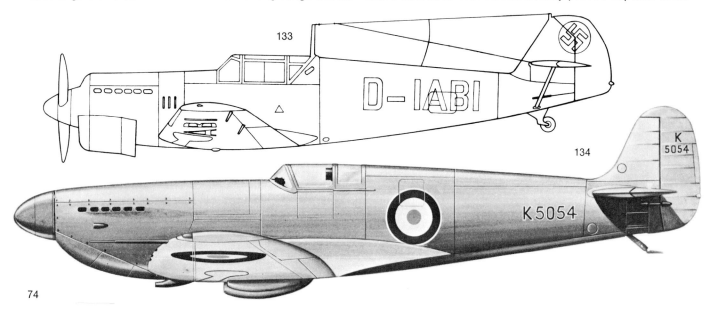

133

134

K 5054

K5054

other fighters except the Russian monoplane. It was as a result of combat experience that the improved E-series was developed with 20-mm cannon in place of the light machine-guns and drop tanks so that range of action could be increased. With one of these machines Werner Molders, the Condor Legion's top scorer in Spain, shot down fourteen Republican airplanes in the last months of the war. Another single-seat fighter monoplane to see combat in Spain at the end of the war was the Fiat G.50 *Freccia* (Arrow) (145) powered by an 840 hp Fiat A.74 RC 38 engine and armed with twin Breda-SAFAT 12.7-mm machine-guns in the upper engine decking, which later replaced the C.R. 32 biplane fighters in the Italian Air Force.

By trial and error the German pilots had gradually learned new tactics and re-discovered others that had been forgotten. It was found for instance that the best formation was a pair of fighters flying abreast and about two hundred yards apart so that each could cover the other from attack, a method incidentally that was eventually adopted by all other countries and survived into the jet age. It had also been Oswald Boelke's tactic in the First World War, except that his spacing was about sixty yards, reflecting the smaller turning radius of the Albatros. Dog-fighting was not in fact over, it merely meant that combats would take place over a wider area of air space. Larger formations from four aircraft to whole squadrons were built up on the pair system, flying at varying heights to give cross-cover. Radio telephones enabled pilots to communicate with each other in flight so that squadrons acting as a unit could make sweeps covering several miles of sky. But by far the most valuable lesson that the Spanish Civil War taught the Germans was the effectiveness of a combined air and a ground plan of attack, in which tactical air forces comprising bomber, reconnaisance, fighter and ground-

attack squadrons were concentrated to make lightning strikes against opposing ground forces. From the success of such methods in Spain were created massive air fleets, *Luftflotten,* and the new concept of Lightning War, *Blitzkrieg,* that was to make such a devastating impact when Germany began its territorial expansion in Europe.

While the Messerschmitt Bf 109s were being given invaluable testing under war conditions in Spain and produced in such quantities that Germany could even afford to export machines to other countries in 1939, Britain was at last waking up to the Nazi threat. During the mid-1930s, public apathy and political irresponsibility had allowed the RAF to fall to fifth position among the world's air forces, equipped mainly with obsolete biplane fighters. Even the last and best of these, the Hawker Fury Mk II and the Gloster Gladiator (138) which began to enter service in 1937, were outclassed by the new monoplane fighters with which other nations were equipping themselves. But two British monoplane fighters were in fact under development as a result of the decision in 1934 to expand the RAF. The first was the famous Supermarine Spitfire, probably the greatest combat aircraft ever built. It was largely due to the effors of Supermarine's chief designer, R. J. Mitchell, that the Spitfire came to be what it was, based on his S6B racing seaplane which had won the Schneider Trophy outright for Britain in 1931. He was one of the few people who took the German threat seriously and although seriously ill he designed a single-seat fighter that was well ahead of its time and a great improvement even on the Air Ministry's specifications. The prototype Spitfire (134) which first flew in 1936 was Britain's first all-metal fighter, a small, clean design with distinctively curved wings and pointed wing-tips, built around the new 1,030 hp Rolls-Royce Merlin PV.12 engine. It was so advanced both structurally and aerodynamically that few modifications

133   **Messerschmitt Bf 109 prototype,** built 1935 around the 610 hp Junkers Jumo 210A engine. As this was not available for the first flights, a Rolls-Royce Kestrel V was temporarily installed. Over 35,000 109s of various types were produced, more than any other single-seat fighter in aviation history. It accounted for nearly two-thirds of Germany's output of fighters from 1939 to 1945 and equipped the air forces of several other countries; examples were still in use up to the mid-1960s.

134   **Supermarine Spitfire prototype,** developed 1936 from the Supermarine S6B racing seaplane which won the Schneider Trophy outright for Britain in 1931 and the most famous fighter of the Second World War. It was the only Allied fighter to remain in continuous production throughout the war. Over 20,000 of a large number of variants were built. The Spitfire was best known for its role in the Battle of Britain, when it was the one fighter which was superior to the Bf 109.

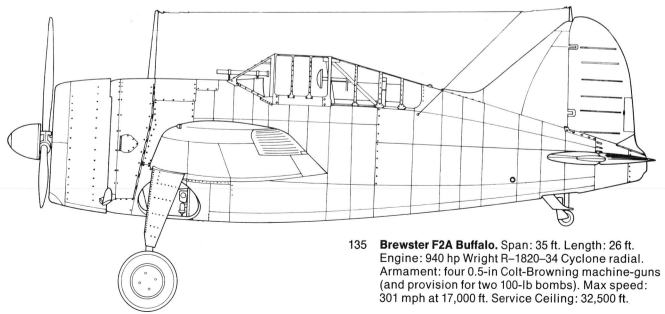

135   **Brewster F2A Buffalo.** Span: 35 ft. Length: 26 ft. Engine: 940 hp Wright R–1820–34 Cyclone radial. Armament: four 0.5-in Colt-Browning machine-guns (and provision for two 100-lb bombs). Max speed: 301 mph at 17,000 ft. Service Ceiling: 32,500 ft.

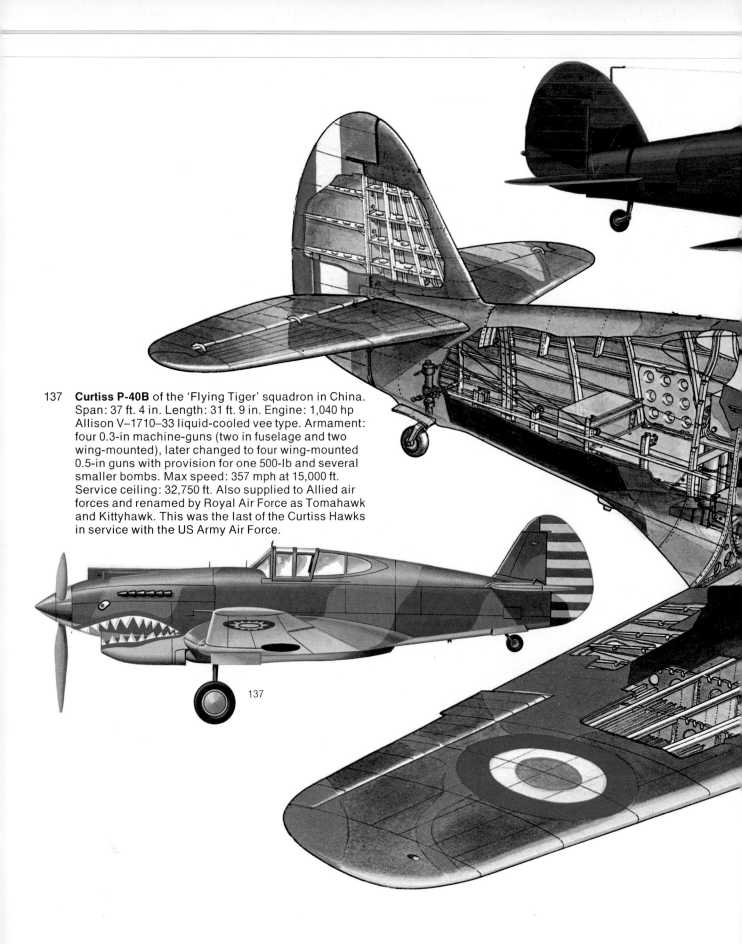

137 **Curtiss P-40B** of the 'Flying Tiger' squadron in China.
Span: 37 ft. 4 in. Length: 31 ft. 9 in. Engine: 1,040 hp
Allison V–1710–33 liquid-cooled vee type. Armament:
four 0.3-in machine-guns (two in fuselage and two
wing-mounted), later changed to four wing-mounted
0.5-in guns with provision for one 500-lb and several
smaller bombs. Max speed: 357 mph at 15,000 ft.
Service ceiling: 32,750 ft. Also supplied to Allied air
forces and renamed by Royal Air Force as Tomahawk
and Kittyhawk. This was the last of the Curtiss Hawks
in service with the US Army Air Force.

137

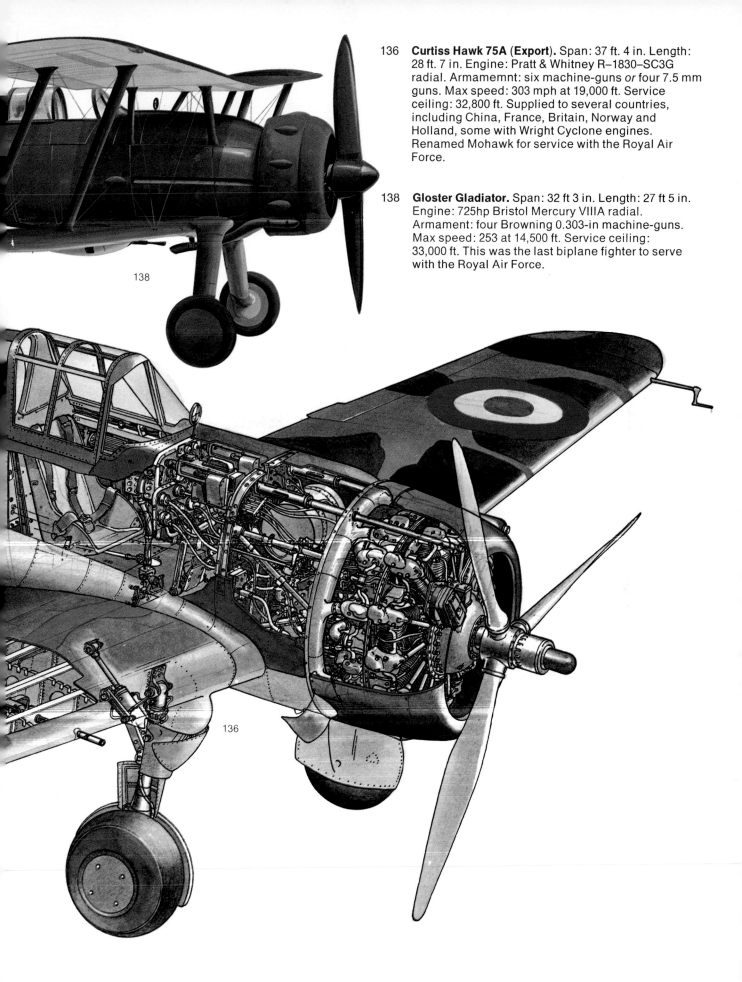

136 **Curtiss Hawk 75A (Export).** Span: 37 ft. 4 in. Length: 28 ft. 7 in. Engine: Pratt & Whitney R–1830–SC3G radial. Armamemnt: six machine-guns *or* four 7.5 mm guns. Max speed: 303 mph at 19,000 ft. Service ceiling: 32,800 ft. Supplied to several countries, including China, France, Britain, Norway and Holland, some with Wright Cyclone engines. Renamed Mohawk for service with the Royal Air Force.

138 **Gloster Gladiator.** Span: 32 ft 3 in. Length: 27 ft 5 in. Engine: 725hp Bristol Mercury VIIIA radial. Armament: four Browning 0.303-in machine-guns. Max speed: 253 at 14,500 ft. Service ceiling: 33,000 ft. This was the last biplane fighter to serve with the Royal Air Force.

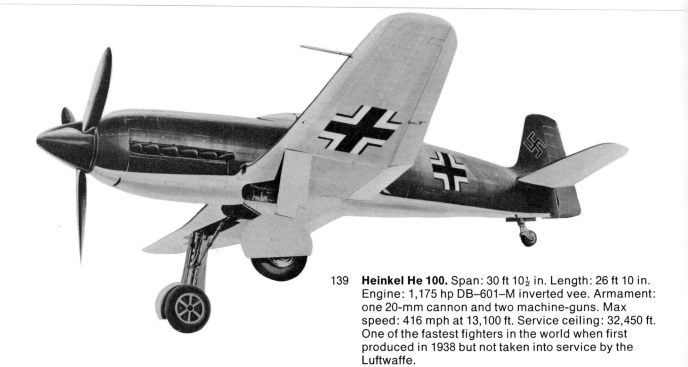

139 **Heinkel He 100.** Span: 30 ft 10½ in. Length: 26 ft 10 in. Engine: 1,175 hp DB–601–M inverted vee. Armament: one 20-mm cannon and two machine-guns. Max speed: 416 mph at 13,100 ft. Service ceiling: 32,450 ft. One of the fastest fighters in the world when first produced in 1938 but not taken into service by the Luftwaffe.

were required and a production order of 450 machines was given that same year. Another advantage was the availability of the reliable Browning .303 machine-gun which carried 1,200 rounds, sufficient for fifteen seconds' fire. These were mounted in the wings, four to begin with but later increased to eight. The first Spitfire Mk 1s (182) went into service with No. 19 Squadron in mid-1938. The original Air Ministry specification had called for a speed of not less than 275 mph at 15,000 feet and a ceiling of 33,000 feet, which was itself a considerable advance on the RAF's fastest fighter of that time, the Hawker Fury Mk II with a top speed of 223 mph. Mitchell produced an airplane with a speed of 355 mph at 19,000 feet and a ceiling of 34,000 feet that was soon increased with the fitting of three-blade variable-pitch propellers in place of the original two-blade fixed-pitch type. He died in 1937, having seen only his first prototype fly.

The other single-seat fighter forever associated with the Spitfire in the Battle of Britain was the Hawker Hurricane which began its development in 1933 as a monoplane version of the Hawker Fury. The prototype first flew in 1935, a few months before the Spitfire, and it first entered service in 1937. Like the Spitfire it was powered by the Rolls-Royce Merlin engine and was armed from the beginning with eight wing-mounted Browning machine-guns, unprecedented at that time and one reason for Messerschmitt increasing the armament on his fighters. Although sometimes confused with the Spitfire it was in fact considerably different. It was rather larger and heavier and while covered at the front with detachable metal panels, the aft section of the tubular-metal fuselage was fabric over wooden formers. Its undercarriage retracted outwards. Top speed of the Hurricane Mk I (148) was 324 mph at 17,500 feet and it did not have quite the ceiling or rate of climb of the Spitfire. Nevertheless it was one of the great fighters of the war and equipped more RAF squadrons in 1939 than the Spitfire.

The main single-seat fighter in service with the French Air Force at the outbreak of war was the Morane-Saulnier

406 (160) a low-wing monoplane powered by the 850 hp Hispano 12 Y-31 engine which gave it a top speed of 305 mph at 16,400 feet, armed with a Hispano 9 cannon firing through the propeller shaft and two machine-guns in the wings. Some of the Dewoitine D 500s and D 501s were still operational although this type had largely been withdrawn. The more advanced Bloch 151 and 152 (150) all-metal low-wing monoplanes had been delivered but were not ready for flying owing to shortages of some equipment, the French Air Force having suffered the same neglect during the 1930s as the RAF. This fighter had made its first flight in 1937 and was armed either with four machine-guns in the wings or two cannon and two machine-guns. A later model, the Bloch 155, was powered by the 1,180 hp Gnôme-Rhône radial engine which gave it a top speed of 348 mph at 18,000 feet and a ceiling of 33,500 feet. It had armour protection for the pilot and two additional machine-guns.

The interest in twin-engined fighters that led to the development of the Messerschmitt Bf 110 had originated largely in France. In addition to the lightweight type of fighter the French had in the early 1930s turned their attention to large twin-engined multi-seat aircraft which were intended to perform in a triple role as bomber, fighter and reconnaissance. A number built by Breguet and Potez (130) were essentially bombers but from this requirement was developed the Potez 630 monoplane series, a three-seat day and night fighter which began entering service in 1938, powered by two Gnôme-Rhône 14 Mars engines. It was of all-metal construction, except for the fabric-covered control surfaces, and had a tailplane with two fins and rudders. Various versions were made for different purposes but as a fighter the Potez 631 was formidably armed with two nose-mounted Hispano 9 or 404 cannon, six MAC machine-guns mounted under the wings, and another for rear defence. In the Netherlands Fokker also produced a twin-engined fighter, the mid-wing G.1 with the tail assembly carried on two booms extending back from the 750 hp Hispano-Suiza radial engines. The

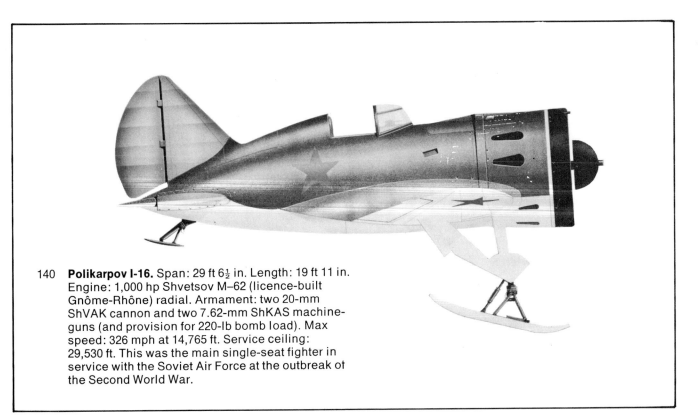

140 **Polikarpov I-16.** Span: 29 ft 6½ in. Length: 19 ft 11 in. Engine: 1,000 hp Shvetsov M–62 (licence-built Gnôme-Rhône) radial. Armament: two 20-mm ShVAK cannon and two 7.62-mm ShKAS machine-guns (and provision for 220-lb bomb load). Max speed: 326 mph at 14,765 ft. Service ceiling: 29,530 ft. This was the main single-seat fighter in service with the Soviet Air Force at the outbreak of the Second World War.

two crew sat in a central nacelle. This unusual aircraft created immense interest when it was first displayed at the 1936 Salon de l'Aeronautique, especially in view of its intended armament of no less than nine machine-guns, eight of them concentrated in the nose, or two cannon and three machine-guns. It was the last of the great line of Fokker fighters and a three-seat version, the G.IA, ordered by the Dutch Air Force, was the most effective military aircraft in the Netherlands at the outbreak of war. As an 'aircraft destroyer' type of fighter it had a certain affinity both in concept and design with the Vickers F.B.5 'Gunbus' developed before the First World War. It was a revival of interest in the same idea in Britain that led to the introduction of the two-seat Boulton Paul Defiant with its rear gun turret.

The Americans on the other hand had abandoned the two-seat fighter along with the biplane type, and with the Curtiss P-36 embarked on a new line of single-seat monoplane fighters. Built as a private venture in 1935, the P-36 had an enclosed cockpit and retractable undercarriage and could achieve almost 300 mph at 10,000 feet with the 1,050 hp Pratt and Whitney radial engine. In common with most American fighters at that time, armament consisted of one 0.30-inch and one 0.50-inch machine-gun in the engine cowling while two more 0.30-inch machine-guns were mounted in the wings of later models. Deliveries to the US Army Corps began in 1938 and a few saw action during the Japanese attack on Pearl Harbour in December 1941. But it was the export version of the P-36, known as the Curtiss Hawk 75 (136) and thus reviving the famous name that had always been associated with biplanes in the United States, that saw more operational use. Originally this version had a fixed undercarriage and a lower-powered 875 hp Wright radial engine in order to keep costs down, but so successful was the type in world markets that more of the higher-powered standard models were bought. French versions, equipped with four or six 7.5-mm machine-guns, were later transferred to the RAF where they were known as 'Mohawks' and saw service in Burma

and the Far East. Other purchasing countries included Argentina, Siam, Norway and the Netherlands, whose air force used them operationally against the Japanese during the invasion of the Netherlands East Indies.

But perhaps the best known area of operations in which Hawks flew was in China, where they comprised the main fighter type in the tiny Chinese Air Force following the Japanese invasion from Manchuria in July 1937. Like the Germans in the Spanish Civil War this conflict gave the Japanese a chance to try out new tactics for the much greater war of expansion they were planning. The new Mitsubishi and Nakajimi monoplane fighters quickly established air superiority over China, enabling Japanese bombers to raid defenceless cities virtually at will, but they never succeeded in wiping out all air resistance. This was largely due to the efforts of Captain Claire L. Chennault, a retired American Army Air Corps officer who in 1937 became air adviser to the Chinese government. He organised a highly efficient warning network throughout China by means of thousands of simple radio sets distributed to the peasants who reported on the movements of Japanese aircraft, and at the same time trained the Chinese pilots to harass the invaders both in the air and on the ground. With only a few aircraft and even fewer trained pilots these were little more than guerrilla tactics in a war that was being lost but they held the enemy for a while until the conflict became a much wider issue with Japan's invasion of South-East Asia. The worst moment came in 1940 when the Japanese decided to use the war in China to try out the new Mitsubishi A6M Zero-Sen (169), a sleek low-wing monoplane with two 7.7-mm fuselage-mounted machine-guns and two 20-mm wing cannon and long-range fuel tanks which enabled bombers to be continuously escorted on thousand-mile round trips. The Zero was one of the best fighters in the world at that time and developed into the most famous of all Japanese warplanes. The threat to the main supply route of the Burma Road on which China's survival depended caused President Roosevelt in 1941 to declare all-out aid for China

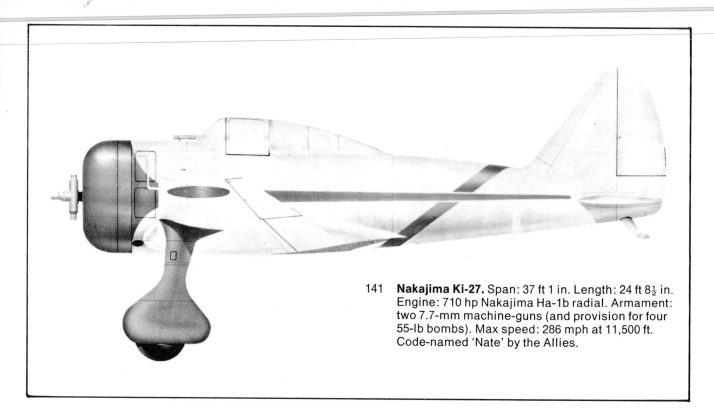

141 **Nakajima Ki-27.** Span: 37 ft 1 in. Length: 24 ft 8½ in. Engine: 710 hp Nakajima Ha-1b radial. Armament: two 7.7-mm machine-guns (and provision for four 55-lb bombs). Max speed: 286 mph at 11,500 ft. Code-named 'Nate' by the Allies.

and led to the formation of an American Volunteer Group of recently discharged military pilots who would fight under Chennault's command. They were supplied with the new Curtiss P-40 'Tomahawk' low-wing monoplane (137), the last of the Hawk fighters. Although no match against the faster and more manoeuverable Zero they could take a greater amount of punishment from machine-gun and anti-aircraft fire and had the asset of armour-plating to protect the pilots. The American volunteers painted rows of teeth on the engine covers which were unusually long to encompass the new liquid-cooled in-line Allison engine, as a result of which they came to be known as 'The Flying Tigers'. Together with RAF Buffalo fighters and Hurricanes operating from Burma they fought a grim four-months battle until May 1942 when the Japanese defeated the Allied ground forces in Burma, cutting off the Burma Road, and Chennault had to return to bases in China.

In Europe at the end of the 1930s other fighters were lining up in the air forces of those countries that would be involved in the threatening hostilities. In addition to those already mentioned Czechoslovakia had also produced its own fighter which became the standard air force type in 1938. This was the Avia B534 (143), a biplane but one of the finest of its kind with a Hispano-Suiza in-line engine giving 249 mph at 13,000 feet and armed with two machine-guns in the fuselage sides and a third firing through the propeller hub. Yugoslavia had a small number of the Ikarus IK-2, an all-metal monoplane with high braced wing that had been designed in 1934 to equip the Yugoslavian Air Force in addition to its foreign-built fighters. It was powered by the 860 hp Hispano-Suiza liquid-cooled engine with a built-in 20-mm *moteur canon* firing through the propeller hub and two 7.92-mm Darne machine-guns in front of the cockpit.

But the fighter that would see most of the early action against the Messerschmitt 109s was the P.Z.L. gull-wing single-seater which equipped the Polish Air Force. This series of graceful airplanes, the parasol wing so formed in order to give the pilot a better view over the engine, had

begun in 1929 with the P.1 which was one of the best fighters in the world at that time, powered by the 600 hp Hispano-Suiza V-type engine. Later models used radial engines and with the P.7 of 1933 the Polish Air Force was the first in the world to have a first-line fighter force of all-metal monoplanes. By 1939 most of its fighter squadrons were equipped with the P.11c (147), powered by the 645 hp Mercury VI S.2 engine which gave a top speed of 242 mph at 18,000 feet and a ceiling of 36,000 feet, but by then the type was already obsolete. The final development of this Pulawski-designed fighter was the P.24, adapted for Turkish, Bulgarian and Roumanian requirements and which, with a 970 hp Gnôme-Rhône 14 N7 engine giving 267 mph at 13,900 feet, constituted the main fighter strength of the Greek Air Force in 1939. When it had first appeared in 1934 it was the world's fastest radial-powered fighter at that time with a top speed of 257.2 mph and also the world's first twin-cannon interceptor, with two cannon mounted in the wing strut fairings in addition to two machine-guns on top of the fuselage. This was one answer to the problem of where to mount the modern-type 20-mm cannon for fighter aircraft that was introduced by the French in the early 1930s. Wing-mountings proved difficult at first because the wings lacked sufficient structural rigidity at that time; it was not until early 1939 for instance that an experimental installation was made in the wing of a Hurricane. In the meantime the *moteur canon* had been preferred by most designers, firing through the hollow propeller shaft. The other solution of course was to mount cannon in the nose of twin-engined fighters, such as the Messerschmitt 110, and this was the form later taken by the first British fighter expressly designed for cannon armament, the Westland Whirlwind, which was also the world's first twin-engined single-seater.

142 **Mitsubishi A5M4.** Span: 36 ft 1 in. Length: 24 ft 9½ in. Engine: 710 hp Nakajima Kotobuki 41 radial. Armament: two 7.7-mm machine-guns (and provision for two 66-lb bombs). Max speed: 273 moh at 9,800 ft. Service ceiling: 32,100 ft. The first monoplane fighter to enter service with the Japanese Navy, code-named 'Claude' by the Allies.

The Second World War

One of the great lessons of the Second World War was the overriding importance of air power, although not always in the ways that might have been envisaged. The bombing of cities for instance often produced the opposite result of what was intended by increasing the morale of civilian populations instead of decreasing it, while military-industrial targets showed a remarkable ability to recover and continue production even after apparently devastating attacks. On the other hand, the laying of mines from the air was found to be far more effective against merchant shipping in the North Sea and English Channel than direct bombing. Air power could be a decisive factor in itself, such as in the Pacific where the carrier-based torpedo bomber made the battleship virtually obsolete. But generally speaking the most effective use of air power was in combination with other forces, as shown by the early German *blitzkriegs* and the Allied combined operations assault on Normandy in 1944.

The fighter airplane played a vital role throughout the war both for offensive and defensive day fighting, night fighting, long-range bomber escort, ground attack, bombing and reconnaissance. Tremendous strides were made in its technology, just as in the First World War. While there were still a few biplane fighters in service in 1939, the first jets had arrived by 1945. Speeds increased from 300 to 600 mph, fighting heights rose to 40,000 feet, and the first early-warning system of visual signals gave place to airborne radar. Armament progressed from mostly machine-guns to cannon (20-mm, 30-mm and even 50-mm) and then on to the first rocket missiles. It had been thought before the war that aerial combat between fighters was a thing of the past, in view of their increased weight and speed. The early air battles showed that fighters only needed more space to be able to engage in the same kind of dog-fighting as their predecessors, but by the end of the war that prediction had largely come true. Manoeuvre-ability decreased with higher speeds until the day of massive air battles between hundreds of fighters was indeed over.

In 1939 the *Luftwaffe* had a first-line force of 3,609 aircraft, together with 552 transports, and a strength of over half a million officers and men. It was with this formidable air force, the biggest in the world at that time and grouped into large tactical Air Fleets, *Luftflotten,* that Germany embarked on territorial expansion in Europe. Having annexed Austria, the Rhineland and Czechoslovakia without a shot being fired, Hitler turned his attention on Poland. Early in the morning of September 1st the German Army crossed the Polish frontier, spearheaded by tanks and heavy air attacks. The Second World War had begun and a new name came to terrorize the peoples of Europe, *blitzkrieg.* Against a force of 1,581 aircraft in *Luftflotten* I and IV, including 210 fighters, the Polish Air Force could muster only 279 aircraft of which 159 were P.Z.L. single-seat fighters. The German plan was to destroy the Polish Air Force on the first day by bombing airfields and hangars so that the *Luftwaffe* could then concentrate on helping the army. But the Poles, forewarned of the attack by the usual German propaganda campaign, had hidden their fighters on special landing strips while obsolete and unserviceable machines were left on the airfields to deceive the Germans that the bombers were succeeding in their objective. Three days later the Polish fighters took off from their hiding-places to fight the first air battles of the Second World War. The Germans were taken by surprise initially but the Messerschmitt 109s were more than a match for the out-dated P.Z.L.s. Nevertheless, for two weeks the Poles fought courageously to intercept enemy bombers and strafe the advancing Wehrmacht, shooting down 126 German aircraft for a loss of 114 of their own. On September 17th the fight ended, with total aircraft losses on both sides being German 285, Polish 333. Ten days later, after the massive air and artillery bombardment of Warsaw, Poland surrendered. Apart from shooting the tiny Polish Air Force from the skies, the *Luftwaffe's* greatest contribution to the German victory was in the use of Junkers Ju 87 dive bombers to aid the army on the ground. Developing the tactics he had employed in Spain General von Richthofen, the *Luftwaffe's* field commander,

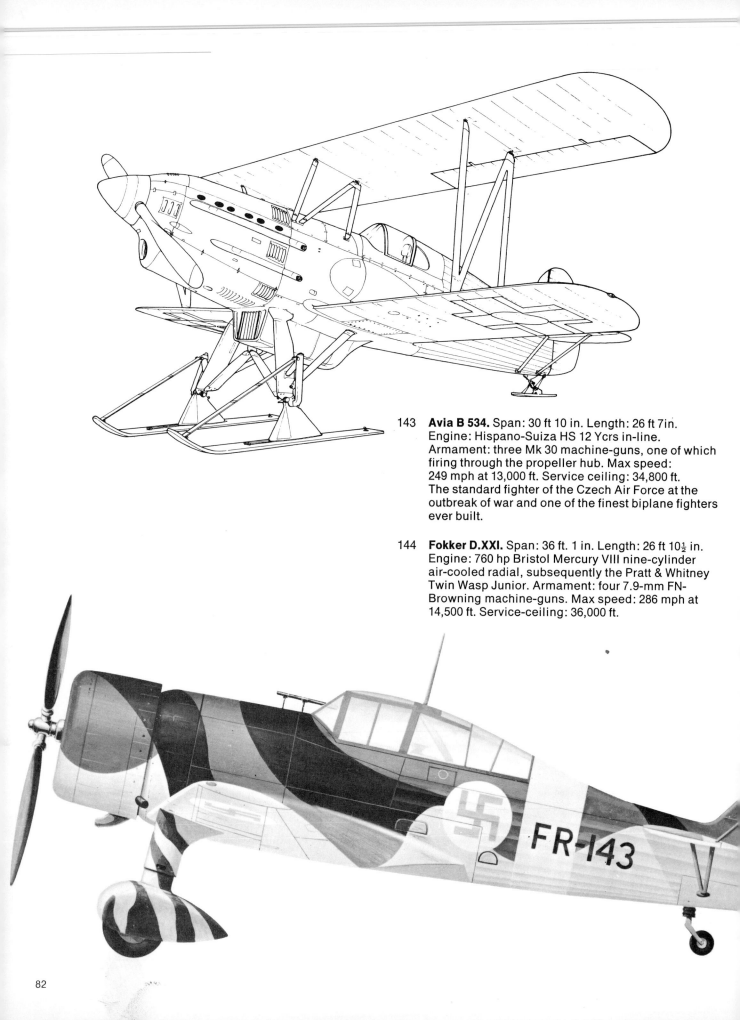

143 **Avia B 534.** Span: 30 ft 10 in. Length: 26 ft 7in.
Engine: Hispano-Suiza HS 12 Ycrs in-line.
Armament: three Mk 30 machine-guns, one of which
firing through the propeller hub. Max speed:
249 mph at 13,000 ft. Service ceiling: 34,800 ft.
The standard fighter of the Czech Air Force at the
outbreak of war and one of the finest biplane fighters
ever built.

144 **Fokker D.XXI.** Span: 36 ft. 1 in. Length: 26 ft 10½ in.
Engine: 760 hp Bristol Mercury VIII nine-cylinder
air-cooled radial, subsequently the Pratt & Whitney
Twin Wasp Junior. Armament: four 7.9-mm FN-
Browning machine-guns. Max speed: 286 mph at
14,500 ft. Service-ceiling: 36,000 ft.

145 **Fiat G.50** **Freccia** (**Arrow**). Span: 36 ft 1 in. Length: 25 ft 7in. Engine: 870 hp Fiat A.74 RC 38 radial. Armament: two 12.7-mm Breda-SAFAT machine-guns. Max speed: 293 mph at 16,400 ft. Service ceiling: 32,500 ft. The first all-metal single-seat fighter monoplane to enter Italian Air Force service.

used reconnaissance aircraft to spot targets for the army and dive-bombers as long-range artillery. The steep diving attack enabled a high degree of accuracy to be achieved while the scream made by the Ju 87s devastated the morale of the ground troops. It was in Poland that the 'Stuka' legend was born, the name taken from the German word for dive-bomber.

In Britain meanwhile, war had been declared on September 3rd as an inevitable consequence of Germany's invasion of Poland. The vulnerability of British cities and military targets to bomber attacks, especially with the advanced aircraft being built in the mid-1930s, had been only too apparent and was one reason for the decision in 1934 to expand the RAF. British strategy hinged on the creation of a fighter force of Hurricanes and Spitfires to intercept enemy bombers, while at the same time a force of heavy bombers was building up to strike into the heart of industrial Germany. The former Air Defence of Great Britain was split up into various groups, including Fighter Command under Air Marshal Sir Hugh Dowding who reckoned that fifty-three squadrons were essential for the defence of the United Kingdom. By September 1939 the re-equipment programme was still under way and was not expected to be completed until 1942, whereas German production had then reached its peak. First-line strength of the Metropolitan RAF amounted to 1,476 aircraft and that of the Air Force overseas to 435, about half the total available to the *Luftwaffe*. But of more immediate importance, against the German long-range striking force of some 1,500 bombers, Fighter Command could muster only some 350 modern eight-gun fighters formed into twenty-two squadrons, mostly Hurricanes for the Spitfires were only just coming into service, and a further thirteen squadrons of out-dated biplanes. This defence force was depleted still further by the decision to send Hurricane squadrons to France to provide air cover for the British Expeditionary Force, initially four but later increased by another nine.

However, partly off-setting this deficiency, Britain had organised an effective warning system that would give the fighters time to get off the ground to intercept enemy raiders. Methods of detecting airplanes by means of reflected radio waves which could be transmitted and seen on a cathode-ray tube had been studied before the war by scientists in the United States, Germany and France, but it was in Britain, thanks largely to the work of R. A. Watson-Watt of the National Physics Laboratory, that radar was most highly developed. A chain of coastal stations built in the southern and eastern areas could detect medium-altitude formations up to 100 miles away and indicate their strength, course and speed. Friendly aircraft were distinguished by the transmission of a special signal. Radar provided a scientific means of interception which greatly increased the efficiency of Britain's woefully low fighter strength, while improved radio communication enabled close control to be maintained from the ground.

During the so-called 'phoney war' of the winter of 1939/40, the *Luftwaffe* withdrew to its bases in Germany to refit while the British and French prepared for the campaigns of the coming summer. The French Air Force was even further behind in its re-equipment programme than the British. Of a first-line strength of 549 fighters over 130 were obsolete, as were seventy-five of its hundred bombers. In an attempt to rectify this situation ten squadrons of Fairey Battle day-bombers from RAF Bomber Command were sent to France early in September as an Advanced Air Striking Force. This three-seat single-engine bomber weighed twice as much as a Hurricane although powered by the same engine. With a top speed of 240 mph and armament of only one fixed and one moveable machine-gun, it soon proved to be a death-trap for its crews when up against the 354 mph Messerschmitt Bf 109E fighters armed with two 20-mm cannon and two machine-guns. It was withdrawn from daytime missions and used for night reconnaissance instead. A better performance was expected from the more heavily armed

146 **Fiat C.R.32.** Span: 31 ft 2 in. Length: 24 ft 5½ in.
Engine: Fiat A.30 liquid-cooled in-line. Armament:
two 12.7-mm and two 7.7-mm machine-guns (and
provision for 220-lb bomb load). Max speed:
233 mph at 9,850 ft. Service ceiling: 29,500 ft.
One of the most agile biplane fighters of the 1930s.
Equipped General Franco's *La Cucaracha* squadron
in Spanish Civil War and was main fighter type in
service with the Italian Air Force, together with its
successor the C.R.42, at the outbreak of the Second
World War.

146

147 **P.Z.L. P.11c.** Span: 35 ft 2 in. Length: 24 ft 9 in.
Engine: 560 hp Polish-built Bristol Mercury VI radial.
Armament: four 7.7-mm machine-guns. Max speed:
242 mph at 18,000 ft. Service ceiling: 36,000 ft.
Although obsolete by September 1939, the Polish
Air Force scored initial success with this fighter
against the Luftwaffe and the invading German
armies.

148 **Hawker Hurricane Mk I.** Span: 40 ft. Length:
31 ft 5 in. Engine: 1.030 hp Rolls-Royce Merlin II.
Armament: eight 0.303-in Browning machine-guns.
Max speed: 324 mph at 17,500 ft. Service ceiling:
34,200 ft. Developed in 1934 from the Hawker Fury
and best known for its part in the Battle of Britain,
when it shot down more enemy aircraft than all other
air and ground defences combined. In 1942 it was
outclassed as an interceptor and was used increasingly for ground-attack duties. In this role, the Mk IV
carried two Browning machine-guns for sighting
purposes, two 40-mm cannon, eight rocket
projectiles with 60-lb warheads, and a 500-lb bomb
load.

149 **Boulton Paul Defiant Mk I** Span: 39 ft 4 in.
Length: 35 ft 4 in. Engine: 1.030 hp Rolls-Royce
Merlin III. Armament: four 0.303-in Browning
machine guns in power-operated turret. Max speed:
303 mph at 16,500 ft. Service ceiling: 30,350 ft. This
two-seater used most successfully as a night fighter
equipped with interception radar.

147

twin-engined bombers such as the Blenheim and
Wellington, operating from eastern Britain. It was a
generally held theory by most of the major powers that
such aircraft flying in tight formations could break through
an enemy's defence on daylight raids. Since the Battle
have proved incapable of striking against industrial
targets in Germany, and in any case the British and
French were not anxious during this period to provoke
retaliation by bombing Germany, Bomber Command
switched its attack to German shipping and naval bases
in the North Sea. It was only by painful experience that
the RAF relearned the RFC's lesson in the First World War
that bomber formations alone, unescorted by fighters,
could not survive in daylight raids against well-equipped
fighter opposition, no matter how many guns and gun-
turrets they carried. This was made abundantly clear on
December 18th 1939 when a formation of twenty-two
Wellingtons without fighter screen or escort set out to
bomb German warships at Wilhelmshaven. They were

spotted by an experimental German radar unit and intercepted by a force of sixteen Bf109s and thirty-four Bf110s.
Ten Wellingtons were shot down, two ditched in the sea,
and three crash-landed after returning across the English
shore, for a loss of only two German fighters. The idea of
unescorted daylight bombing was temporarily abandoned.

The 'phoney war' ended on April 9th 1940 with Germany's
invasion of Denmark and Norway. Denmark could offer no
resistance and surrendered at the end of the day. Norway's
small and out-dated fighter force was quickly destroyed
and all known airfields were in enemy hands by the time
Britain decided to despatch a small expeditionary force to
help the Norwegians. One RAF fighter squadron was
included with this force, equipped with obsolete Gloster
Gladiators which were chosen because they could take off
from the aircraft-carrier *Glorious* and operate from small
landing grounds such as frozen lakes. A few enemy
airplanes were shot down but little could be done to stem

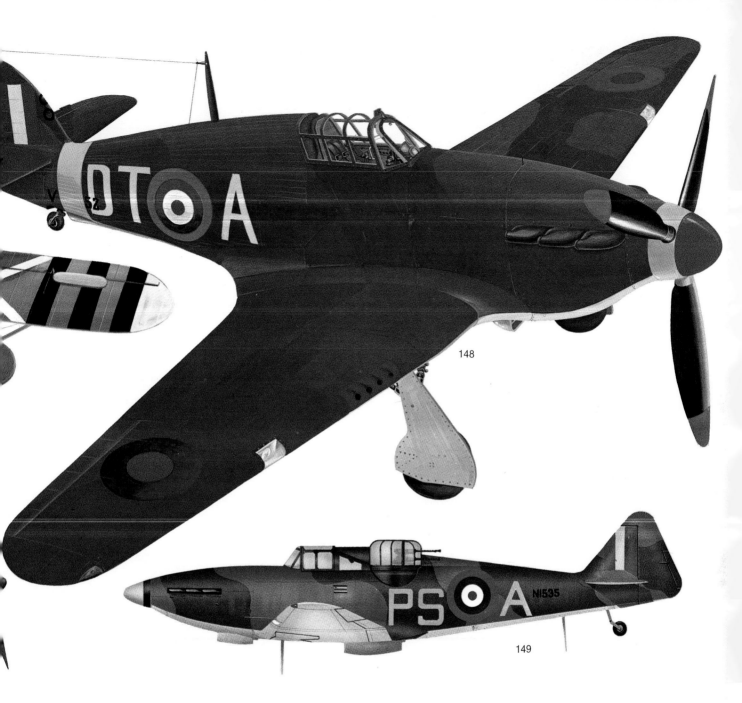

148

149

the relentless German advance through Norway, even after the arrival of a Hurricane squadron as reinforcement. The *Luftwaffe* was the decisive factor on the German side by providing air-to-ground support in difficult terrain and by dropping paratroops. Upon evacuation the remaining Gladiators and the Hurricanes, which had never before landed on an aircraft-carrier, were successfully flown to *Glorious,* but the vessel was sunk by German battleships on the voyage home.

On May 10th Germany launched the now familiar *blitz-krieg* onslaughts against Holland, Belgium and Luxem-bourg, including air attacks on airfields both in those countries and in France. The Dutch and Belgian air forces were virtually wiped out and only the Hurricanes of the seven RAF fighter squadrons then in France and the Morane-Saulnier 406s and Dewoitine D 250s of the ill-organised French Air Force could put up any resistance. The Hurricanes in particular took a tremendous toll of the

enemy in assisting the forward movement of the British Expeditionary Force, aided by long-range fighters from England. But at the same time the British bombers of the Advanced Air Striking Force suffered heavily from the marauding Messerschmitt fighters as daylight raids were resumed against the enemy, losing over half the strength of 135 Battles and Blenheims within three days. As the German armies swept through the Low Countries and across France, contemptuously by-passing the 'impreg-nable' Maginot Line, desperate calls were made to Fighter Command for more Hurricanes. Air Marshal Dowding resisted as best he could, realising that the decisive air battle would be fought over Britain and seeing his machines being thrown away in a hopeless battle in France, but he was forced to part with several more squadrons until a total of thirteen were stationed on French soil. The Hurricanes were not as fast as the Bf109Es, nor did they have as good a rate of climb although they were not so badly out-classed as the French Moranes.

Rolls-Royce Merlin II engines being installed in Spitfire Mk Is at Eastleigh, Hampshire. *Flight International*

But what often proved a vital factor was that the German pilots could open fire at a longer range with their 20-mm cannon against the Hurricanes' machine-guns. The Hurricane squadrons achieved considerable success at first against the Stuka dive-bombers until the Germans began flying in large formations, heavily escorted by twin-engined Bf 110s with 109s roving overhead and on the flanks. Sometimes there were as few as eight Hurricanes against sixty Stukas and thirty Messerschmitts. Many were destroyed before they could get through to the bombers.

After ten days fighting, with the fall of France imminent, the remnants of the Hurricane squadrons were ordered back to England. Out of a total of 261 aircraft sent to France, only sixty-six returned. The others had either been destroyed or were so badly damaged that they had to be left behind. Something like a quarter of Britain's entire strength in modern fighters had been written off. Then came the evacuation of the B.E.F. from Dunkirk in which, against all odds, some 340,000 British and French troops were ferried across the Channel to England from May 27th to June 4th. Hitler had made a great mistake in deciding to let the *Luftwaffe* deliver the final blow against the beleaguered Allied armies instead of the German Army for Dunkirk was within range of fighters based in southern England. Some 200 Hurricanes and Spitfires flew no less

than 2,739 sorties during the nine days of the evacuation, providing vital air cover over the beaches, but they were too few to prevent German bombers reducing the town and port of Dunkirk to rubble. Because of fuel limitations British fighters could only spend about forty minutes over the area and there were inevitably times when the ground troops were unprotected. But without their presence the evacuation would have been impossible. It was at Dunkirk that Messerschmitt 109s met Spitfires and found themselves for the first time outclassed in manoeuverability and turning although they had a higher service ceiling and a better rate of climb. Another British fighter used for the first time at Dunkirk was the two-seater Boulton Paul Defiant (149). From a distance it looked like a Hurricane and the Germans at first attacked from the rear as usual, only to receive an unpleasant shock from the four-gun power-operated turret. But the Defiant's success was short-lived. The Germans learned to attack it from ahead or below where its inferior performance soon showed. So many losses were inflicted that the Defiant was later withdrawn from front-line service; in 1941 the type was fitted with radar and used as a night fighter.

With the evacuation from Dunkirk over, the *Luftwaffe*

150 **Bloch 152.** Span: 34 ft. 7 in. Length: 29 ft 8½ in. Engine: 1,060 hp Gnôme-Rhône 14N-49 radial. Armament: two 20-mm cannon and two 7.5-mm machine-guns *or* four machine-guns. Max speed: 323 mph at 13,000 ft. Service ceiling: 32,800 ft.

151 **Arsenal VG-33.** Span: 35 ft 5¼ in. Length: 28 ft 4¼ in. Engine: 860 hp Hispano-Suiza 12Y-21. Armament: one 20-mm cannon and four 7.5-mm machine-guns. Max speed: 347 mph at 17,000 ft. Service ceiling: 36,280 ft.

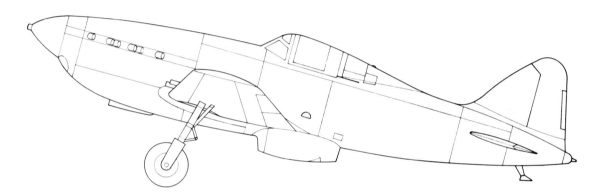

turned its attention to helping the German Army strike towards Paris. British fighters and bombers continued to harrass the advancing enemy but on June 25th France capitulated and the German campaign in the west was over. Within forty-six breathtaking days Germany, joined by Italy on June 10th now that victory seemed certain, had occupied most of western Europe. Only Britain now stood in the Nazi path. Much of Germany's success had been due to overwhelming air superiority which proved the lessons learned earlier in Spain. The air battles had produced the first fighter aces of the war; Adolph Galland and Werner Molders on the German side with seventeen and twenty-five victories respectively while the RAF's top scorer at that time was Flying Officer E. J. Kain, a New Zealander flying with No. 73 Squadron who shot down fourteen enemy aircraft. During May and June the RAF had lost 959 aircraft, including 477 of Dowding's precious fighters, against *Luftwaffe* losses of 1,284.

The Battle of Britain

It was now time for Germany to turn her attention on Britain. From the fighting that had already taken place and especially the superior performance of the Spitfire, the German General Staff realised that air supremacy was essential before the massive invasion armada being assembled could transport the German Army across the Channel. Goering reckoned he would need only two weeks to destroy the RAF as a fighting force. The Battle of Britain was about to begin.

During the month of July the *Luftwaffe* assembled three great Air Fleets for the task, totalling 2,800 aircraft. *Luftflotten* 2 and 3 were based along the Channel coast, their bombers within one hour's flight of London, while *Luftflotte* 5 was poised to intervene in the battle over Britain from bases in Norway and Denmark. The British aircraft industry had been making tremendous strides in production during 1940, producing about 1,600 machines a month by August of which 476 were fighters. Nevertheless, against the German first-line strength of over 1,200 long-range bombers, 280 dive-bombers and 1,000 fighters, Fighter Command could muster only 700 fighters of which 620 were Spitfires and Hurricanes. The RAF by itself, which had already lost nearly 300 fighter pilots over France and the Low Countries, could not have supplied the full strength to fly the sixty squadrons that had been formed, in spite of the loan of fifty-eight pilots from the Fleet Air Arm. But Fighter Command had the invaluable help not only of pilots from the Commonwealth and American volunteers but also those who had escaped from Poland, Czechoslovakia, France, Belgium and Holland.

Radar and an efficient fighter control system operating from the various Group headquarters scattered throughout Britain could hope to make up some of the material deficiency by avoiding the need for standing patrols so that the maximum number of aircraft would be available when most needed. But night attacks could also be expected, for which the Germans had developed a radio-beam system to guide bombers onto their targets. It was for this reason that the RAF brought night-fighters into service, carrying a new and at that time highly secret form of interception radar in order to locate bombers in darkness. The first airplane ever to be so equipped was the Bristol Blenheim with the armament of one fixed .303-inch

Messerschmitt Bf 110

152 **Bf 110 A-O.** Span: 53 ft 4¾ in. Length: 39 ft 8½ in. Engine: two 610 hp Jumo 210 B. Armament: five 7.9-mm machine-guns.

153 **Bf 110 C-4.** Span: 53 ft 4¾ in. Length: 39 ft 8½ in. Engine: two 1,100 hp DB 601 A twelve-cylinder inverted vee with direct fuel injection. Armament: two 20-mm cannon and three machine-guns. Max speed: 349 mph at 22,965 ft. Service ceiling: 32,000 ft.

154 **Bf 110 B-1.** Span: 53 ft 4¾ in. Length: 39 ft 8½ in. Engine: two 690 hp DB 600 A inverted vee. Armament: two 20-mm cannon and three machine-guns.

155 **Bf 110 D-3.** A fighter-bomber version of the C-series with long-range fuel tanks in place of the two 20-mm cannon and able to carry two 1,100-lb bombs.

156 **Bf 110 G-2/R1.** Span: 53 ft 4¾ in. Length: 41 ft 6¾ in. Engine: two 1,475 hp DB 605 B. Armament: one 37-mm Flak 18 gun, two 20-mm cannon and four machine-guns. Max speed: 342 mph at 22,900 ft. Service ceiling: 26,000 ft. The G-2 series were primarily fighter-bombers.

157 **Bf 110 G-4/R3.** A four-seat night-fighter version which was the first to carry airborne interception radar, the Lichtenstein SN-2 system.

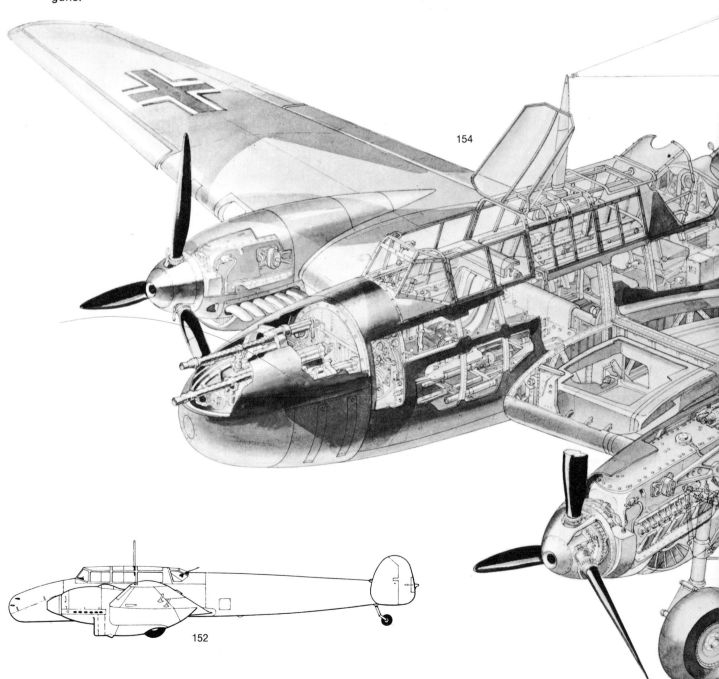

154

152

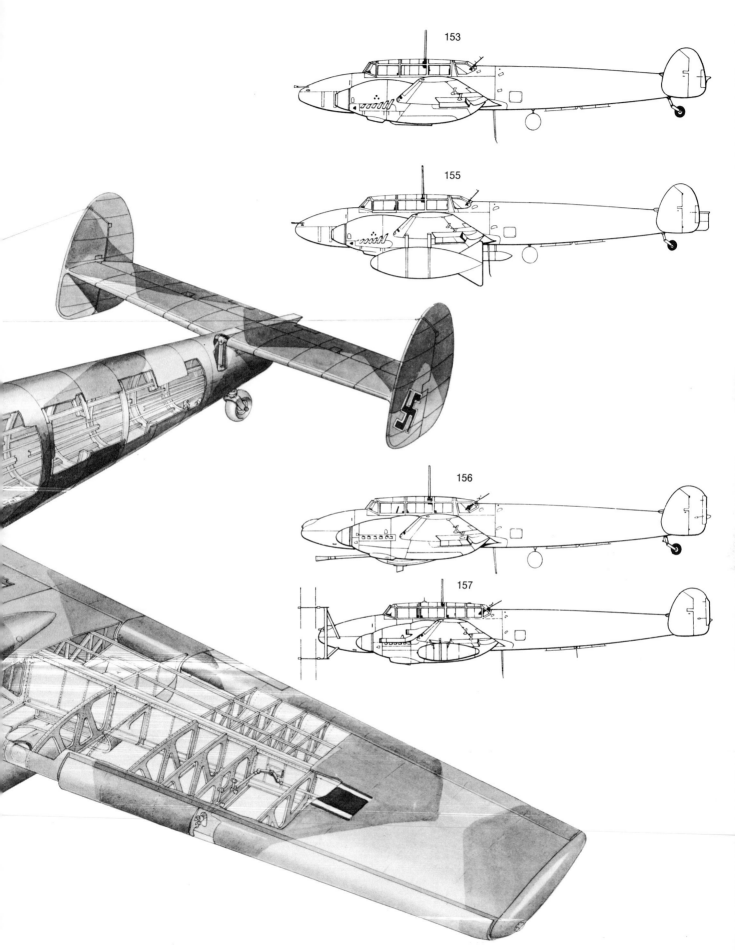

153

155

156

157

forward-firing Browning and one Vickers K gun in a semi-rotating turret augmented by four Brownings firing forward from an under-fuselage gun pack. Powered by two 840 hp Bristol Mercury radial engines the Blenheim had created a sensation when it first flew in 1935 by achieving 280 mph in level flight, considerably faster than the best fighters of that time. This was far below the fighter speeds of 1940 of course, but the Mk IF was a reasonably effective stop-gap until specifically designed night-fighters were available. Two other conversions from existing bomber types were also used for night-fighting at the start of the Battle of Britain, their twin engines leaving the nose free for the radar installation. First was the two-seat Bristol Beaufighter, many of its parts identical with those of the Beaufort torpedo-bomber but powered by more powerful 1,590 hp Hercules XI air-cooled radial engines giving speeds of about 330 mph. Its standard armament of four 20-mm cannon in the nose and six machine-guns in the wings made it the most heavily armed fighter in the world when it began production. The second was an American adaptation of the Douglas DB-7 light bomber known as the Havoc I, a single-seater armed with eight fixed forward-firing machine-guns. A number built in France before the German invasion were transferred to the RAF, which also bought direct from the United States. Some were equipped with powerful 2,700-million-candlepower Helmore Turbin-lite searchlights in addition to radar, the batteries being stowed in the bomb compartment. They carried no armament but special lights were fitted above the wings so that Hurricanes flying in formation with them could remain in contact. The idea was for a Havoc to track an enemy bomber, then suddenly illuminate it so that the Hurricane could go in for the kill. It was not very successful however, and neither was another night-fighting device fitted to the Havoc known as 'Pandora' which consisted of an explosive charge trailed 2,000 feet below in the path of the enemy.

On the German side the new D series of the twin-engined Messerschmitt Bf 110 (155) was coming into service in the spring of 1940, equipped with long-range fuel tanks which was something the British had not developed at that time. One version, the D-4, was equipped as a night-fighter to combat the growing number of raids by RAF heavy bombers as they tried to hinder preparations for the German invasion by attacking airfields in the occupied countries and industrial targets in Germany. The D-4 was not a great success for the Germans did not then have any system of airborne interception radar. Not until 1942 when radar was first introduced with the G-series (156) did the Bf 110 show itself in its true colours as Germany's most successful night-fighter. Before that however it had to suffer the ignominy of a crushing defeat in the Battle of Britain.

The first phase of the battle opened with German attacks on coastal shipping in the English Channel, partly in an attempt to lure the British fighters into the air. Fighter patrols had to be provided, wearing to both men and machines, for the Germans could pounce from their newly-won bases in France before being intercepted by radar-alerted reinforcements. Six hundred sorties a day were flown by Fighter Command and although greatly out-numbered, the Spitfires and Hurricanes shot down 227 enemy aircraft between July 10th and August 10th for a loss of ninety-six of their own. The Ju 87 dive-bombers were particularly vulnerable to the eight-gun British fighters. It was during this period, when many RAF pilots had to bale out into the sea, that an efficient air/sea rescue service was developed.

The main *Luftwaffe* offensive began on August 12th with daylight raids aimed at destroying fighter airfields and the vital south coast radar stations, followed by night raids from August 13th onwards against industrial centres. With growing intensity hundreds of bombers and dive-bombers would strike at five or six major targets each day, taxing in particular the resources of No. 11 Group (commanded by Air Vice-Marshal K. R. Park) which covered south-eastern England with thirteen squadrons of Hurricanes, six of Spitfires and two of Blenheims. But although heavily outnumbered the British fighters, with the help of radar and an efficient control system to ensure interception, scored heavily against the enemy. On August 15th for instance, when 520 bombers escorted by 1,270 fighters took part in raids in southern, south-eastern and north-eastern England, the score at the end of the day was seventy-six German losses against thirty-four by the RAF.

As the huge formations were shattered by skillful and determined attacks the bomber crews became so demoralized that accurate bombing was impossible and little damage was done on the ground. After ten days Fighter Command had shot down 367 enemy aircraft against a loss of 183 in combat and thirty on the ground. The *Luftwaffe* was certainly not succeeding in its lightning blow, but the British also could not face such losses with only a hundred fighters a week being supplied by the hard-pressed aircraft factories. In addition, 154 of the 1,000 fighter pilots available at the start of the battle had been killed or were severely wounded and only sixty-three replacements had come from the training establishments. Some of the key fighter control bases had been put out of action and many airfields damaged. By the end of the month each German bomber was being escorted by four fighters, instead of two as in the early days. The battles were now primarily between fighters in a grim war of attrition which over a period of four days saw 106 German aircraft lost to 101 by the RAF. The bombers were beginning to succeed in their objective of destroying Fighter Command airfields and control centres, especially as most were now protected by armour-plate which was difficult to penetrate with macine-guns. Heavy calibre cannon was required but these were in short supply at that time and only one Spitfire squadron was so equipped. A crisis point was reached in the first week of September when Fighter Command's reserve of aircraft to replace losses was down to 125 and the wastage of pilots was putting an even greater strain on those who were left. A concerted attack to eliminate the essential radar towers and control centres would give the *Luftwaffe* the air supremacy it sought. The German invasion armada was gathering strength across the Channel to strike when such a moment arrived.

And then, on September 7th at Hitler's insistence, the *Luftwaffe* switched its attack from the airfields and sector stations to London, as a reprisal for RAF Bomber Command raids on Berlin. It was the beginning of the 'Blitz' which saw large areas of London and other cities destroyed. But it saved the day by enabling Fighter Command to continue operations and to build up its strength. Goering and his staff had convinced themselves that Fighter Command was just about finished and barely had any aircraft left. It was wishful thinking. On September 15th, no less than twenty-one RAF squadrons took part in battles that raged all day against over 600 heavily escorted German bombers. Fifty-six were shot down and many more badly damaged, their crews killed or wounded, for a loss of twenty-six RAF fighters. Only slight damage was done to London and at the end of the day it was finally realised by the Germans that the RAF, far from being defeated, was showing signs of increased activity. The

158 Dewoitine D 520S. Span: 33 ft. 6 in. Length: 28 ft 9 in. Engine: 930 hp Hispano-Suiza 12Y–45 vee type with Szydlowski supercharger. Armament: one Hispano 20-mm cannon firing through the propeller hub and four 7.5-mm machine-guns. Max speed: 342 mph at 19,700 ft. Service ceiling: 34,500 ft. One of the most successful French fighters at the outbreak of war but never achieved the performance for which it was designed, owing to the non-availability of high-powered engines.

159   Cockpit of a Dewoitine D 520.

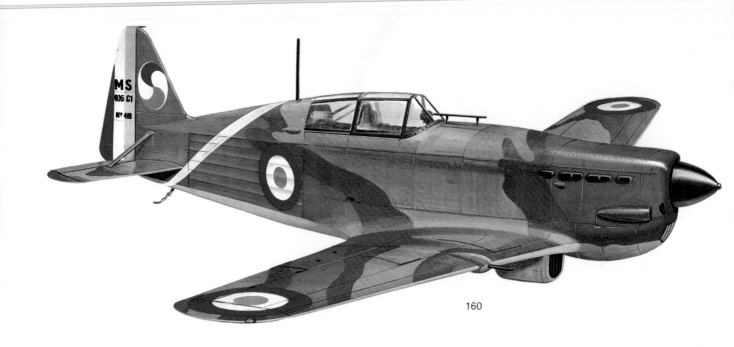

160

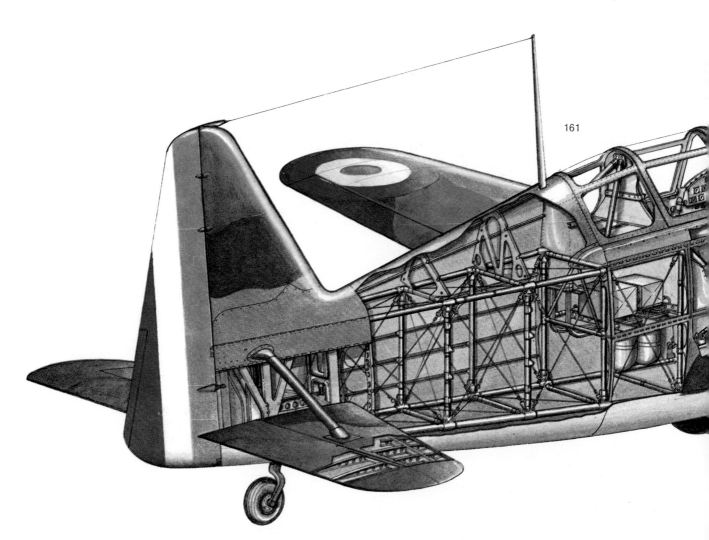

161

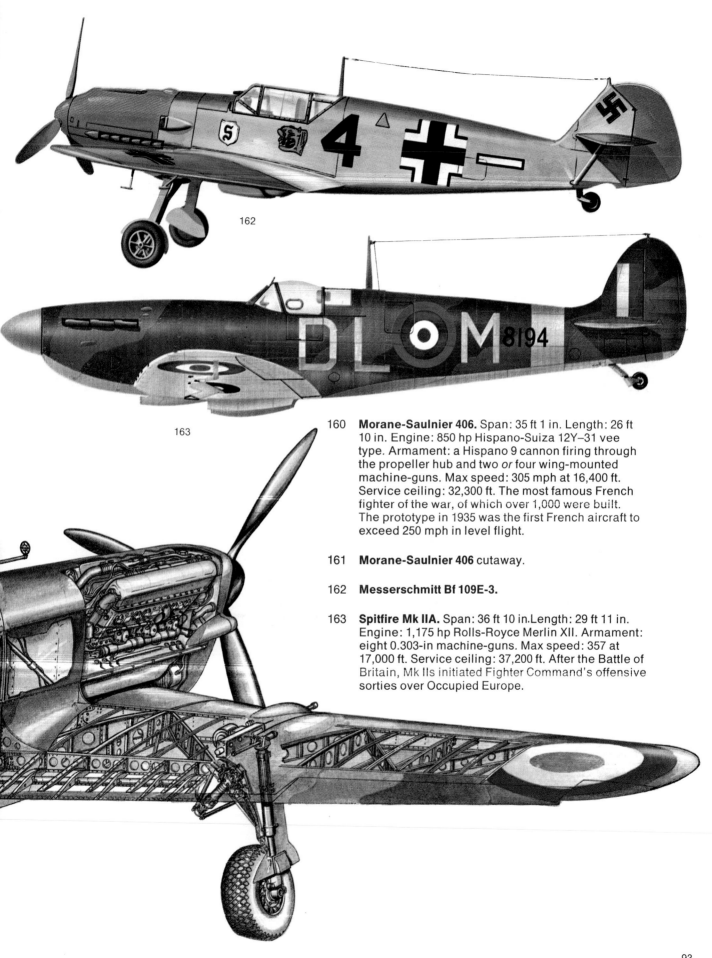

162

163

160 **Morane-Saulnier 406.** Span: 35 ft 1 in. Length: 26 ft 10 in. Engine: 850 hp Hispano-Suiza 12Y–31 vee type. Armament: a Hispano 9 cannon firing through the propeller hub and two *or* four wing-mounted machine-guns. Max speed: 305 mph at 16,400 ft. Service ceiling: 32,300 ft. The most famous French fighter of the war, of which over 1,000 were built. The prototype in 1935 was the first French aircraft to exceed 250 mph in level flight.

161 **Morane-Saulnier 406** cutaway.

162 **Messerschmitt Bf 109E-3.**

163 **Spitfire Mk IIA.** Span: 36 ft 10 in. Length: 29 ft 11 in. Engine: 1,175 hp Rolls-Royce Merlin XII. Armament: eight 0.303-in machine-guns. Max speed: 357 at 17,000 ft. Service ceiling: 37,200 ft. After the Battle of Britain, Mk IIs initiated Fighter Command's offensive sorties over Occupied Europe.

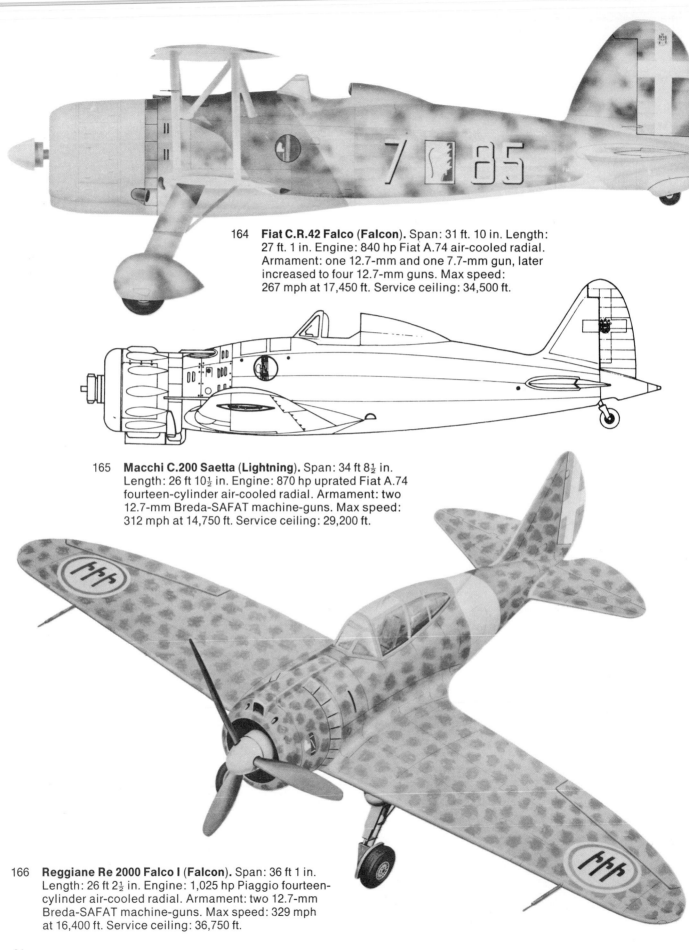

164 **Fiat C.R.42 Falco (Falcon).** Span: 31 ft. 10 in. Length:
27 ft. 1 in. Engine: 840 hp Fiat A.74 air-cooled radial.
Armament: one 12.7-mm and one 7.7-mm gun, later
increased to four 12.7-mm guns. Max speed:
267 mph at 17,450 ft. Service ceiling: 34,500 ft.

165 **Macchi C.200 Saetta (Lightning).** Span: 34 ft 8½ in.
Length: 26 ft 10½ in. Engine: 870 hp uprated Fiat A.74
fourteen-cylinder air-cooled radial. Armament: two
12.7-mm Breda-SAFAT machine-guns. Max speed:
312 mph at 14,750 ft. Service ceiling: 29,200 ft.

166 **Reggiane Re 2000 Falco I (Falcon).** Span: 36 ft 1 in.
Length: 26 ft 2½ in. Engine: 1,025 hp Piaggio fourteen-
cylinder air-cooled radial. Armament: two 12.7-mm
Breda-SAFAT machine-guns. Max speed: 329 mph
at 16,400 ft. Service ceiling: 36,750 ft.

plan to invade Britain was postponed indefinitely. Although it was not immediately apparent, the Battle of Britain had been won. The raids continued but by the end of October the Germans had lost a total of 1,733 aircraft against 915 RAF losses. Even the *Luftwaffe* could not take such a beating for so little return. In mid-November the bombing raids petered out as Hitler turned his eyes eastwards towards Russia and his second fatal mistake of the war.

The Battle of Britain was important not only because it saved Britain from invasion and possible defeat but because it taught many lessons in the use of fighter aircraft which held true for the rest of the war. It proved once again, as RAF Bomber Command had discovered during the Battle of France, that daylight raids stood little chance against determined fighter opposition. Interesting comparisons could be made between the fighters that took part. The Spitfire's engines gave a maximum performance at about 18,000 feet which made it ideal for attacking bombers which seldom flew above 17,000 feet. The Hurricane's optimum performance was at around 15,000 feet. The Bf 109E had better fighting qualities than either of the British fighters above 25,000 feet and since it took a Spitfire twenty minutes to climb to that altitude, the 109s invariably had the initial advantage of height. But as the dog-fighting circled lower the tighter turn of the Spitfire gave it the advantage. In the early days of the battle the *Luftwaffe* positioned their fighter escorts at about 4,000 feet higher and a mile behind the bomber formations, ready to pounce down on attacking British fighters. Because of the accurate information provided by radar, the British found they could exploit this gap by attacking the bombers and turning away before the 109s could interfere. The *Luftwaffe* replied by increasing the support for each bomber wing to three fighter wings, one flying ahead to clear the target area, one providing high escort cover, and a third flying level as close escort which meant reducing speed and weaving to keep in contact. The tactics employed by Fighter Command consequently were for the faster Spitfires to engage the escort fighters while the Hurricanes, slower but possessing excellent qualities as steady gun platforms, concentrated their attacks on the bombers. For that reason they actually scored more victories than the Spitfires. The enemy escorts were engaged at the earliest possible moment so that they would use up their fuel in combat and be forced to return to base, leaving the bombers to their fate. This was especially critical for the 109s which, like their British counterparts, had a radius of action of only about 125 miles. They could only remain for half-an-hour or so over Britain whereas the British fighters could stay in the air longer, then land to re-fuel, re-arm, and rejoin the battle. This was not such a problem for the long-range Bf 110s, but they were found to be hopelessly outclassed by the agile single-engined British fighters. Even their longer-ranging 20-mm cannon armament was not the advantage it might have been in combats that were usually fought at very close range. The point of convergence of the eight machine-guns mounted in the Spitfires and Hurricanes for instance was reduced from 450 yards to 250 yards for that very reason. The point was reached where the Bf 110 fighter escorts had themselves to be escorted by 109s. By the end of the battle over 300 had been destroyed and the 110 was from then on developed as a night-fighter.

There were bitter recriminations on the German side between the bomber crews and fighter pilots. There was no radio communication between the two, nor of course control from the ground, and it sometimes happened that the bombers became separated from their escorts because of bad weather or a failure to meet at the rendezvous point. The unescorted bombers would then suffer heavily from the British interceptors. The Stuka dive-bombers were a special problem. Their dive-brakes enabled them to dive at a steady speed while the escorting 109s could not hold back and soon overtook them, again leaving them at the mercy of the British fighters. Stuka losses were so great that they were temporarily withdrawn from the battle in mid-August. There was little agreement between the bomber crews and fighter pilots to the best escort tactics to employ. The former preferred a close escort while the latter wanted a free hand to seek out and engage the British fighter squadrons. They accused the bombers at times of wandering off course and exceeding their planned time over Britain which meant that the short-range 109s either had to leave them early or ditch in the sea on the way back. Neither group was helped by the conflicting orders and counter-orders issued by Goering who unfairly criticised his pilots for not pressing the attack hard enough. There were differences of opinion on the British side as well, such as the argument between small fighter wings or the large formations which Douglas Bader supported, but nothing like as great as on the German side. The tight vee formation of three was still being flown by some British squadrons when the battle opened, as against the superior loose four-abreast pattern flown by the Messerschmitts who could guard each others' tails. The vee gave way to four fighters flying in an open line-astern pattern, which was an improvement, but it was not until the following spring, mainly at Bader's instigation, that the abreast 'finger-four' formation was adopted. Other RAF 'aces' who did much to develop fighter tactics during the Battle of Britain included the great South African Sailor Malan, who scored thirty-two victories, Standford Tuck and John Cunningham.

Fighter Development

Meanwhile, Italy had entered the war with a first-line strength of just over 1,500 aircraft. Fiat C.R.32 and C.R.42 biplanes still constituted about two-thirds of the single-seat fighter strength but they were rapidly being replaced by monoplane types. The Fiat G.50 Arrow had already seen service during the Spanish Civil War, powered by an 840 hp Fiat radial engine, and an excellent development of this fighter was the Fiat G.55 Centaur with a Daimler-Benz in-line engine instead. Another major type was the Macchi C.200 Lightning (165), developed from the famous Macchi racing seaplane of the 1920s and 1930s with two 12.7-mm Breda-SAFAT machine-guns in the upper engine decking. This was also powered by a radial engine, the 870 hp Fiat A.74 in production machines, and again a later development, the C.202 Thunderbolt (248), used the Daimler-Benz liquid-cooled in-line engine.

In the early stages of the war in Africa, the Middle East and Mediterranean, the fighting between the twenty-nine RAF squadrons based throughout that entire area and the Italian Air Force was mainly between biplane fighters, the Gloster Gladiator on the one hand and the Fiat C.R.42 on the other. The British quickly established an air supremacy which was only threatened when the *Luftwaffe* intervened but even then was never entirely lost. Malta was the vital key as a British naval and air base from which to attack enemy convoys and as a refuge for Allied convoys supplying the armies in North Africa. As soon as the war

168 **De Havilland Mosquito.** Span: 54 ft 2 in. Length: 40 ft 11 in. Engine: two 1,460 hp Rolls-Royce Merlin 21/23 vee type. Armament: four 20-mm cannon and four 0.303-in machine-guns (and provision for 2,000-lb bomb load *or* adapted to carry one 4,000-lb 'block-buster'). Max speed: various types from 370 mph at 14,000 ft to 415 mph at 28,000 ft. Service ceiling: various types from 28,800 ft to 40,000 ft. This all-wood fighter-bomber was the most versatile aircraft to serve with RAF Bomber Command and was adapted for many different purposes. For interception it was mainly used as a night-fighter with interception radar.

began, the full weight of more than 200 Italian aircraft based in Sicily was hurled against Malta, whose only air defences to begin with consisted of four Sea Gladiator biplanes. One was destroyed early in the fight but the other three, immortalized as Faith, Hope and Charity, withstood the onslaught until Hurricane reinforcements could be sent. The Italians faced defeat on the sea, in the air and on land, and it was only the intervention of Germany towards the end of 1940, following her *blitzkriegs* into the Balkans, that saved her Axis ally from greater embarrassment. Greece capitulated on April 21st 1941 after the RAF squadrons based there and the small Greek Air Force had been wiped out, and in the following month the Germans launched an airborne assault on Crete which Hitler saw as the other key to the whole area. Although the attack succeeded, the Germans lost a great many aircraft and of even greater importance some of her most

experienced air crews, just as in the west in 1940. This had a marked effect when Germany attacked Russia at the end of June. Although the *Luftwaffe* established an early supremacy on the Eastern Front, helped by the surprise of the attack and the superiority of the new Messerschmitt Bf 109F (204), generally agreed to be the finest fighter of the series, the Germans were never again in the position of being able to launch a large scale airborne assault. Crete had become the grave of the German paratroop force.

Against the Bf 109F, powered by the new 1,300 hp DB 601E engine which gave it a maximum speed of nearly 400 mph and armed with a 20-mm cannon firing through the spinner and two 7.9-mm machine-guns above the engine cowling, the Russian fighters were heavily outclassed. Most squadrons were still equipped with Poli-

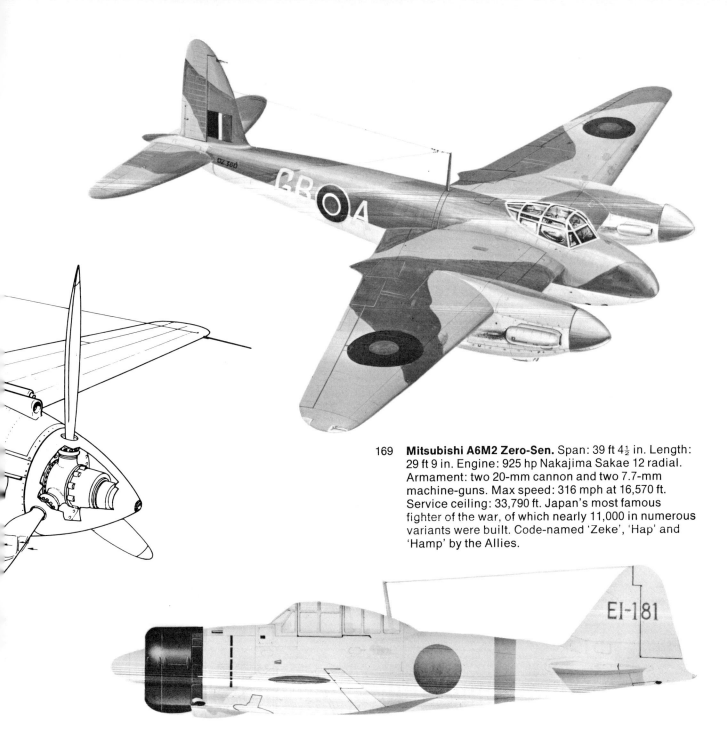

169 **Mitsubishi A6M2 Zero-Sen.** Span: 39 ft 4½ in. Length: 29 ft 9 in. Engine: 925 hp Nakajima Sakae 12 radial. Armament: two 20-mm cannon and two 7.7-mm machine-guns. Max speed: 316 mph at 16,570 ft. Service ceiling: 33,790 ft. Japan's most famous fighter of the war, of which nearly 11,000 in numerous variants were built. Code-named 'Zeke', 'Hap' and 'Hamp' by the Allies.

karpov I-16s of various types, with a maximum speed at sea level of 326.2 mph and a service ceiling of only 29,500 feet. In fact it was the slower 270 mph Polikarpov I-153 biplane, whose manoeuvrability compensated to some extent for the speed of the Messerschmitts and whose ceiling height was over 35,000 feet, that gave a slightly better account of itself. But a new generation of Russian fighters was coming into service in 1941, all low-wing monoplanes with liquid-cooled in-line engines and, unlike the mostly all-metal airplanes of other countries, partly constructed of wood. The first to be used extensively in combat was the Lavochkin LaGG-3 whose armament combinations included a 20-mm or 23-mm cannon firing through the propeller shaft and one heavy or two light machine-guns. Five machine-guns, of which three were 12.7-mm and two 7.62-mm, together with auxiliary fuel tanks, were fitted for escort duties with the Ilyushin

Stormovik (255) armoured ground-attack aircraft. It was at this time also that the first of the famous MiG fighters appeared, designed by a team under the leadership of A. I. Mikoyan and M. I. Gurevich. The MiG-1 prototype which appeared at the end of 1940 was very fast, 390 mph at 23,000 feet, and had a high ceiling of nearly 40,000 feet, but it lacked manoeuvrability. The MiG-3 (179) was a considerable improvement, over 7 mph faster and easier to handle with long-range fuel tanks and a sliding canopy. It was outstanding at above 16,400 feet, better than any fighters the Germans possessed until 1942, and formed the backbone of Russia's high-altitude fighter force. At lower altitudes speed and climb were inferior however, and the armament of one heavy and two light machine-guns was inadequate. Two additional heavy 12.7-mm machine-guns were later added under the wings.

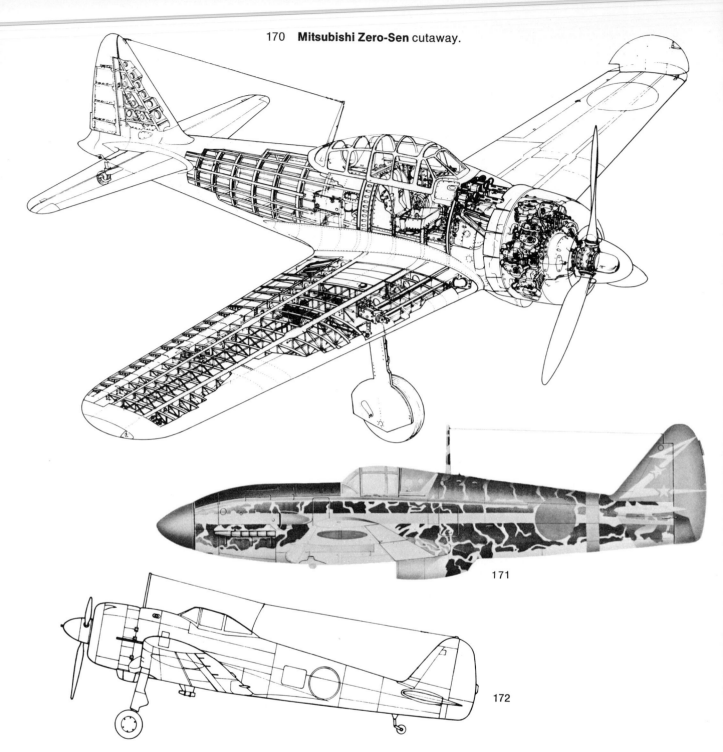

170 **Mitsubishi Zero-Sen** cutaway.

171

172

171 **Kawasaki Ki-61 Hien (Flying Swallow).** Span: 39 ft 4½ in. Length: 29 ft 4 in. Engine: 1,175 hp Ha–40 liquid-cooled inverted vee, based on the German DB 601 A. Armament: two 20-mm cannon and two 7.7-mm machine-guns. Max speed: 379 mph at 19,680 ft. Service ceiling: 36,000 ft. Developed for the Japanese Army Air Force and code-named 'Tony' by the Allies.

172 **Nakajima Ki-43 Hayabusa (Peregrine Falcon).** Span: 37 ft 6½ in. Length: 29 ft. Engine: 975 hp Sakae Ha–25 radial. Armament: two 12.7-mm and one 7.7-mm machine-guns. Max speed: 308 mph at 13,100 ft. Service ceiling: 38,500 ft. Code-named 'Oscar' by the Allies.

173 **Bell P-39 Airacobra.** Span: 34 ft. Length: 30 ft 2 in. Engine: 1,150 hp Allison V–1710–35 vee type. Armament: one 37-mm cannon firing through the propeller hub, two 0.5-in machine-guns mounted on the fuselage and four 0.3-in wing-mounted machine-guns. Max speed: 368 mph at 13,600 ft. Service ceiling: 33,000 ft. The only American fighter of the war to have its engine buried in the centre-fuselage. This was a turbo-supercharged Allison in the prototype but was changed to an ordinary in-line engine for production models which restricted their performance.

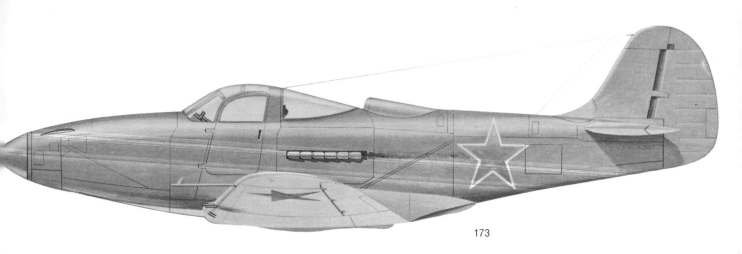

173

By far the best of the new Russian fighters was the Yak-1, designed by A. S. Yakovlev in 1938 to meet the monoplane fighter specification. Its wooden wing was built in one piece and together with a fuselage of welded steel tubes covered with fabric-faced plywood, it was notable for its lightness and graceful lines, ranking with the Spitfire, Messerschmitt BF 109 and Zero as one of the great fighters during the first two years of the war. The undercarriage and tailwheel were fully retractable and the 1,240 hp twelve-cylinder in-line engine gave it a maximum speed of 372 mph at 11,500 feet and a service ceiling of 33,000 feet. It was not as fast as the MiG-3 but more than made up for this by its manoeuvrability and rate of climb. Armament consisted of a 20-mm cannon firing through the propeller shaft and two wing-mounted 7.62-mm machine-guns, later replaced by a single 12.7-mm machine-gun. Although in production at the time of the German invasion the Yak-1 had not reached front-line service. As a safety precaution the factories manufacturing the fighter were moved far to the east and within a month had resumed production. Over 37,000 Yak fighters of various types were produced during the war.

The return by the Russians to the use of wood in aircraft construction was paralleled in Britain by the most famous wooden aircraft of all, the de Havilland Mosquito (168). Originally conceived in 1938 as a private-venture light bomber, it did not attract official interest until 1940 when several prototypes were ordered. The first demonstration flight showed the Mosquito to be a very special aircraft indeed, with a speed of nearly 400 mph and the manoeuvrability of a fighter, capable of upward rolls with one of its two engines stopped. The cantilever midwing and monocoque fuselage were of all-wood construction with plywood skinning, these materials being used for lightness and to conserve metal which was in short supply. By using two powerful Rolls-Royce Merlin engines it was intended to rely on speed to escape interception and for that reason was originally unarmed. As a high-altitude bomber, flying at between 30,000 and 40,000 feet, it was the fastest type in Bomber Command for nearly ten years until the advent of the Canberra jet. But it was seen early that such an aircraft could have many other uses and it became in fact the RAF's most versatile type. As a fighter with four 20-mm cannon and four .303-in machine-guns in its nose, together with a bullet-proof windscreen and other modifications, it was designated the Mk II. A night-fighter version went into service in May 1942 to replace the Bristol Beaufighter, equipped with radar and a distinctive arrowhead antenna and painted in a matt black finish, all of which reduced the speed to about 370 mph at 14,000 feet with the 1,460 hp Merlin 21 or 23 engines. Performance was gradually increased however by the installation of more powerful Merlins. The arrowhead antenna was later replaced by a spinning disc scanner which enabled the nose to be kept smooth. Many Mosquito variants were produced for such specialised purposes as photo-reconnaissance and dropping 'blockbuster' bombs. They were built in Canada and Australia as well as in Britain, some adapted to take American equipment. It became the RAF's major specialized nightfighter type but in numbers produced it was used mainly as a fighter-bomber, escorting some of Bomber Command's massive raids for which 50-gallon drop tanks were installed to extend the range to 1,800 miles.

The Mosquito's versatility was surpassed only by the Junkers Ju 88 (254), used for a greater variety of duties than any other combat airplane of the Second World War. This again started its career in the late 1930's as a fast twin-engined medium bomber for the *Luftwaffe*, a number of which took part in the Battle of Britain. Powered by two 1,200 hp Jumo engines which gave about 290 mph at 18,000 feet it did not of course have the speed of the Mosquito but carried armament and a heavier bomb load. Various versions of the bomber A-series were built for medium and dive-bombing, shipping attack, long-range reconnaissance, ground-attack (mainly against tanks on the Russian front), and conversion training. A parallel development was the Ju 88C heavy fighter which also became the most widely used of the German night-fighters until the appearance of the specialised Ju 88G nightfighter. The C-series mounted one 20-mm cannon and three or five machine-guns in a solid nose, plus a single machine-gun behind the cockpit for rear defence. Higher powered Jumo engines gave an increased speed of 310 mph at 19,500 feet, with a ceiling of 32,500 feet, and the fighter's strong construction and manoeuvrability made it an excellent 'aircraft destroyer'. Its appearance was somewhat encumbered by the Lichtenstein radar aerials projecting from the nose when used for night fighting. In a different form these were also characteristic of the G-series which emerged in 1944 with enlarged, squarer tail surfaces, but performance was greatly improved with more powerful engines which gave 390 mph at 29,800 feet and four or six forward-firing cannon and sometimes an additional two cannon firing upwards and forwards.

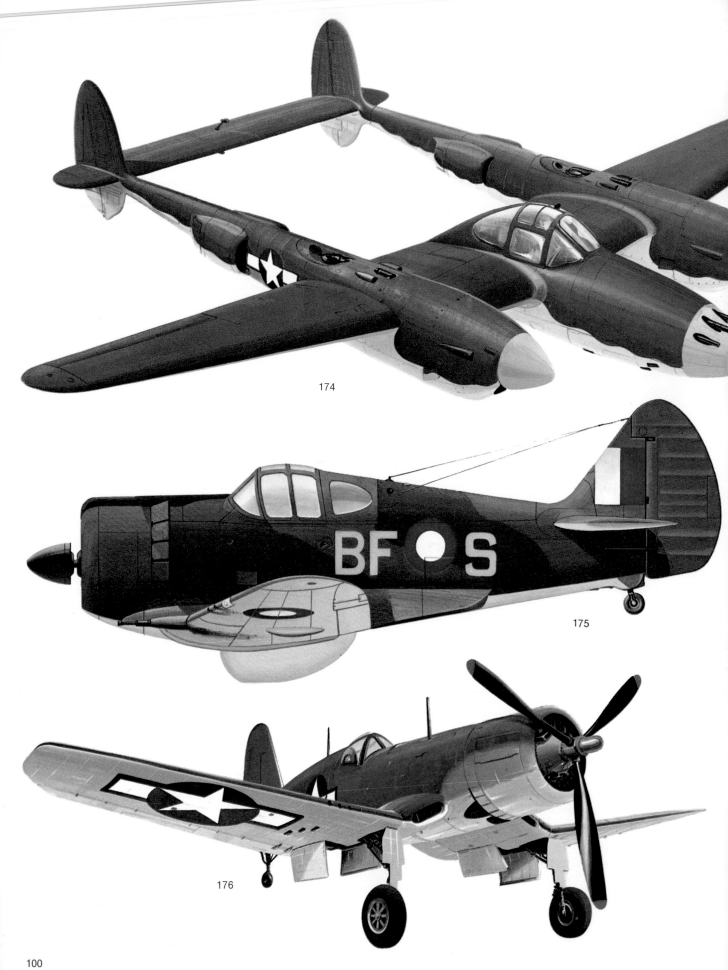

174

175

176

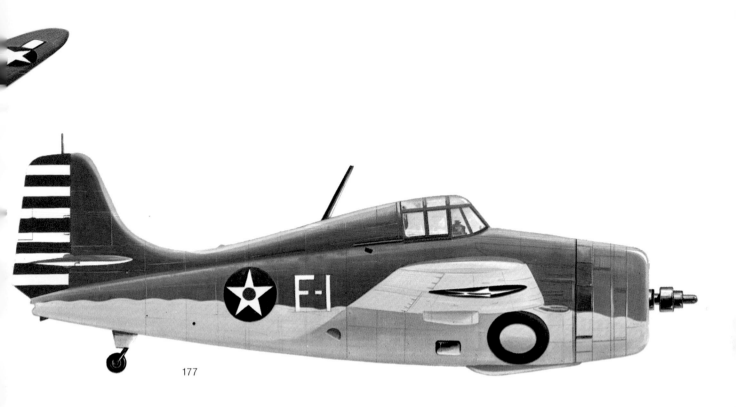

177

174 **Lockheed P-38 Lightning.** Span: 52 ft. Length: 37 ft 10 in. Engine: two 1,425 hp Allison V–1710–89/91 vee type. Armament: one 37-mm cannon, two 0.5-in and two 0.3-in machine-guns (and provision for two 1,600-lb bombs). Max speed: 405 mph at 20,000 ft. Service ceiling: 38,000 ft. A P–38 was the first American fighter to shoot down a German aircraft in the war. The type was developed in a number of variants, including a two-seater fighter-bomber version.

175 **CA-12 Boomerang.** Span: 36 ft 3 in. Length: 25 ft 6 in. Engine: 1,200 hp Pratt & Whitney Twin Wasp fourteen-cylinder radial. Armament: two 20-mm Hispano cannon and four 0.303-in Browning machine-guns. Max speed: 296 at 7,600 ft. Service ceiling: 29,000 ft. The only Australian-designed and built fighter of the war, developed as a stop-gap requirement for the Royal Australian Air Force after the Japanese attack on Pearl Harbour.

176 **Vought Corsair F4U-1.** Span: 34 ft 4 in. Length: 24 ft 5 in. Engine: 2,000 hp Pratt & Whitney R–2800–8 Double Wasp radial. Armament: six 0.5-in machine-guns. Max speed: 417 mph at 19,900 ft. Service ceiling: 36,900 ft. The best American naval fighter of the war, the Corsair remained the longest in production and was the last American piston-engined fighter.

177 **Grumman F4F Wildcat.** Span: 38 ft. Length: 28 ft 9 in. Engine: 1,200 hp Wright radial. Armament: four 0.5-in machine-guns. Max speed: 330 mph at 21,000 ft. Service ceiling: 37,500 ft. Re-named Marlet when used by the British Fleet Air Arm.

While the Messerschmitt Bf 109 was the fighter produced in the largest numbers in Germany and the Junkers Ju 88 was the most versatile aircraft, a claim could be made that the Focke-Wulf Fw 190 (213) was the outstanding single-seat interceptor fighter of the war, possessing the best all-round fighting capabilities in terms of speed and manoeuvrability, low and high operational altitudes, good handling characteristics and an excellent gun and bomb platform. Other fighters might have had the edge in any particular one of these capabilities but the Fw 190 had perhaps the least faults of all. It was first flown in June 1939 and production machines in the A-series were built around the 1,600 hp BMW 801 air-cooled radial engine which gave a speed of 390 mph at 18,000 feet. The remarkably neat installation reduced the diameter of the nose cowling to less than usual for the radial type of engine and careful attention was paid to the cooling fan and exhaust system. Armament varied considerably but was usually four 20-mm cannon and two 7.9-mm machine-guns. Six cannon were used for attacking bombers when it was found that the single cannon and two machine-guns of the Bf 109 did not have sufficient hitting power to bring down larger aircraft which by this time were strongly armour-plated.

When the Fw 190 first began to be used in low-altitude hit-and-run missions over southern England in the summer of 1941, RAF Fighter Command was alarmed to find it superior to the Spitfire. By then the Spitfire had passed several stages of development, including models equipped for photo-reconnaissance and air/sea rescue duties. The Mark V was in general use at that time, powered by the 1,440 hp Merlin and usually armed with two 20-mm cannon and four machine-guns. Tropical machines manufactured for operations in the Western

178 **Lavochkin La-7.** Span: 32 ft 2 in. Length: 27 ft 10½ in.
Engine: 1,510 hp ASh–82FN radial. Armament:
three 20-mm ShVAK cannon. Max speed: 422.5
at 21,000 ft. Service ceiling: 34,450 ft. Achieved a
top speed of 461 mph when fitted with an
experimental liquid-fuel rocket motor in its tail.

Desert had a large fairing under the nose to incorporate a special filter. With little to do after the Battle of Britain had been won Fighter Command, now under Air Chief Marshal Sholto Douglas, had initiated offensive fighter sweeps over Occupied Europe which were known as 'Rhubarbs'. These did not provoke the *Luftwaffe* to the extent intended, and then came the threat of the new Fw 190, its 390 mph at 18,000 feet out-classing the Mk V's 374 mph at 13,000 feet. One answer which partly redressed the balance was found to be 'clipping' the pointed wing tips of the Mark V to improve its rolling characteristics at low altitudes while the Mk VI (184) was given an increased wing span and pressurised cockpit for better high-altitude performance. With the Mk IX (187), fitted with the new 1,660 hp Merlin engine and a two-speed two-stage supercharger which gave speeds of up to 416 mph at 27,500 feet and a service ceiling of 45,000 feet, the Spitfire turned the tables again and established superiority over the Fw 190. The Mk IX was in fact the most widely used of all the Spitfire variants, with a longer fuselage to take the new engine, an additional radiator mounted under the port wing, and built respectively with clipped, standard and extended wings for low, medium and high altitude operations.

The Germans countered by derating the Fw 190 from a high-altitude fighter to a low-level fighter-bomber, for which purpose it proved a formidable weapon. Against this Rolls-Royce and Vickers collaborated in the installation of the 1,735 hp Griffon engine in a specially strengthened airframe, rated to deliver its maximum power at 1,000 feet; this was the Mark XII Spitfire (188). As competition between the two types continued, in 1943 the Germans produced the Fw 190D with a 1,776 hp in-line Jumo engine, liquid-cooled by a radiator mounted in the nose which gave it the appearance of a radial type. The fuselage was lengthened to balance the larger cowling and the fin area was also increased. While less aesthetically pleasing this fighter had an excellent performance, including a maximum speed of 426 mph at 22,000 feet. The final Fw 190 model was the G-series fighter-bomber, after which production ended in favour of the Ta 152 (225) designed by Kurt Tank.

Meanwhile the Spitfire continued in a succession of variants, more than for any other single type in fact and the only Allied fighter to remain in continuous production throughout the war. By the time the Mark XIV (189) high-altitude type had been introduced, its 2,050 hp Griffon engine giving 448 mph at 26,000 feet and a ceiling of 44,500 feet, so many changes had been incorporated that

it was virtually a new airplane. It had a five-bladed propeller which rotated in the opposite direction to those driven by Merlin engines, so that flying it had quite a different feel. The Mark XVI was the last to use the Merlin engine, Packard-built, before the Griffon became standard. With the Mark 21, the last variant in production at the end of the war, the wing was completely re-designed so that the Spitfire was no longer distinctive for its eliptical wing shape. Some were fitted with contra-rotating propellers. The last machine of the final production version, the Mark 24, was produced in October 1947. Over the ten years of its development the Spitfire's speed had been increased 35 per cent to 454 mph, its weight by 40 per cent and its rate of climb by 80 per cent. It was still able to compete on equal terms with much later piston-engined fighters. Over 20,000 machines of various types were produced.

Sea-based Air Power

Although land-based air power played a vital role in the war at sea in the Atlantic and Mediterranean, best illustrated perhaps by the value to the British of Malta as an air base, the European nations had not fully appreciated before the war the significance of sea-based air power, in spite of the lessons that might have been learned from the First World War. Neither Germany nor Italy developed aircraft carriers or specialised naval aircraft, other than the conversion of a few German types for catapulting from cruisers and other ships. The French had one carrier in 1939 but it played little part in the conflict and by the fall of France in 1940 only the British were left with operational carriers. But they were mostly equipped with obsolete biplanes as a result of the policy by which, until 1937, purchasing for the Fleet Air Arm was handled by the Air Ministry. Some of these, such as the Sea Gladiator which was the main fighter type, were conversions of RAF models. When the success of the Spitfires and Hurricanes coming into service with the RAF was apparent, the Royal Navy expressed the need also for a monoplane fighter armed with eight machine-guns to combat the cannon-armed Bf 109s and Italian Macchi 202s which were its usual opponents. The first answer in 1940 was the Fairey Fulmar, a two-seater of all-metal construction with a monocoque fuselage and folding wings for stowage on board carriers. Like the Defiant it suffered from a relatively low performance and lack of rearward defensive armament which, as in the case of most European multi-seat aircraft, had not kept pace with the increase in fire-power of single-seat fighters. The decision was taken to use specially strengthened Spitfires and Hurricanes for naval use. The first single-seat monoplanes to reach the Fleet Air Arm were former Battle of Britain Hurricanes, converted in 1941 for launching by catapult from the decks of merchant ships and known as 'Hurricats.' Their pilots usually had to ditch in the sea after a sortie and hope they would be rescued by other ships. Then came the Sea Hurricane, fitted with deck arrester gear for operation from carriers, and the Supermarine which was produced in a number of variants.

The prime need was for carrier-borne fighters to provide air cover over the British Fleets and other convoys and also for torpedo-bombers to attack enemy surface ships and submarines. Because of a lack of foresight before the war little had been done to develop the specialised type of aircraft required. The effectiveness of carrier operations had clearly been demonstrated in November 1940 when a force of Swordfish biplane torpedo-bombers from HMS *Illustrious* struck at the Italian naval base at Taranto, sinking two battleships and damaging a third and two destroyers for the loss of only two aircraft. Fleet Air Arm Swordfish were instrumental in the sinking of the new German battleship *Bismarck* in May the following year. A similar success might have been gained against the battlecruisers *Scharnhorst* and *Gneisenau* when, together with *Bismarck*'s consort *Prinz Eugen,* they made a dash up the English Channel in February 1942. But this time the Swordfish biplanes, which were already obsolescent at the beginning of the war, came up against a German fighter cover of Fw 190 and Bf 109s, as well as intensive naval anti-aircraft fire. All the Swordfish were shot down, in spite of the gallantry of their crews, without scoring a single hit. It was at this point, after the humiliation of German warships passing unharmed within a few miles of Dover (although they later struck mines laid by the RAF off the Dutch coast), that the neglect of naval aircraft before the war became truly apparent. The companies that specialized in naval aircraft, who had produced for instance some of the best fighters of the First World War, had been allowed to fall behind in the technological revolution from fabric-covered biplanes to all-metal monoplanes through a lack of orders. They were now given a greater priority by the Admiralty, following a public enquiry on the incident, but with such a leeway to make up it was not until the end of the war that suitable naval aircraft were being produced by British manufacturers. In the meantime the only solution was to buy aircraft from America where the US Navy had consistently, from the early 1930s, been developing specialized carrier types. These formed the bulk of the Royal Navy's air force for the rest of the war, including the Grumman F4F Wildcat (177) which, known as the Martlet, was one of the main carrier-borne fighter types to serve with the Fleet Air Arm.

If sea-based air power had been neglected in Europe during the inter-war years, this was certainly not the case in the United States and Japan. Facing a possible conflict over the vast expanse of the Pacific both countries had concentrated their efforts on building large carrier fleets and the specialized naval aircraft to go with them, although the lead had been taken by Japan. It was in the Pacific that the biggest naval battles of the war took place, often between carrier fleets that were not within direct range of each other but relied on their aircraft to press the attack from distances of up to 200 miles. Naval fighters played an essential role in these battles, as escorts, interceptors, and fighter-bombers.

At the time of the Japanese surprise attacks on Pearl Harbour, Hong Kong and Malaya on December 7th/8th 1941, the total first-line strength of the US Army Air Corps and US Navy was about 5,000, divided more or less equally between the two services, of which only slightly over 2,000 were modern combat aircraft. Most were engaged on training programmes in the United States in preparation for the war against Germany, and American air strength in the Pacific numbered only 688 aircraft. The Dutch had about 200 in the Netherlands East Indies and the British some 332 in Malaya and Singapore, but these were mostly obsolete types. The Japanese on the other hand possessed a formidable first line strength of 1,500 army and 1,500 navy aircraft. They were superior not only in numbers but also in fighter types. The Mitsubishi Zero had already proved its supremacy in the skies over China and now the Japanese Navy was equipped with the improved model A6M2 (169), powered by the 925 hp Nakajima Sakae engine which gave 332 mph at 17,000 feet and a ceiling of 34,000 feet, with folding wingtips and new-type ailerons which gave it better manoeuvrability. Armament consisted of two 7.7-mm fuselage-mounted machine-guns and two 20-mm wing cannon. Against this deadly fighter which suffered from few of the defects of specialized carrier-borne aircraft as compared with those land-based and consequently less encumbered, the standard US Navy type was the Grumman F4F Wildcat with folding wings and a 1,200 hp Wright radial engine which gave 330 mph at 21,000 feet and a ceiling of 37,500 feet. Whereas the Axis powers at this time favoured the use of cannon as the main armament on fighters while the British preferred eight light-calibre machine-guns, the Americans had answered the need for more effective armament by turning to .50-in machine-guns, four of which were mounted in the wings of the Wildcat. Although somewhat slower and less manoeuvrable than the Zero, the Wildcat was faster in a dive and had an important advantage in its more rugged construction and the armour plate built around the pilot's seat to give him protection. The Zeros were more vulnerable when hit, as had already been discovered during the fighting in China, partly because they lacked armour plate and the heavier type of petrol tank which self-sealed if perforated by gunfire. These were normal protective measures on most fighters by that time. But with the Zero's speed and manoeuvrability, the Japanese pilots could count on receiving fewer hits. The Curtiss P-40 Tomahawk (167) which was then coming into service with the US Army Air Corps also had four .50-in wing mounted machine-guns. It was basically a modification of the P-36 to take the new Allison liquid-cooled in-line engine, super-charged for combat at medium altitudes.

Japanese strategy aimed at taking over China and the rich territories of South-east Asia, was a kind of *judo blitzkrieg* based on air supremacy to cover land operations down the mainland and seaborne invasions of the various island groups. The attack on Pearl Harbour by 353 bombers and fighters from the six carriers of Vice-Admiral Chuichi Nagumo's First Air Fleet was intended to destroy the US Pacific Fleet before it could interfere with this aggressive territorial expansion. Once the Japanese had established a defensive perimeter of island strongholds in the Central and South-west Pacific they hoped the Allies would find it too difficult to free the conquered territories and would make peace. Fighters played an essential part in the raid by strafing American aircraft on the ground before they could take off to intercept the dive-bombers attacking the ships moored in the harbour. Only

179 **Mikoyan-Gurevich Mig-3.** Span: 33 ft 9½ in. Length:
180 26 ft 9 in. Engine: 1,350 hp AM–35A vee type.
Armament: three 12.7-mm and two 7.62-mm
machine-guns (and provision for one 220-lb bomb).
Max speed: 397.6 mph at 25,600 ft. Service ceiling:
39,370 ft. Production only lasted from 1940 to 1941
but the MiG–3 was an outstanding fighter at high-
altitudes.

181 **Yakovlev Yak-3.** Span: 30 ft 2 in. Length: 27 ft 10½ in.
Engine: M–105PF in-line. Armament: one 20-mm
ShVAK cannon and two 12.7-mm Beresin machine-
guns. Max speed: 399 mph at 16,400 ft (447 mph
at 18,850 ft when fitted with VK–107A engine).
Service ceiling: 35,450 ft.

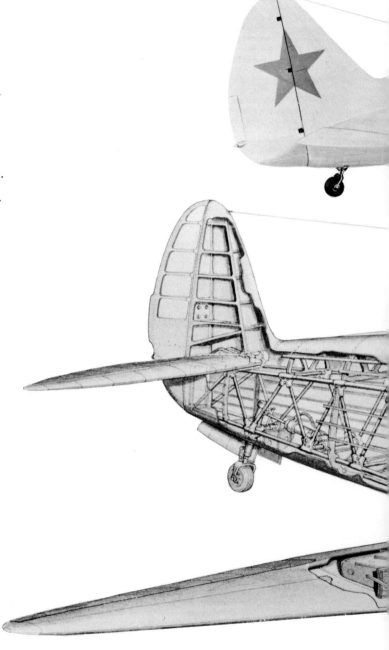

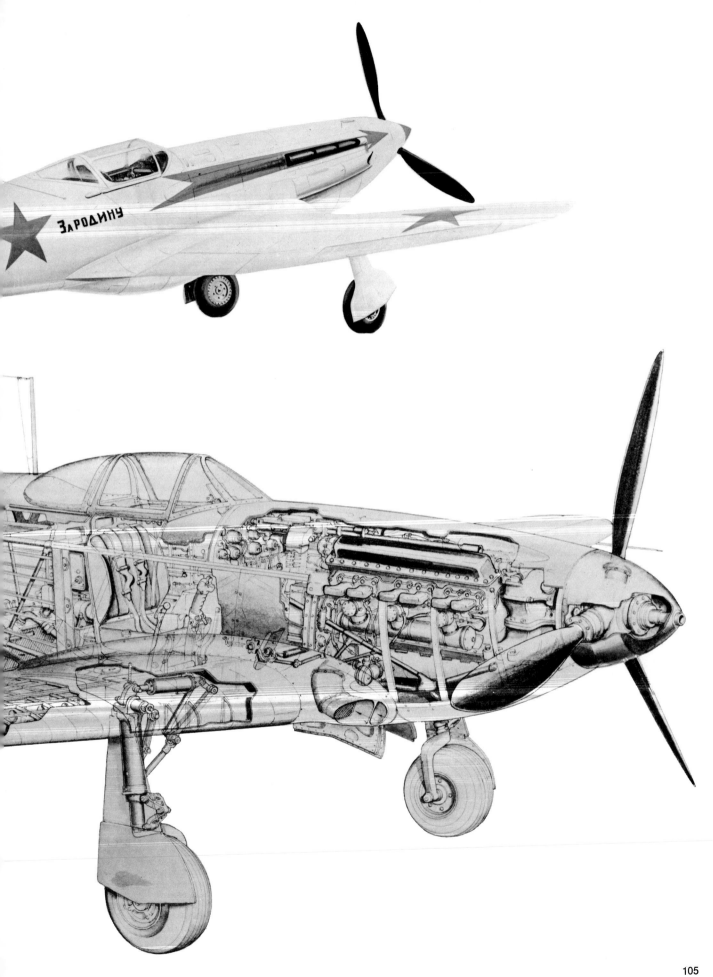

Supermarine Spitfire

182 **Spitfire Mk I.** Span: 36 ft 10 in. Length: 29 ft 11 in. Engine: 1,030 hp Rolls-Royce Merlin II. Armament: four wing-mounted 0.303-in Browning machine-guns, later increased to eight *or* two 20-mm Hispano cannon and four machine-guns. Max speed: 355 mph at 19,000 ft. Service ceiling: 34,000 ft. This was the main version which fought in the Battle of Britain. Early models had two-bladed fixed-pitch propellers but these were later changed to three-blade variable-pitch or constant-speed propellers.

183 **Spitfire Mk II.** The 1,175 hp Merlin XII engine gave 357 mph at 17,000 ft and a service ceiling of 37,200 ft.

184 **Spitfire Mk VI.** Span: 40 ft 2 in. Length: 29 ft 11 in. Engine: 1,440 hp Merlin 45. Max speed: 364 mph. Extended wing tips and pressurized cockpit for high-altitude performance.

185 **Spitfire Mk VII.** Span: 40 ft 2 in. Length: 31 ft 4 in. Engine: 1,660 hp Merlin 61 with two-speed two-stage supercharger. Max speed: 408 mph at 25,000 ft. Service ceiling: 43,000 ft. Another high-altitude variant, the first type to exceed 400 mph in level flight and to have a retractable tailwheel.

186 **Spitfire Mk VIII.** Span: 36 ft 10 in. Length: 30 ft 4 in. A low-altitude version of the Mk VII with clipped wing tips.

187 **Spitfire Mk IX.** Preceded the Mk VIII and produced with standard, clipped and extended wings. Introduced the 'E' wing, armed with one 20-mm Hispano and one 0.5-in Browning machine-gun in each half.

188 **Spitfire Mk XII.** Span: 32 ft 8 in. Length: 31 ft 10 in. Engine: 1,735 hp Griffon III or IV. Max speed: 393 mph at 18,000 ft. Service ceiling: 40,000 ft. A specially-strengthened low-altitude version with an increased vertical tail area.

189 **Spitfire Mk XIV.** Span: 36 ft 10 in. Length: 32 ft. 8 in. Engine: 2,050 hp Griffon 61 with two-speed two-stage supercharger. Armament: two 20-mm cannon and two 0.5-in machine-guns. Max speed: 448 mph at 26,000 ft. Service ceiling: 44,500 ft. Designed for maximum performance at high altitude, with a five-bladed propeller, lengthened nose and increased fin area, this variant was used successfully against the V.1 flying bombs and the Me 262 jet fighters. Later models had sliding rear-view bubble hoods.

190 **Spitfire Mk XVIII.** Span: 36 ft 10 in. Length: 33 ft 4 in. Production version of the Mk XIV, with strengthened wings and increased internal fuel tankage, the fighter-reconnaissance version fitted with two oblique and one vertical cameras.

191 **Spitfire Mk 21.** Span: 36 ft 11 in. Length: 32 ft 8 in. Engine: 2,050 hp Griffon 61 or the 2,375 Griffon 65 driving contra-rotating propellers. Max speed: 454 mph at 26,000 ft. Service ceiling: 43,500 ft. The last Spitfire in production at the end of the war and

too late to see operational service. Major structural changes were made, particularly to the wings which lost their distinctive elliptical shape.

192 **Supermarine Seafire F.II.** Span: 36 ft 10 in. Length: 29 ft 11 in. Engine: 1,470 hp Rolls-Royce Merlin 45 vee type. Armament: two 20-mm cannon and four 0.303-in machine-guns. Max speed: 352 mph at 12,250 ft. Service ceiling: 33,800 ft. A carrier-borne version of the Spitfire.

193 **Seafire F.45.** Span: 36 ft 11 in. Length: 33 ft 7 in. Engine: Griffon 61/85 driving either five-bladed or six-bladed contra-rotating propellers. Armament: four 20-mm cannon. Max speed: 438 mph at 25,000 ft. Service ceiling: 41,000 ft. A naval version of the Spitfire Mk 21.

194 **Supermarine Seafang F.32.** Span 35 ft. Length: 34 ft 1 in. Engine: Griffon 89 driving contra-rotating propellers. Max speed: 475 mph. A naval version of the Spitfire with folding wings.

195 **Seafire F.3.** Span: 36 ft 8 in. Length: 30 ft. Engine: 1.585 hp Merlin 55M. Armament: four 20-mm cannon (and provision for two 250-lb bombs). Max speed: 352 mph at 12,250 ft. Service ceiling: 33,800 ft. Introduced a manually-operated double-folding wing and could be fitted with rocket-assisted take-off gear.

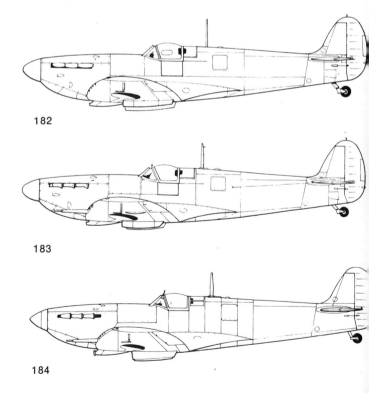

182

183

184

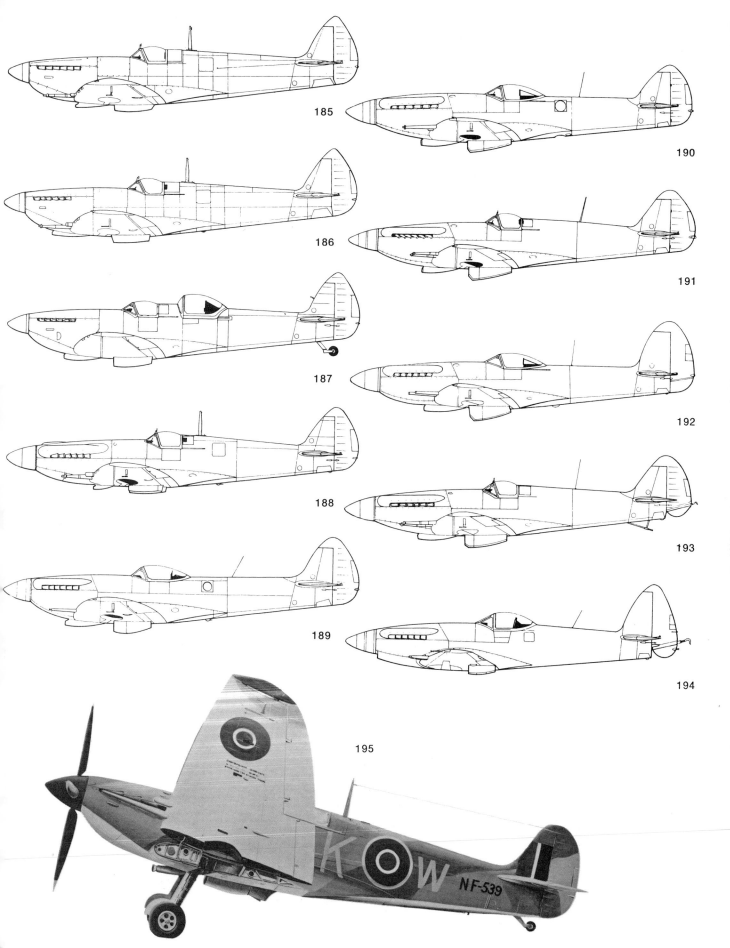

185

190

186

191

187

192

188

193

189

194

195

NF-539

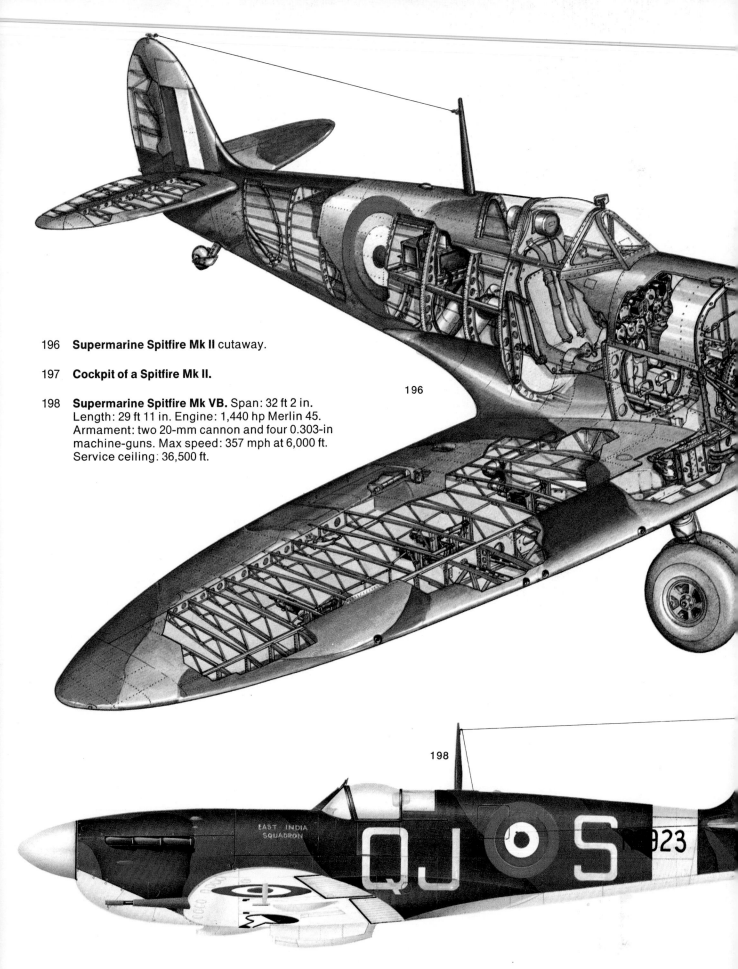

196 **Supermarine Spitfire Mk II** cutaway.

197 **Cockpit of a Spitfire Mk II.**

198 **Supermarine Spitfire Mk VB.** Span: 32 ft 2 in.
Length: 29 ft 11 in. Engine: 1,440 hp Merlin 45.
Armament: two 20-mm cannon and four 0.303-in
machine-guns. Max speed: 357 mph at 6,000 ft.
Service ceiling: 36,500 ft.

196

198

Messerschmitt Bf 109

199 **Bf 109 B-1.** Span: 32 ft 4½ in. Length: 28 ft 6½ in. Engine: 635 hp Jumo 210D. Armament: one 20-mm cannon firing through the propeller shaft and two 7.9-mm machine-guns. Max speed: 292 mph at 13,100 ft. Service ceiling: 26,575 ft. One of the fighter types which equipped the *Condor Legion* during the Spanish Civil War.

200 **Bf 109 V-1.** Prototype of the Bf 109 which first flew in September 1935, powered by a 695 hp Rolls-Royce Kestrel V engine because of the shortage of Jumo 210 units.

201 **Bf 109 D-1.** Powered by the 960 hp Daimler-Benz DB 600 engine which gave an increased speed of 323 mph.

202 **Bf 109 E-3 .** Span: 32 ft 4¼ in. Length: 28 ft 3¾ in. Engine: 1,100 hp DB 601A with direct fuel injection. Armament: three 20-mm cannon and two 7.9-mm machine-guns. Max speed: 354 mph at 12,300 ft. Service ceiling: 36,000 ft. Known throughout the *Luftwaffe* as 'Emil', this was the principal fighter type used during the Battle of Britain.

203 **Bf 109 T-1.** A carrier (Trager) conversion of the E-III for the proposed aircraft carrier *Graf Zeppelin,* with folding outer wing panels, arrester hook and catapult spools. The carrier was not completed and the few T-types produced were later used in operations from Norway.

204 **Bf 109 F-1.** Span: 36 ft 6½ in. Length: 29 ft 0½ in. Engine: 1,200 hp DB 601N. Armament: one 20-mm cannon firing through the spinner and two 7.9-mm machine-guns. Max speed: 390 mph at 22,000 ft. Service ceiling: 37,000 ft. Generally considered the finest of the 109 variants, and the first that was able to out-manoeuvre the Spitfire Mk V, the F-series had increased-span rounded-tip wings, cantilever tailplane, and a retractable tail-wheel.

205 **Bf 109 F-4.** Powered by the 1,300 hp DB 601E engine, this was the first variant to carry a heavier engine-mounted MG 151/20 cannon. The central gun was very effective in the hands of marksmen like Werner Molders, but was not so successful when operated by inexperienced pilots.

206 **Bf 109 F-4/R1.** In place of the F-4's single gun, this type carried two MG 151/20 cannon in underwing gondolas.

207 **Bf 109 H-1.** A high-altitude development of the F-4 with an addition wing section, increasing the span to 40 ft 1½ in.

208 **Bf 109 K-2.** Span: 32 ft 6½ in. Length: 29 ft 7 in. Engine: 1,550 hp DB 605 ASCM/DCM with MW–50 injection. Armament: one 30-mm and two 15-mm cannon. Max speed: 452 mph at 19,685 ft. Service ceiling: 41,000 ft.

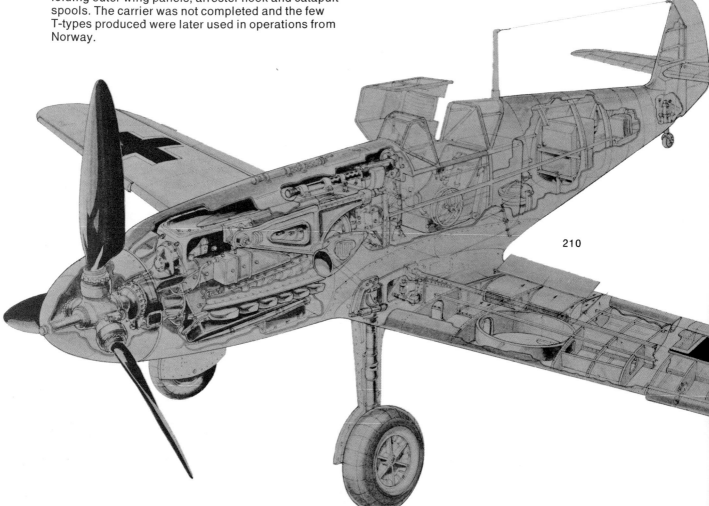

210

209 **Bf 109 G-6/R2.** Span: 32 ft 6½ in. Length: 29 ft 8 in. Engine: 1,475 hp DB 605. Armament: three 20-mm cannon, two machine-guns, and two 210-mm WGr 21 rocket tubes. Max speed: 387 mph at 22,970 ft. Service ceiling: 38,500 ft. The 'Gustav' series were very effective against Allied bombers but the heavier armament severely restricted their performance.

210 **Bf 109 F-1** cutaway.

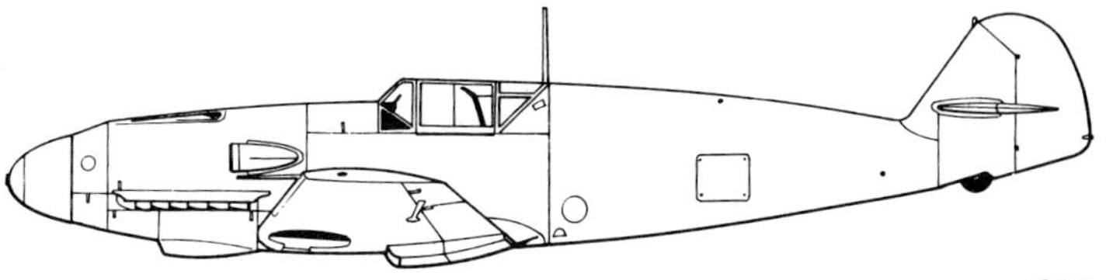

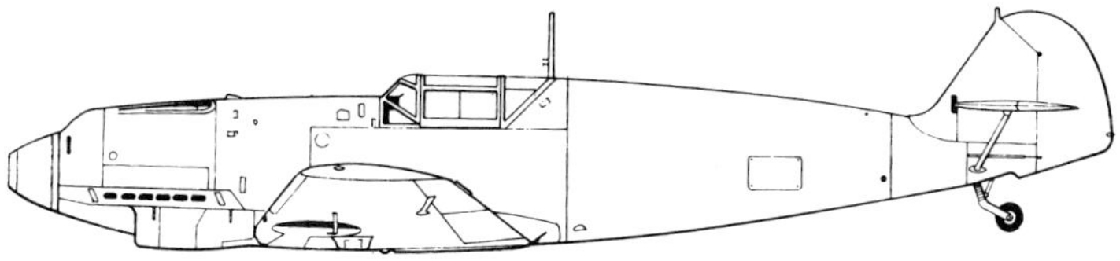

199

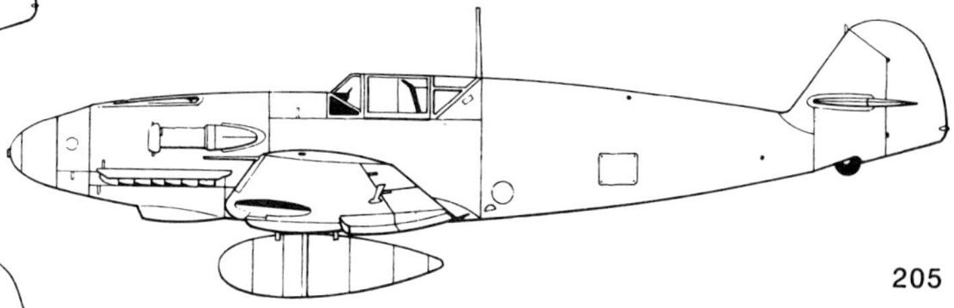

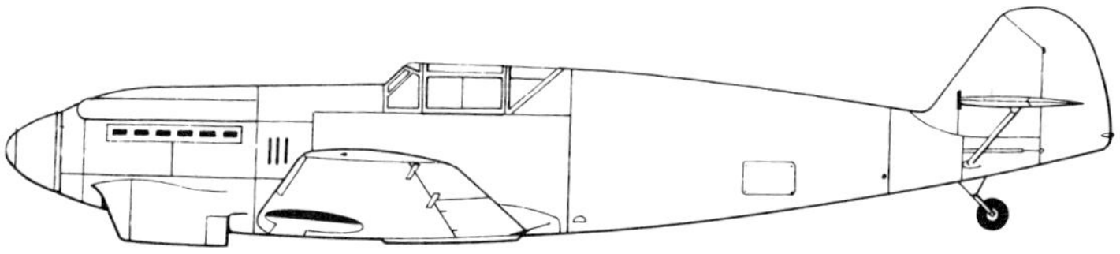

200

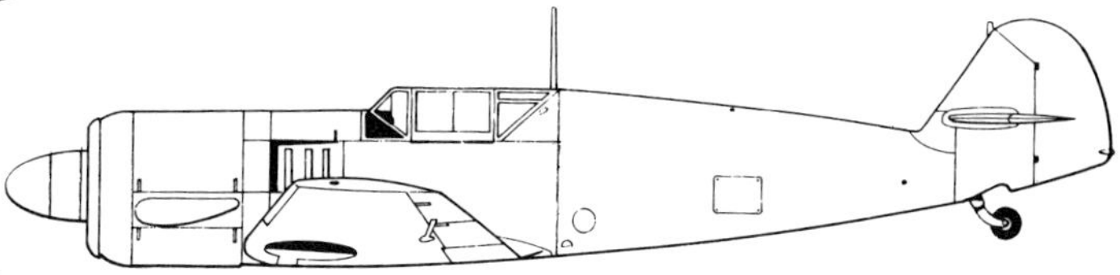

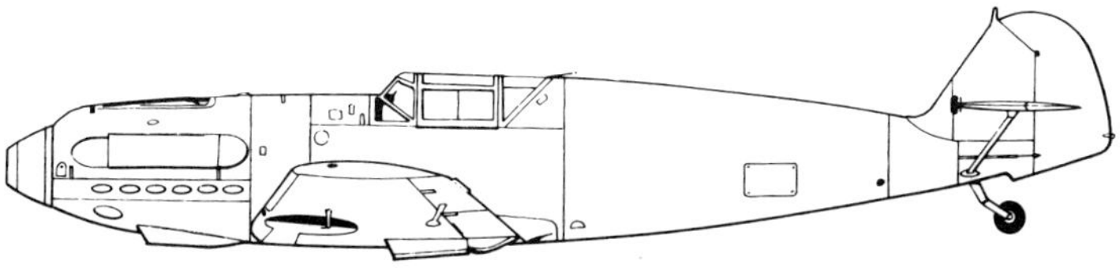

201

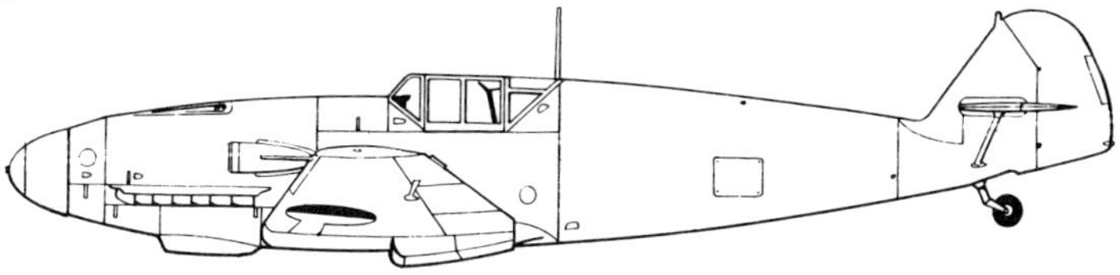

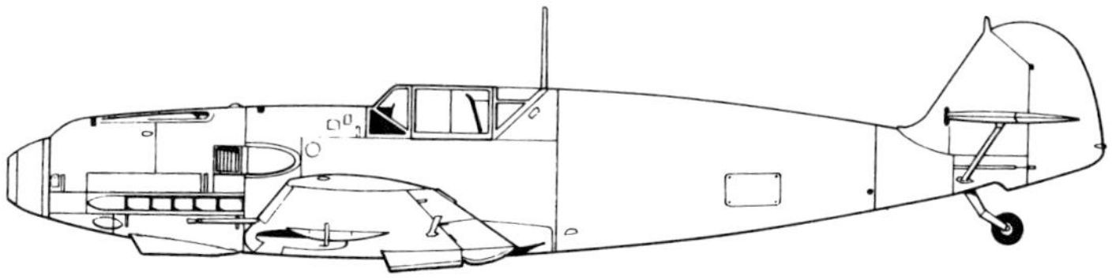

202

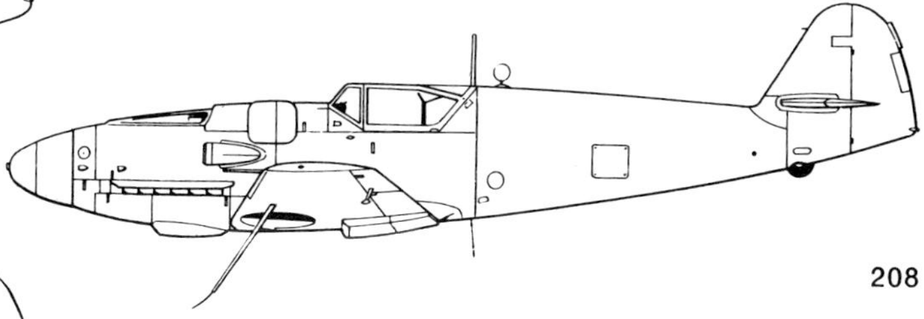

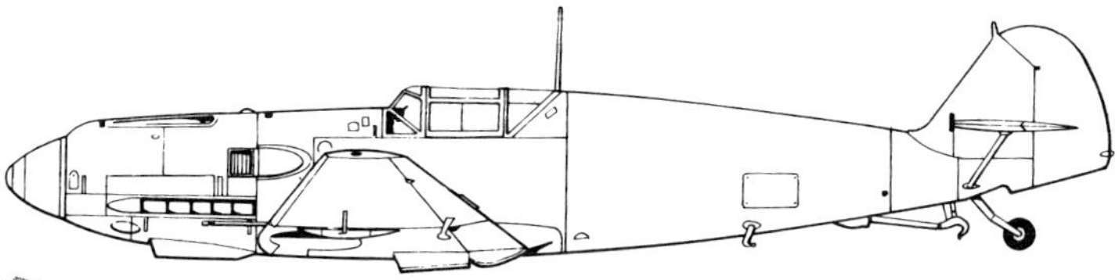

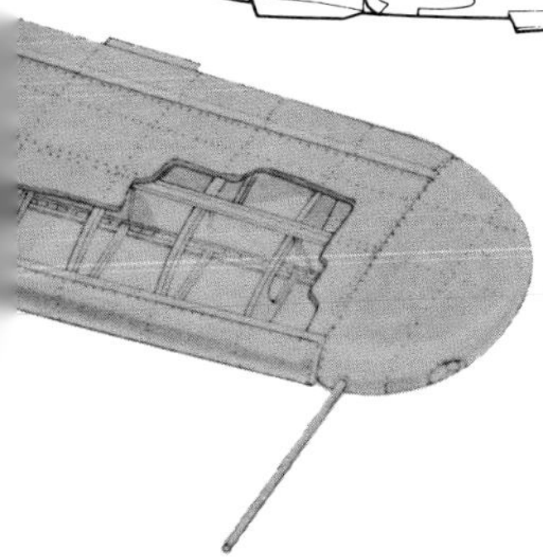

203

204

205

206

207

208

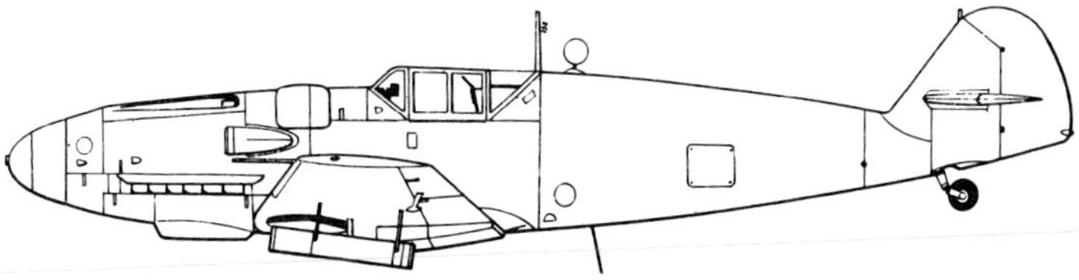

209

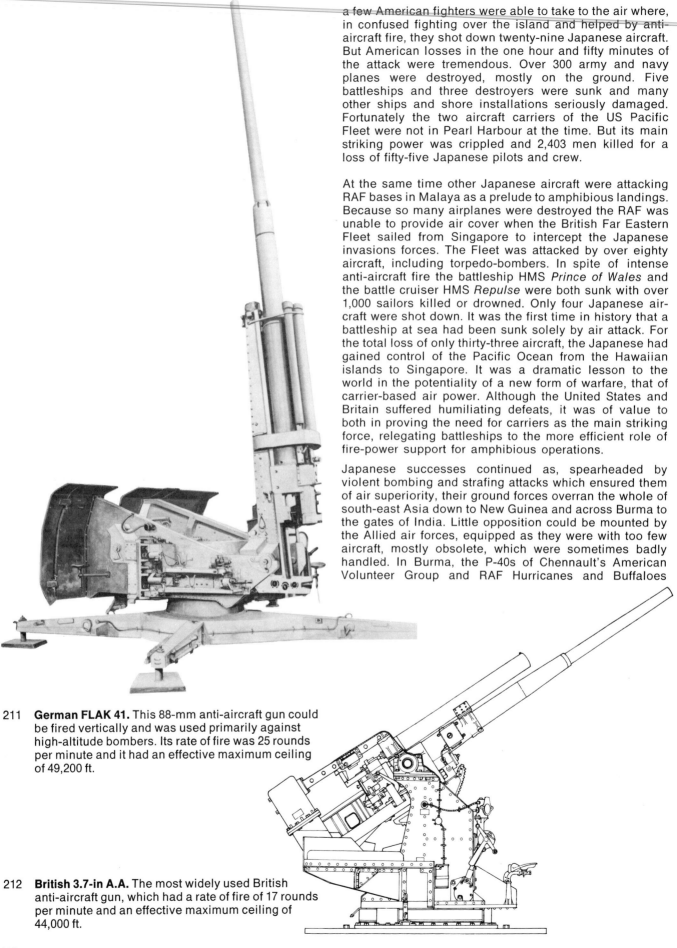

a few American fighters were able to take to the air where, in confused fighting over the island and helped by anti-aircraft fire, they shot down twenty-nine Japanese aircraft. But American losses in the one hour and fifty minutes of the attack were tremendous. Over 300 army and navy planes were destroyed, mostly on the ground. Five battleships and three destroyers were sunk and many other ships and shore installations seriously damaged. Fortunately the two aircraft carriers of the US Pacific Fleet were not in Pearl Harbour at the time. But its main striking power was crippled and 2,403 men killed for a loss of fifty-five Japanese pilots and crew.

At the same time other Japanese aircraft were attacking RAF bases in Malaya as a prelude to amphibious landings. Because so many airplanes were destroyed the RAF was unable to provide air cover when the British Far Eastern Fleet sailed from Singapore to intercept the Japanese invasions forces. The Fleet was attacked by over eighty aircraft, including torpedo-bombers. In spite of intense anti-aircraft fire the battleship HMS *Prince of Wales* and the battle cruiser HMS *Repulse* were both sunk with over 1,000 sailors killed or drowned. Only four Japanese aircraft were shot down. It was the first time in history that a battleship at sea had been sunk solely by air attack. For the total loss of only thirty-three aircraft, the Japanese had gained control of the Pacific Ocean from the Hawaiian islands to Singapore. It was a dramatic lesson to the world in the potentiality of a new form of warfare, that of carrier-based air power. Although the United States and Britain suffered humiliating defeats, it was of value to both in proving the need for carriers as the main striking force, relegating battleships to the more efficient role of fire-power support for amphibious operations.

Japanese successes continued as, spearheaded by violent bombing and strafing attacks which ensured them of air superiority, their ground forces overran the whole of south-east Asia down to New Guinea and across Burma to the gates of India. Little opposition could be mounted by the Allied air forces, equipped as they were with too few aircraft, mostly obsolete, which were sometimes badly handled. In Burma, the P-40s of Chennault's American Volunteer Group and RAF Hurricanes and Buffaloes

211 **German FLAK 41.** This 88-mm anti-aircraft gun could be fired vertically and was used primarily against high-altitude bombers. Its rate of fire was 25 rounds per minute and it had an effective maximum ceiling of 49,200 ft.

212 **British 3.7-in A.A.** The most widely used British anti-aircraft gun, which had a rate of fire of 17 rounds per minute and an effective maximum ceiling of 44,000 ft.

The destruction of a Messerschmitt Bf 109. *U.S. Air Force*

The destruction of a Junkers Ju 88. *U.S. Air Force*

Gun-camera sequences
A photographic record of combats in the air, taken by cameras
fitted to guns and synchronised to operate when the guns fired,
was one advantage that pilots in the Second World War had over
their predecessors in the First War. They were a valuable asset
in devising and testing out offensive tactics.

fought a fierce four-months air battle, destroying 233 Japanese aircraft for a loss of thirty-eight fighters, but could not stem the Japanese advance. The most effective air defence was put up by the RAF and the Fleet Air Arm against bombing attacks on British naval bases in Ceylon, launched from carriers of the Japanese First Air Fleet which had gone on to blitz Port Darwin in north-western Australia after Pearl Harbour. On April 5th 1942 a force of seventy-five bombers escorted by a similar number of fighters attacked Colombo, where it was met by thirty-six Hurricanes and six Fulmars. Eighteen Japanese aircraft were shot down, and although the British lost nineteen, their resistance so demoralized the Japanese pilots that only one destroyer and an armed merchant cruiser were sunk. Four days later they struck at Trincomalee and lost fifteen aircraft for eleven British. During other attacks in the Indian Ocean and the Bay of Bengal, Japanese dive-bombers sunk two heavy cruisers, a light aircraft carrier, a destroyer and many merchant ships, as well as damaging shore installations. Having lost nearly a third of his aircraft, Admiral Nagumo decided to withdraw to rest and refit. Thus it was that his vitally important force was out of action when the Battle of the Coral Sea was fought in May, the first true carrier battle in history.

The Zero-Sen dominated air combat in the Pacific until early 1943 but the Japanese also had several other notable fighters. For the Japanese Army Air Force, Nakajima produced the Ki-43 Hayabusa (Peregrine Falcon) (172) which saw service with the Navy's Zero over Malaya, Burma and the Pacific. Like most of the Japanese fighters it was powered by an air-cooled radial engine which gave it a good speed, range and manoeuvrability, nearly matching that of the Zero. The initial armament was only two 12.7-mm machine-guns but armour plating and self-sealing fuel tanks were fitted to give the pilot greater protection. Another Nakajima fighter, the Ki-44 Shoki (Demon) was developed as an interceptor for defence of the Japanese homeland, sacrificing range and manoeuvrability for high speed (376 mph) and rate of climb. The need for such interceptors became apparent when the Americans took the war to the heart of Japan by bombing industrial targets in Tokyo and other cities, beginning with the famous raid led by James Doolittle on April 18th 1942. It was partly as a result of that first unexpected raid that the Japanese decided to extend their conquests in the Central and Southern Pacific but where, first in the Battle of the Coral Sea in May and then at Midway in June, they were effectively halted for the first time by the Allies. The Battle of Midway in particular was a clearcut American victory and one of the most decisive of the Pacific war for it brought to an end Japanese air superiority over the Pacific Ocean. Although both were naval battles they were fought entirely by air power, with the opposing fleets far out of sight of each other. An even more manoeuvrable Nakajima fighter was the Ki-84 Hayate (Gale) (230) which began to enter service early in 1944 and was in some respects superior to the American escort fighters of that time at heights of up to 30,000 feet. It was powered by a 1,900 hp two-row Homare radial engine with eighteen cylinders which gave a speed of 388 mph at 20,000 feet and armed with twin 12.7-mm machine-guns in the upper engine cowling and two 20-mm wing cannon, later raised to 30-mm. As Japan was experiencing shortages of light metal alloys at that time, a number of experimental airplanes of this type were built of wood. The Nakajima JINI-S Gekko (Moonlight) was originally intended as a twin-engined multi-seat escort fighter with a long range of up to 2,500 miles but it lacked speed and manoeuvrability for this purpose and was eventually used as a night-fighter, equipped with two pairs of upward and downward firing 20-mm cannon to the rear of the cockpit.

With the conquest of the many islands of the South-west Pacific in mind, Japan had an obvious requirement for naval seaplane fighters which could operate independently of carriers or land bases. As an interim measure Nakajima produced the A6M2-N, with a large centre float and two stabilizing floats under the wings, which in 1942 saw service from the Aleutian Islands in the north to the Solomons in the south. It was based on the Nakajima Type 95 observation aircraft and did not have a good combat performance but the following year Kawanishi produced what was probably the best seaplane fighter of its time, the NIKI Kyoju (Mighty Wind) (228). This single-seat mid-wing monoplane of all-metal construction had a speed of nearly 300 mph at 19,000 feet, provided by the two-row Mitsubishi Kasei radial engine fitted with counter-rotating propellers, and a ceiling of 34,600 feet. It was armed with two 20-mm wing cannon and two 7.7-mm machine-guns in the engine cowling. It was specifically designed to accompany amphibious landing forccs in areas where there were no airfields but towards the end of the war it was used, like many other fighters, as an interceptor in defence of the Japanese homeland. So successful was it in its earlier role that it was developed into a land-based fighter, a unique evolution in combat aircraft for the reverse was normally the case. The NIK2-J Shiden (Violet lightning) (232) which was developed from the first NIKI Kyoju was one of the finest fighters to serve in the Pacific theatre in 1944, powered by various Homare radial engines up to 2,000 hp which gave it speeds of up to 370 mph at 18,000 feet.

Mitsubishi's famous Zero-Sen was followed by the J2M Raiden (Thunderbolt) (231), a somewhat less successful type at first but eventually developed into one of Japan's best high-altitude interceptors in the final months of the war when powered by the 1,820 hp Kasei 26a engine. This, like the engines which powered most Japanese fighters, was an air-cooled radial type but one exception was produced by the Kawasaki company, the fourth of the major aircraft manufacturers. In 1937 Kawasaki had secured the manufacturing rights to Germany's DB 601 liquid-cooled in-line engine and from this developed its own 1,100 hp Ha-40 in-line engine, installed in the Ki-61 Hien (Swallow) (171) which came into service in 1943. Various teething problems were encountered with the engine, eventually rated up to 1,450 hp with the Ha-140, as well as with the airframe, although these hardly mattered to the many Hien pilots who chose suicide ramming as a means of intercepting B–29 Superfortresses. The Ki-100 (229) which was next produced by Kawasaki was also designed with a slim airframe to take the in-line engine but at the last minute because of a shortage of such engines, the only type available was the Mitsubishi 1,500 hp fourteen-cylinder radial. In spite of the problems of fitting such an engine, excellent though it was, to a slender airframe, the Ki-100 became in fact the best fighter to serve the Japanese Army Air Force throughout the war. In speed, climb and manoeuvrability it was superior to most American fighters in 1945 although its limited output against the sheer size of the Allied forces could not affect the outcome. Kawasaki also produced two twin-engined fighters, the Ki–45 Toryu (Dragon Killer) which was a two-seat counterpart of the German Bf 110, also used for night interception, and the Ki–102 which was intended for ground-attack purposes, heavily armed with a 57-mm cannon, two 20-mm cannon, and a 12.7-mm machine-gun firing upwards from the rear cockpit.

Zero A6M2's and Aichi (Val) D3AI's line up ready for the
"Turkey Shoot" in which The Imperial Japanese forces lost
one hundred and seven machines for the loss of only six
U.S. fighters. *Source Unknown*

One of the most remarkable features of the Second World War was the tremendous production achieved by the American aircraft industry, supplying both its own armed services in their fight against Germany and Japan and also those of Britain and Russia through the lend-lease programme. Total production rose from about 18,000 machines in 1941 to 48,000 in 1942, over 90,000 in 1943, and a peak of more than 100,000 in 1944. Included among these were some notable fighters which saw service in many different parts of the world, powered in many instances by turbo-superchargers to increase performance at high altitudes which was still the key to air combat. The prototype Bell P-39 Airacobra (173) was an early example, unique in having its turbo-supercharged Allison V-1710 engine buried in the centre of the fuselage to permit a heavy calibre cannon to be installed in the nose, but the turbo-supercharger was deleted from production models. This restricted the Airacobra's usefulness as a fighter when it saw service from 1942 onwards with the US Army Air Corps in the Pacific and in Europe but it was highly successful as a ground-attack aircraft in North Africa. It was the first single-engined fighter with a tricycle undercarriage to enter service with the USAAF. A later development, the P-63 Kingcobra with a completely new wing designed to achieve laminar flow, was used extensively by the Russian Air Force for ground-attack.

The first monoplane fighter to go into service with the

US Navy was the Brewster F2A Buffalo (135) but it saw little combat except briefly in the Battle of Midway and was withdrawn from front-line service when found to be inferior to the Japanese fighters. The Grumman F4F Wildcat was much more successful and in its later form as the FM-2, powered by the Wright R-1820-56 engine which gave greater horsepower for take-off, began at last to equal the performance of Japanese fighters and in 1943 marked a turning point in the Pacific war. Later that year the Wildcat was replaced by the F6F Hellcat which became the main carrier-borne fighter with the US fleet in 1944. It also operated with the British Fleet Air Arm and saw action right to the end of the war. But in spite of its undoubted success it was over-shadowed by the Vought F4U Corsair (176) which in May 1940 became the first American aircraft to exceed 400 mph in level flight. The Corsair, with its distinctive inverted gull-wing, was developed to give the US Navy a carrier-borne fighter with a performance as good as that of land-based fighters but when deliveries began in 1942 it was thought the high landing speed and relatively poor visibility for the pilot would make it unsuitable for carrier operations. It was consequently used by land-based Marine squadrons but

Focke-Wulf Fw 190

213 Fw 190 V-1. Prototype, first flew on June 1st 1939. Span: 31 ft 2 in. Length: 28 ft 10½ in. Engine: 1,550 hp BMW 139. Armament: Two MG 131 and two 7.9-mm MG 17 machine-guns. Max speed: 369 mph at sea level.

217 **Fw 190 F-8.** Span: 34 ft 5½ in. Length 29 ft. Engine: BMW 801 D–2. Armament: four machine-guns (and provision for 24 underwing rocket projectiles or one 3,000-lb armour-piercing bomb). Max speed: 394 mph at 18,000 ft. This type had increased armour protection for the pilot.

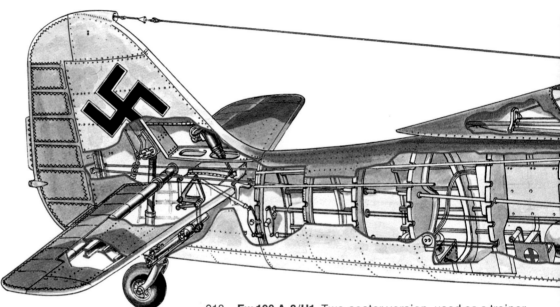

214 **Fw 190 A-O.** Span: 34 ft 5½ in. Length: 28 ft 10½ in. Engine: 1,600 hp BMW 801 air-cooled radial. Armament: four MG 17 machine-guns. Max speed: 389 mph at 18,045 ft.

215 **Fw 190 A-4/R6.** Engine: 1,700 hp BMW 801 D-2, increased to 2,100 hp with MW 50 power boost. Armament: two 20-mm cannon, two 7.9-mm machine-guns and 21-cm rocket tubes. Max speed: 416 mph at 20,590 ft. Service ceiling: 37,400 ft.

216 **Fw 190 A-6/R1.** Span: 34 ft 5½ in. Length: 29 ft 4½ in. Engine: BMW 801 D–2. Armament: six MG 151 cannon and two MG 17 machine-guns. Max speed: 382 mph at 19,000 ft. Service ceiling: 34,700 ft.

218 **Fw 190 A-8/U1.** Two-seater version, used as a trainer for former Ju 87 pilots. Engine: BMW 801 D–2. Armament: four 20-mm cannon and two 13-mm machine-guns. Max speed: 408 mph at 20,600 ft. Service ceiling: 37,400 ft.

219 **Fw 190 A-8/SG 116.** This A–8 type was equipped with the *Vellendusche* gun, a series of three 30-mm barrels firing upwards, used for attacking bombers from underneath.

220 **Fw 190 A-8/Dopple Reiter 1.** An experimental version, equipped with two 55-gallon fuel tanks on the upper wing for increased range. The tanks could be jettisoned.

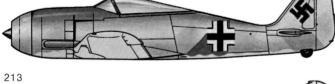

213

214

215

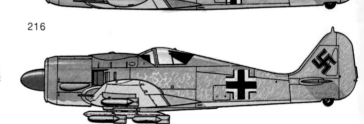

216

217

218

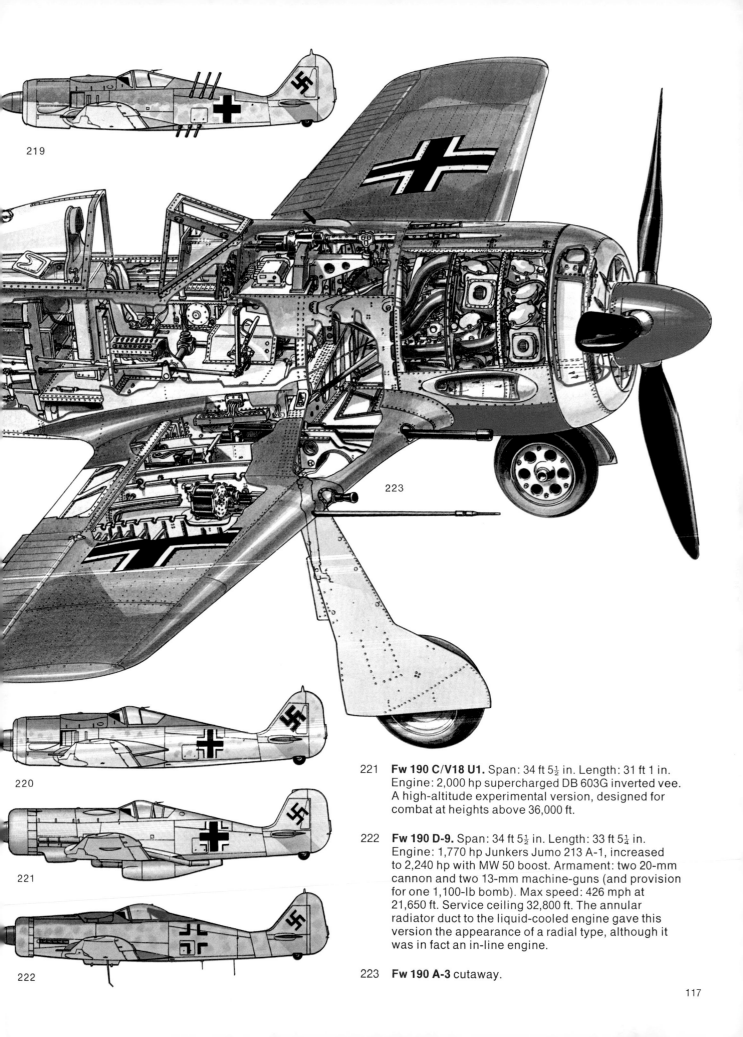

219

223

221 **Fw 190 C/V18 U1.** Span: 34 ft 5½ in. Length: 31 ft 1 in.
Engine: 2,000 hp supercharged DB 603G inverted vee.
A high-altitude experimental version, designed for
combat at heights above 36,000 ft.

222 **Fw 190 D-9.** Span: 34 ft 5½ in. Length: 33 ft 5¼ in.
Engine: 1,770 hp Junkers Jumo 213 A-1, increased
to 2,240 hp with MW 50 boost. Armament: two 20-mm
cannon and two 13-mm machine-guns (and provision
for one 1,100-lb bomb). Max speed: 426 mph at
21,650 ft. Service ceiling 32,800 ft. The annular
radiator duct to the liquid-cooled engine gave this
version the appearance of a radial type, although it
was in fact an in-line engine.

223 **Fw 190 A-3** cutaway.

220

221

222

224

225

226

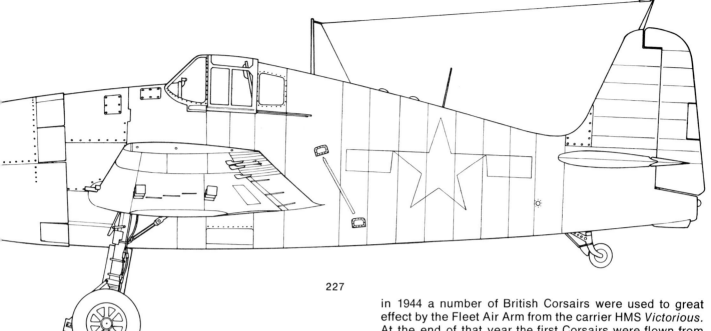

227

224 Focke-Wulf Fw 189 Uhu (Owl). Span: 60 ft 5 in.
Length: 39 ft 4 in. Engine: two 450 hp Argus As 410
twelve-cylinder air-cooled inverted vee. Armament:
four 7.9-mm machine-guns (and provision for a
440-lb bomb load). Max speed: 221 mph at 8,530 ft.
Service ceiling: 27,550 ft.

225 Focke-Wulf Ta 152C. Span: 36 ft 1 in. Length:
35 ft 5½ in. Engine: 2,300 hp DB 603 LA twelve-
cylinder liquid-cooled inverted vee. Armament:
one 30-mm MK 108 cannon and four 20-mm MG 151
guns. Max speed: 439 mph at 37,000 ft. Service
ceiling: 40,350 ft.

226 Grumman F7F Tigercat. Span: 51 ft 6 in. Length:
(type 4N) 46 ft 10 in. Engine: two 2,100 hp R–2800–34W
radial. Armament: four 20-mm cannon and four
0.5-in machine-guns (and provision for two
1,000-lb bombs *or* six rockets *or* a standard Navy
torpedo). Max speed: 430 mph at 21,900 ft. Service
ceiling: 40,450 ft. This was the first twin-engined
fighter to serve on board aircraft carriers. Most were
single-seaters but a two-seat version was developed
for night-fighting.

227 Grumman F6F Hellcat. Span: 42 ft 10 in. Length:
33 ft 7 in. Engine: 2,000 hp Pratt & Whitney R–2800–10
with two-stage supercharger. Armament: six 0.5-in
machine-guns. Max speed: 375 mph at 17,300 ft.
Service ceiling: 37,300 ft.

in 1944 a number of British Corsairs were used to great
effect by the Fleet Air Arm from the carrier HMS *Victorious*.
At the end of that year the first Corsairs were flown from
American carriers and proved themselves to be the finest
carrier-borne fighters of the war, capable of speeds up
to 446 mph at 26,000 feet and a service ceiling of 41,500
feet. In a total of 64,051 missions flown, of which 9,581
were from carriers, over 2,000 Japanese aircraft were
destroyed for a loss of only 189 Corsairs. It was in production for a longer period than any other American fighter,
from 1941 to 1952, and was the last piston-engined fighter
in production for the US forces.

Another radical fighter to serve with US Navy was the
Grumman F7F Tigercat (226), the first twin-engined fighter
in production for operation from aircraft carriers and the
first US Navy type to have a nose-wheel undercarriage.
A number of single-seat versions were delivered in 1944,
armed with four heavy machine-guns in the nose and
four 20-mm cannon in the wings. A later two-seat version
was used for night fighting, equipped with radar in
place of the nose guns.

Air Offensive Against Germany

Following America's entry into the war at the end of 1941
and the battles of the Coral Sea and Midway which
halted Japanese expansion in the Pacific, it was agreed
by the Allied leaders that the defeat of Germany should
be the most immediate objective. One of the first efforts
in achieving this was to be a tremendous bombing offensive against German war industries. These were already
the main targets of RAF Bomber Command which, since
the end of the Battle of Britain, had carried out night raids
with growing intensity to the point where the first 1,000
bomber raid was made against the Cologne marshalling
yards on the night of May 30th/31st 1942. Three months
later the US Eighth Air Force began its own bombing
offensive against Germany from bases in England.

119

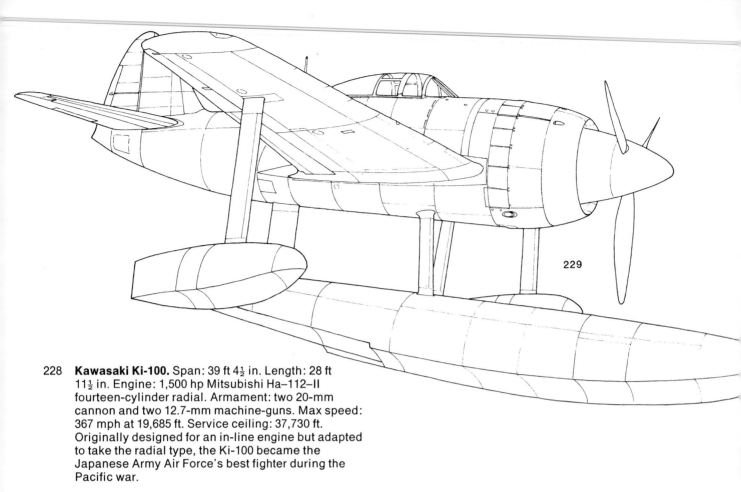

228 **Kawasaki Ki-100.** Span: 39 ft 4½ in. Length: 28 ft
11½ in. Engine: 1,500 hp Mitsubishi Ha–112–II
fourteen-cylinder radial. Armament: two 20-mm
cannon and two 12.7-mm machine-guns. Max speed:
367 mph at 19,685 ft. Service ceiling: 37,730 ft.
Originally designed for an in-line engine but adapted
to take the radial type, the Ki-100 became the
Japanese Army Air Force's best fighter during the
Pacific war.

Equipped with fast, well-armed and armoured bombers
such as the Boeing 'Flying Fortress' and the Consolidated
'Liberator', the Americans felt confident that these could
sufficiently hold their own against German fighters to be
able to make much more accurate daylight raids. As
fighter escorts the USAAF had introduced the Lockheed
P–38 Lightning (174) and the Republic P–47 Thunderbolt
(233).

The Lightning was a twin-boom single-seater powered by
two Allison V–1750 engines, originally of 1,150 hp each,
and with an armament in the nose comprising one 37-mm
cannon, two heavy and two light machine-guns. The first
models were ordered by the RAF but taken over by the
USAAF when America entered the war. A P–38 operating
from Iceland was the first American fighter to shoot down
a German aircraft, an Fw 200 Condor over the North
Atlantic, and from then until the end of the war the type
saw continuous action in all combat areas. Various models
had maximum speeds of up to 414 mph at 25,000 feet and
service ceilings of up to 44,000 feet. The P–38F was fitted
with drop tanks which increased its range to 1,750 miles
with engines throttled back to a cruising speed of 213 mph
and it was mainly this type which accompanied American
bombers on the raids against Germany. In spite of its
fire-power and speed however, the Lightning lacked
manoeuvrability in air combat with single-engined
German fighters.

The Republic P–47 Thunderbolt was in a class of its own,
the largest and heaviest single-seat piston-engined fighter
ever built, powered by a massive eighteen-cylinder Pratt
and Whitney air-cooled radial engine which in its final
2,800 hp version gave a speed of 467 mph at 32,500 feet.
The first P–47s reached USAAF bases in Britain early in
1943 but until drop tanks were fitted to later versions, they
lacked the range to escort bombers and also suffered from
poor manoeuvrability. Towards the end of that year
however, they revealed outstanding characteristics as
fighter-bombers, a form of combat which was
used increasingly towards the end of the Second World
War as bigger and heavier fighters still able to retain their
high speeds, carried small bomb-loads. Standard armament was six or eight heavy wing-mounted machine-
guns and up to 2,500 lbs of bombs. Turbo-supercharging
increased its effectiveness at high altitudes. One variant
achieved 504 mph in level flight, the highest speed ever
achieved by a piston-engined aircraft. Larger numbers
were used by the USAAF than any other single fighter type.

Neither the USAAF nor the RAF possessed sufficient
long-range fighters to escort American bombers when they
began their daylight raids on Germany in August 1942.
The Americans believed that speed and armour would be
sufficient protection for their bombers and they had to
learn the hard way, as the British and Germans before
them, that unescorted day bombers were extremely
vulnerable when up against a determined fighter opposition. The USAAF underrated the defensive capabilities
of the *Luftwaffe,* just as the Germans had underrated that
of Fighter Command in the Battle of Britain. The further
into Germany penetrated by the American bombers, the
more aircraft were lost. The climax came in October 1943
when sixty out of 300 bombers raiding the ball-bearing
factory at Schweinfurt were shot down with only minimal
German losses. For the rest of that year the Americans
limited their daylight bombing to targets in occupied
countries until the arrival of a really suitable long-range
high-performance fighter that could escort bombers into
the heart of Germany.

229 Kawanishi N1K1 Kyofu (Mighty Wind). Span: 39 ft 4½ in. Length: 34 ft 9 in. Engine: Mitsubishi Kasei 1,460 hp two-row radial. Armament: two 20-mm cannon and two 7.7-mm machine-guns. Max speed: 299 mph at 18,700 ft. Service ceiling: 34,645 ft.

230 Nakajima Ki-84 Hayate (Gale). Span: 36 ft 10½ in. Length: 32 ft 6½ in. Engine: 1,900 hp Homare Ha–45 eighteen-cylinder air-cooled radial. Armament: two 20-mm cannon and two 12.7-mm machine-guns (and provision for two 550-lb bombs). Max speed: 388 mph at 19,685 ft. Service ceiling: 34,450 ft. Code-named 'Frank'.

231 Mitsubishi J2M3 Raiden (Thunderbolt). Span: 35 ft 5 in. Length: 31 ft 10 in. Engine: 1,820 hp Kasei 23a radial. Armament: four 20-mm wing-mounted cannon. Max speed: 380 mph at 19,685 ft. Service ceiling: 37,800 ft. Code-named 'Jack'.

232 Kawanishi N1K2-J Shiden (Violet Lightning). Span: 39 ft 3 in. Length: 30 ft 8 in. Engine: 1,990 hp Homare 21 radial. Armament: four 20-mm cannon (and provision for two 550-lb bombs). Max speed: 369 mph at 18,370 ft. Service ceiling: 35,400 ft. Code-named 'George'.

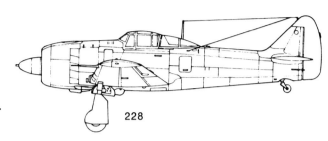

228

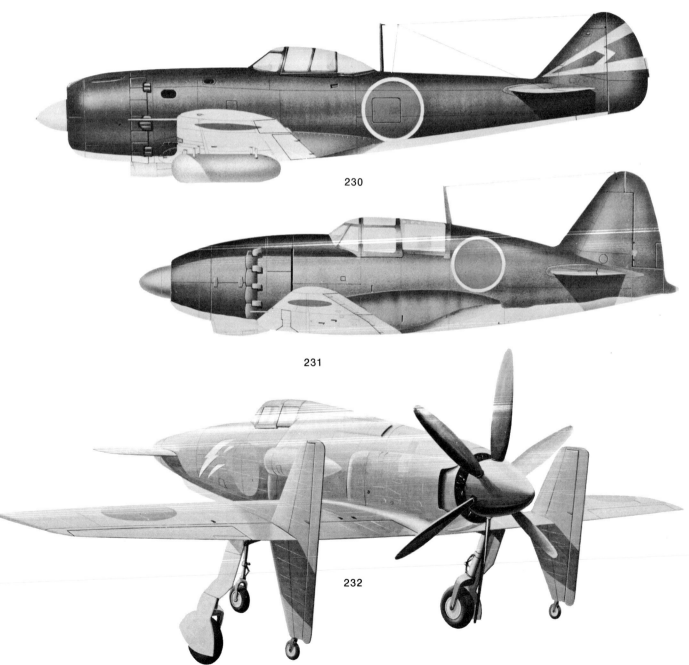

230

231

232

With a 500 lb bomb slung underneath their bellies, a squadron of U.S. Marine ''Corsair'' fighter planes is ready to take off at a central Pacific base for another attack on the Japanese. *Keystone*

Large Italian wine casks filled with earth and topped by sandbags forms an effective revetment for protection against German shells and bombs at the Allied Fifth Army beachhead at Anzio. *U.S. Army Air Corps*

U.S. Navy "Hellcat" fighters line up for take off on an aircraft carrier in the Pacific. *U.S. Navy*

Bell "Aircobras" (P39) of the U.S. Army Air Force.
This plane was reported to have a top speed during a dive of 620 mph. *U.S. Army Air Corps*

234

235

236

237

Heraldry

Following the practice which had become generally established towards the end of the First World War, many fighter squadrons in all the major air forces had their own markings which were displayed on fuselage sides. The ostensible reason was for ease of recognition when in the air but it was also a morale-booster which reflected the pilots' pride in their own squadrons. Some aircraft had individual markings, when permitted by squadron commanders.

234 1st unit of *Jagdgeschwader* 54 – 'Grunherz'. (German)

235 2nd unit of *Jagdgeschwader* 3. (German)

236 36th Pursuit Squadron, U.S.A.A.F. (American)

237 G.C. 111/6 of *Escadrille* 5. (French)

238 37th Fighter Group. (Japan)

239 77th Pursuit Squadron, U.S.A.A.F. (American)

240 Spitfire IIA flown by Pilot Officer A.S.C. Lumsden of No. 118 (F) Squadron, R.A.F. (British)

241. Squadron 54 – Stormo. (Italian)

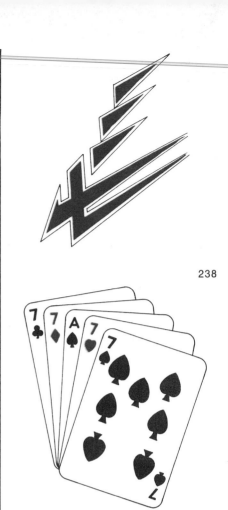

238

239

240

241

233 Republic P-47D Thunderbolt. Span: 40 ft 9 in. Length: 36 ft 1 in. Engine: 2,300 hp Pratt & Whitney R–2800–59 radial. Armament: eight 0.5-in machine-guns (and provision for 1,500-lb bomb load). Max speed: 428 mph at 30,000 ft. Service ceiling: 42,000 ft. A total of 15,660 Thunderbolts were built for America and the Allied powers. It was the most widely used fighter type by the US Army Air Force. The P–47M was basically a P–47D airframe with rocket tubes, used primarily for operations in Europe against the German V–1 flying-bomb.

242 North American P-51B Mustang. Span: 37 ft. Length: 32 ft. 3 in. Engine: 1,200 hp Allison V–1710–81. Armament: four 0.5-in machine-guns (and provision for two 1,000-lb bombs). Max speed: 390 mph at 20,000 ft. Service ceiling: 31,350 ft. A better ratio of enemy aircraft destroyed than any other US fighter. The last piston-engined fighter in US Air Force service.

243 Douglas A-26B Invader. Span: 70 ft. Length: 50 ft. Engine: two 2,000 hp R–2800–27 radials. Armament: six 0.5-in machine-guns (and provision for 4,000-lb bomb load). Max speed: 355 mph at 15,000 ft. Service ceiling: 22,100 ft. Three-seater night-fighter and attack bomber.

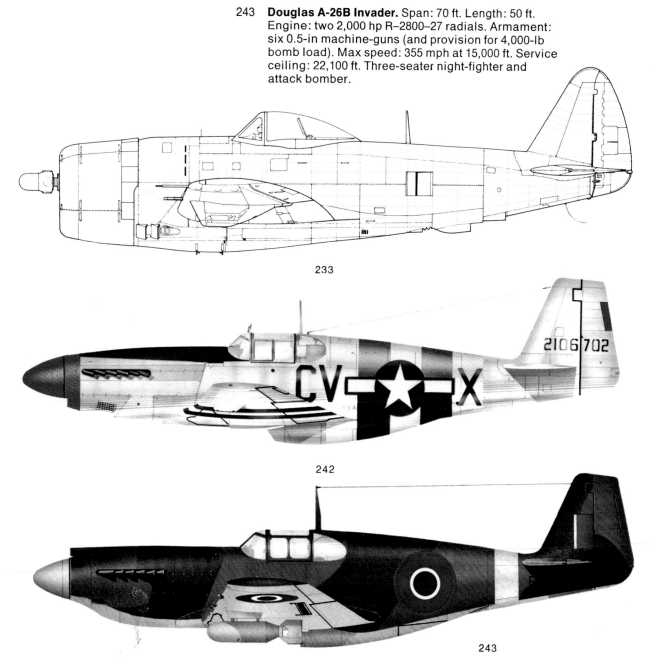

233

242

243

244 **North American P-51D Mustang.** Span: 37 ft. Length: 32 ft 3 in. Engine: 1,490 hp Packard-built V–1650–7 (Rolls-Royce Merlin) vee type. Armament: six 0.5-in machine-guns (and provision for two 1,000-lb bombs). Max speed: 437 mph at 25,000 ft. Service ceiling: 41,900 ft. Distinguished from previous versions by a 'tear-drop' canopy with all-round vision and a re-designed rear fuselage.

245 **North American P-51 Mustang** cutaway.

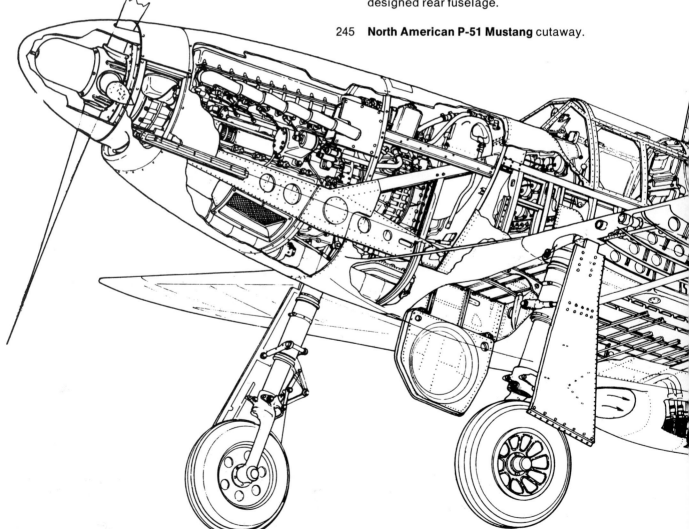

That fighter was the North American P–51 Mustang (242), one of the finest of the war and for speed, range and manoeuvrability the most effective over Europe in 1944 and 1945. It was first ordered by the RAF in 1940 to incorporate many of the lessons Fighter Command had learned in air combat and was required to have an in-line engine and eight machine-guns, according to British practice. The first machines to arrive in Britain at the end of 1941 were faster than any other fighter then in service but their 1,100 hp Allison engines were found to be unsuitable for high-altitude combat. A much improved performance was achieved with the Rolls Royce Merlin 60 engine, for which the Mustang was extensively re-designed late in 1942. This increased its top speed from 380 mph at 13,000 feet to about 440 mph at 30,000 feet. Fitted with 150 gallon drop tanks and armed with four .50-in machine-guns in the wings, this P–51B began operations with the US Eighth Air Force in December 1943 as a bomber escort and contributed greatly to the eventual success of daylight bombing. Towards the end of the war the P–82 Twin Mustang was developed, made from two standard P–51 fuselages joined by a centre-wing panel and tailplane, intended as a long-range bomber escort in the Pacific area, but the war ended before it came into service. It was later converted into a night-fighter to replace the twin-engined, twin-boom Northrop P–61 Black Widow (252) which had been in service in Europe and the Pacific since 1944.

In Britain meanwhile, the production of improved models enabled the Spitfire to be used effectively as fighter throughout the war but by 1942 the Hurricane was becoming outclassed as an interceptor. It was used instead in a ground-attack role with heavier armament. Air-to-surface rocket projectiles were tried at first, giving a single Hurricane the fire-power equal to a destroyer's broadside, then two 40-mm cannon were installed under the wings for anti-tank strikes in North Africa and Burma. The final Mark VI version carried no less than two light machine-guns for sighting purposes, either two 40-mm cannon or long-range fuel tanks, eight rocket projectiles with 60-lb warheads, two 250-lb or 500-lb bombs and smoke curtain equipment. The most effective use of rockets however was made by the Hawker Typhoon (256), originally designed as a replacement for the Hurricane. Its performance was poor at high altitudes but for low-level ground-attack it was one of the outstanding fighter-bombers of the war, capable of carrying two 1,000-lb bombs. During the bitter fighting after the Normandy landings, RAF Typhoons equipped with rocket projectiles destroyed over 130 German tanks in one attack, opening the way for the Allied advance through France and Belgium.

In order to overcome the early problems of the Typhoon, Hawker designed a new thin-section laminar-flow wing for a type which was original to be known as the Typhoon II but which was then given the new name of Tempest. Powered by the Napier Sabre II 24-cylinder H-type engine which gave it a maximum speed of 427 mph at 18,500 feet, a service ceiling of 36,000 feet, and a range of 1,500 miles with drop tanks, the Tempest was one of the most effective

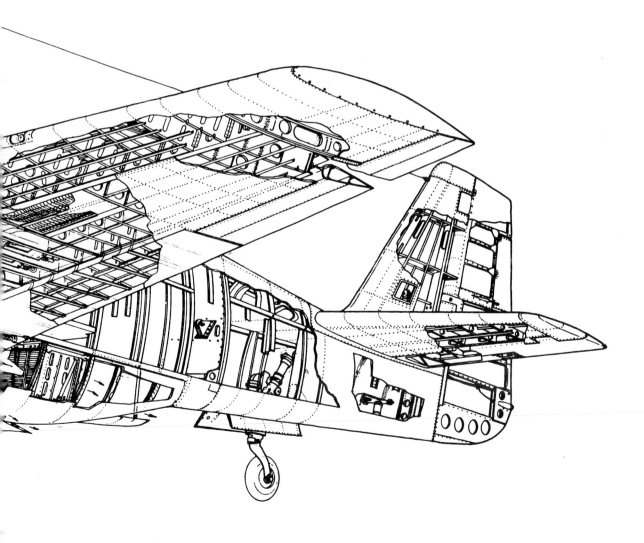

The pilot of a Focke-Wulf FW 190 clears his damaged machine before opening his parachute. *Source Unknown*

fighters during the last months of the war in Europe, contributing greatly to the destruction of V–1 flying bombs. A later development of the Tempest, the Hawker Sea Fury, was the main single-seat fighter in service with the Fleet Air Arm from 1947 to 1953.

The Italians ended the war, upon their surrender in September 1943, with two excellent single-seat fighters which in other circumstances might have made a much greater impact. The Reggiane Re 2005 Sagittario (Archer), the last of a series built by a subsidiary of the Caproni group, had first-rate handling characteristics and, powered by the German 1,475 hp DB 605A liquid-cooled in-line engine, a maximum speed of 390 mph at 23,000 feet and a ceiling of 40,000 feet. It arrived too late to see much combat but at the time of Italy's surrender a new engine project was under way which would have boosted its speed to 450 mph by means of a piston-engined compressor, in fact an early form of turbojet. The Macchi C.205V Veltro (Greyhound) was a development of the M.C. 202 which had shown itself at least the equal of the Hurricane in the Western Desert. The M.C. 205V was a marked improvement with the 1,475 hp DB 605A engine which gave it a top speed of nearly 400 mph. Again this arrived too late to affect the outcome of the war.

In Russia meanwhile, the Yak–1 had given place to the Yak–3 (181), designed to combat the Messerschmitt Bf 109G–2. It had in fact a better climb rate and turning circle than the German fighter and was faster at altitudes below 20,000 feet, eventually improved in 1944 with a new VK–107A engine to give a speed of 447 mph at 19,000 feet. The Yak–3 was the finest piston-engined fighter in service with the Soviet Air Force at the end of the war. The fighter that was used in largest numbers, flown also by Polish and French units ,was the Yak–9, a modification of the Yak–7 two-seater trainer, made of metal and wood construction and used both as a bomber escort with long-range fuel tanks and in a ground-attack role, equipped with up to 45-mm cannon. The relatively poor performance of the LaGG–3 with its in-line engine was considerably improved in the later Lavochkin La–5 and La–7 (178) by installing radial engines. The La–5 in 1942 was able to meet the Messerschmitt Bf 109G–2 on equal terms, being 28 mph faster at 390 mph but lacking the German's rate of climb. This was improved with the La–7 which could climb to 16,400 feet in four minutes twenty-seven seconds and had a top speed of 422 mph at 21,000 feet. It could equal the performance of either the Bf 109G–6 or the Fw 190 A–8. As an experiment, a liquid-fuel rocket motor was installed at the rear to increase speed to 460 mph for some three minutes during flight, but the fumes were found to weaken the fuselage structure.

246   Messerschmitt Me 309. Span: 36 ft 3 in. Length: 31 ft 0½ in. Engine: 1,750 hp DB 603 A. Armament: two 30-mm and two 20-mm cannon and four machine-guns. Max speed: 455 mph. An unsuccessful attempt to produce an improved version of the Bf 109, not developed beyond the prototype stage and abandoned when the Bf 109G proved to have superior turning abilities.

247   Messerschmitt Me 410. Span: 53 ft 8 in. Length: 40 ft 8½ in. Engine: two 1,900 hp DB 603 G. Armament: one 50-mm BK 5 gun, two 30-mm and two 20-mm cannon. Max speed: 388 mph at 22,000 ft. Service ceiling: 32,800 ft.

248   Macchi C.202 Folgore (Thunderbolt). Span: 34 ft 8½ in. Length: 29 ft 0½ in. Engine: 1,075 hp licence-built Daimler-Benz DB 601 A–1 liquid-cooled inverted-vee. Armament: two 12.7-mm and two 7.7-mm machine-guns. Max speed: 370 mph at 16,400 ft. Service ceiling: 37,730 ft.

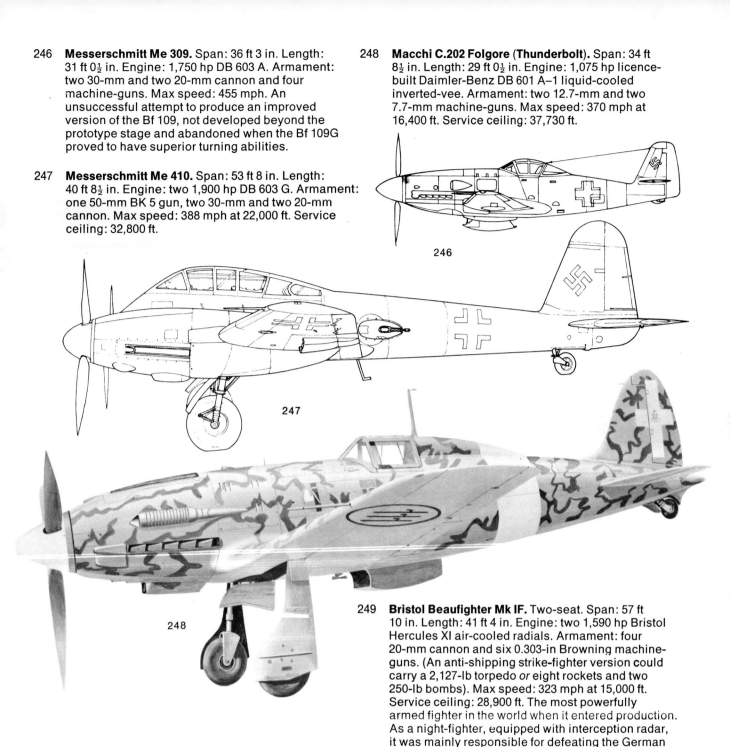

246

247

248

249   Bristol Beaufighter Mk IF. Two-seat. Span: 57 ft 10 in. Length: 41 ft 4 in. Engine: two 1,590 hp Bristol Hercules XI air-cooled radials. Armament: four 20-mm cannon and six 0.303-in Browning machine-guns. (An anti-shipping strike-fighter version could carry a 2,127-lb torpedo or eight rockets and two 250-lb bombs). Max speed: 323 mph at 15,000 ft. Service ceiling: 28,900 ft. The most powerfully armed fighter in the world when it entered production. As a night-fighter, equipped with interception radar, it was mainly responsible for defeating the German night blitz on London in the winter of 1940–41.

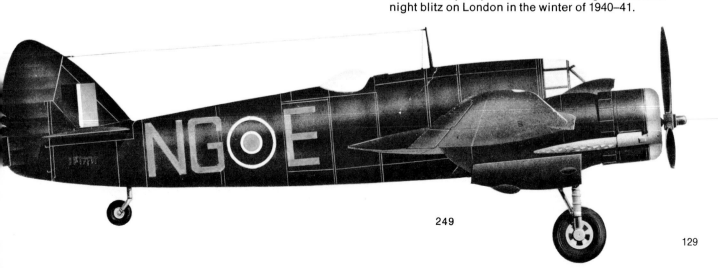

249

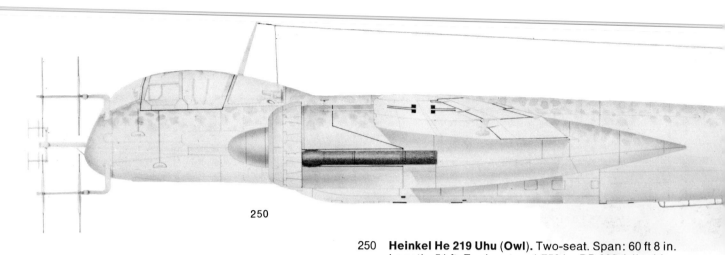

250

250 **Heinkel He 219 Uhu (Owl).** Two-seat. Span: 60 ft 8 in. Length: 51 ft. Engine: two 1,750 hp DB 603 A liquid-cooled inverted-vee. Armament: two 30-mm cannon and four machine-guns. Max speed: 416 mph. at 23,000 ft. Service ceiling: 41,660 ft. Intended originally as a multi-purpose aircraft destroyer, one version carried a crew of three.

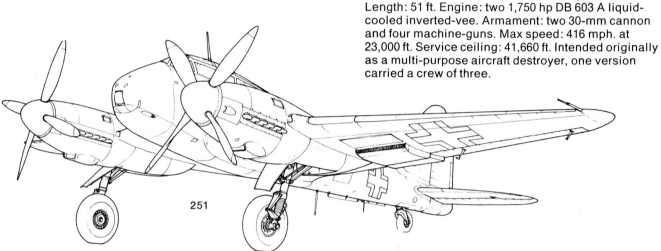

251

251 **Messerschmitt Me 210A.** Span: 53 ft 7 in. Length: 40 ft 3 in. Engine: two 1,395 hp DB 601 F twelve-cylinder inverted-vee. Armament: two 20-mm cannon, two 13-mm guns remotely-controlled, and two 7.9-mm machine-guns (and provision for a 4,400-lb bomb load). Max speed: 385 mph. Service ceiling: 23,000 ft.

253

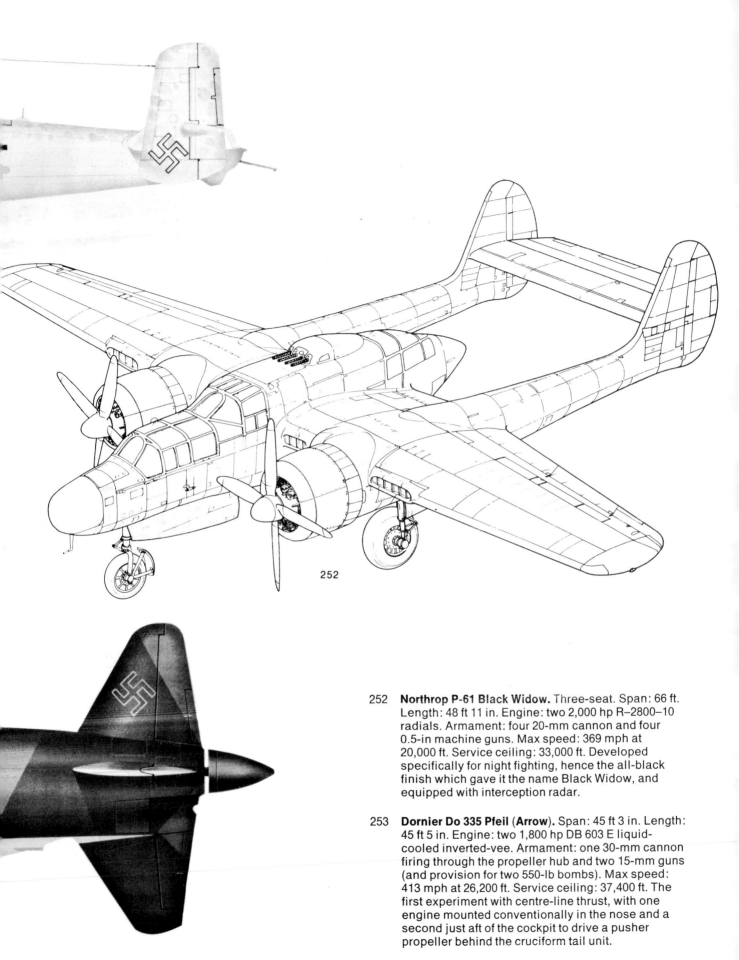

252

252 **Northrop P-61 Black Widow.** Three-seat. Span: 66 ft. Length: 48 ft 11 in. Engine: two 2,000 hp R–2800–10 radials. Armament: four 20-mm cannon and four 0.5-in machine guns. Max speed: 369 mph at 20,000 ft. Service ceiling: 33,000 ft. Developed specifically for night fighting, hence the all-black finish which gave it the name Black Widow, and equipped with interception radar.

253 **Dornier Do 335 Pfeil** (Arrow). Span: 45 ft 3 in. Length: 45 ft 5 in. Engine: two 1,800 hp DB 603 E liquid-cooled inverted-vee. Armament: one 30-mm cannon firing through the propeller hub and two 15-mm guns (and provision for two 550-lb bombs). Max speed: 413 mph at 26,200 ft. Service ceiling: 37,400 ft. The first experiment with centre-line thrust, with one engine mounted conventionally in the nose and a second just aft of the cockpit to drive a pusher propeller behind the cruciform tail unit.

254 **Junkers Ju 88 (G-6c).** Three-seat. Span: 65 ft 10½ in. Length: 54 ft 1½ in. Engine: two 1,750 hp Jumo 213A radials. Armament: two 20-mm cannon and six machine-guns. Max speed: 344 mph at 19,700 ft. Service ceiling: 32,800 ft. Developed originally as a fast medium bomber, the Ju 88 became the most versatile aircraft of the war. The G-series was produced in mid-1944 as a night-fighter, equipped with sophisticated interception radar.

255 **Ilyushin Il-2 Stormovik.** Span: 47 ft 11 in. Length: 38 ft 3 in. Engine: 1,770 hp AM–38 liquid-cooled vee type. Armament: two 23-mm cannon, two 7.62-mm machine-guns and one rearward firing 12.7-mm machine-gun (and provision for eight 82-mm rocket missiles and four 220-lb bombs). Max speed: 262.8 mph at sea level. Service ceiling: 24,600 ft. Produced in single and two-seat versions as a heavily armed and armoured low level ground-attack fighter.

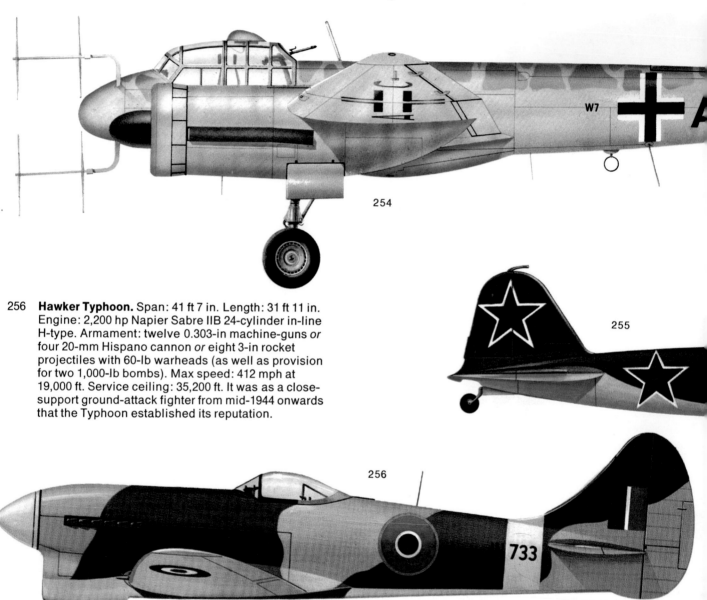

254

255

256

256 **Hawker Typhoon.** Span: 41 ft 7 in. Length: 31 ft 11 in. Engine: 2,200 hp Napier Sabre IIB 24-cylinder in-line H-type. Armament: twelve 0.303-in machine-guns *or* four 20-mm Hispano cannon *or* eight 3-in rocket projectiles with 60-lb warheads (as well as provision for two 1,000-lb bombs). Max speed: 412 mph at 19,000 ft. Service ceiling: 35,200 ft. It was as a close-support ground-attack fighter from mid-1944 onwards that the Typhoon established its reputation.

733

257 **Henschel Hs 129.** Span: 46 ft 7 in. Length: 32 ft. Engine: two 690 hp Gnôme-Rhône 14M fourteen-cylinder radials. Armament: two 20-mm cannon and two 7.9-mm machine-guns with provision for two 110-lb bombs *or* the addition of a 30-mm cannon instead of the bombs *or* in the final version, as here, a 75-mm BK 7.5 cannon in a large housing under the fuselage which could be jettisoned. This was used particularly against tanks but its weight reduced the maximum speed at sea level to 199 mph. Max speed: 253 mph at 12,500 ft. Service ceiling: 29,500 ft. A highly effective ground-attack fighter.

Improvements in German Fighters

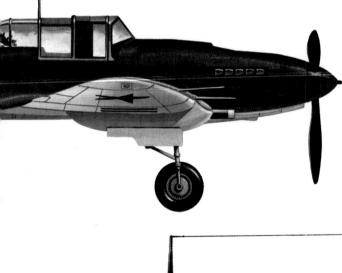

Developments in Germany on piston-engined fighters towards the end of the war included improved versions of the Bf 109 which went from the E and F (Emil and Frederich) series to G (Gustav) which was the last major production series. The heavier DB 605 engine made them less manoeuvrable than their predecessors although they could carry heavier armament of two heavy machine-guns and three cannon. Some Gs from 1943 onwards had pressurized cockpits as did other German and Allied fighters, necessary at the 40,000-foot altitudes at which fighters were then flying. They served in a variety of roles including day and night fighting, fighter-bombing and reconnaissance. An H-series with long-span wings was developed for high-altitude combat while the K-series achieved 452 mph at 19,500 feet although very few of these saw combat. Priority for high-altitude fighter development had by that time been given to Focke-Wulf for the Ta–152, a potential successor to the remarkable Fw 190 which had remained in production for more than five years, over 20,000 machines having been built. The Ta–152, designed by Kurt Tank, would have been one of the outstanding fighters of the war but its arrival in front-line service, delayed by political confusion in Germany and the effects of Allied bombing, was too late for it to make any significant contribution. The only operational type was the C-series which, with a DB 603 LA inverted-Vee liquid-cooled engine that had a radial appearance because of the cowling fitted to it, gave 439 mph at 37,000 feet. A booster could increase the horsepower to 2,300, giving speeds of up to 443 mph at 44,300 feet.

Messerschmitt meanwhile had replaced the Bf 110 with two more twin-engined two-seaters, the Me 210 (251) and Me 410 (247). Neither of them were outstanding aircraft although they were used in large numbers. Armament included remotely-controlled rearward-firing heavy machine-guns, and for bomber interception no fewer than six cannon and two heavy machine-guns were carried. One type of Me 410 had a single 50-mm cannon. But the main effort in Germany, as a desperate attempt was made to fight a war already lost, was directed towards the development of 'secret weapons' in which jet fighters and rockets played a large part.

257

The First Jet Aircraft

Experimental work on jet-propulsion had been going on in both Britain and Germany before the war, based on the principle of opposite reaction in which a mixture of hot gases created by the ignition of compressed air and fuel is forced backwards through a nozzle at the rear of the airplane and thus moves it forwards. Early attempts used a conventional piston-engine to drive the compressor but this soon gave way to the turbojet idea. Air taken in through a duct in front of the airplane was compressed in a revolving compressor, ignited with fuel (originally kerosene) in one or more combustion chambers, and the heat-expanded gases forced back through a turbine also drove the compressor in front before being thrust from the rear. Sir Frank Whittle in Britain was the first to run such an engine successfully, in April 1937, but the first jet-propelled airplane to fly was the German Heinkel He 178 (259) research aircraft which made its maiden flight on August 27th 1939. The experimental He 280 was the first fighter in the world powered by a turbojet; it was not put into production, but it was significant as the first airplane to be equipped with an ejector seat for the pilot, an necessary requirement at the high speeds being contemplated.

The basic difference between the work going on in both countries was that the Germans favoured the axial-flow type of compressor in which the air was thrust directly backwards whereas the British preferred the centrifugal-flow type, thrusting the air outwards before being ducted back. This meant a difference in external design, the German engines being long and slender while the British were shorter and thicker. The Whittle type was developed early on by the Americans whose first jet fighter, the experimental Bell XP–59A Airacomet, made its maiden flight in October 1942, only one year after work on its design had begun. Three other jet fighters were developed in the United States before the war ended; the Lockheed XP–80 Shooting Star and the Ryan XFR–1 Fireball in 1944 and the McDonnell XFH–1 Phantom in 1945. None of them saw service during the war but were the basis of major developments afterwards.

The first jet fighter in the world to go into squadron service was the Messerschmitt Me 262 towards the end of 1944 after six years of development. It could have been introduced as much as one year earlier had it not been for Hitler's insistence on converting it for use as a bomber and delays caused by Allied bombing of the factory which made the turbojet engines. The fighter version was the Me 262A–1a Schwalbe (Swallow) (261) which had a maximum speed of 540 mph at 20,000 feet and a ceiling of 37,500 feet. Its basic armament consisted of four 30-mm short-barrelled cannon mounted in the nose and the fuselage was of triangular-section to enable the greatest amount of fuel to be carried.

While other Me 262s were being converted into a mainly unsuitable fighter-bomber role, the British had also introduced a jet fighter, the Gloster/Armstrong Whitworth Meteor (258) which was in fact the first jet to be used in action. On August 4th 1944 the pilot of a Meteor destroyed a V–1 flying bomb by going alongside and tipping it over with his wing-tip. The Meteor was the only Allied jet fighter to be used operationally during the war. It had two turbojets like the Me 262 but was well over 100 mph slower when first introduced. With more powerful Rolls Royce Derwent 8 engines however its top speed was eventually increased to 590 mph at sea level with a ceiling up to 50,000 feet. In addition to its primary role as a single-seat fighter, armed with four 20-mm cannon, the versatile Meteor was also developed into a two-seat all-weather night-fighter, a two-seat trainer, a high-altitude photo-reconnaissance machine, and also performed many second-line duties. An even more advanced design was the de Havilland Vampire (276) with speeds of up to 540 mph and excellent manoeuvrability, but although it first flew in September 1943 it was too late to see service during the war.

As well as the turbojet engine, the Germans also developed a rocket motor, powered simply by the thrust from a liquid oxygen fuel, which was the forerunner of the rockets that eventually took man into space. This work had started in 1938 and by August 1941 the V–1 flying bomb prototype had made its first flight at 620 mph, using T-Stoff (hydrogen peroxide and water) propellant. This success led to the development of a manned fighter, the

258 **Gloster E.28/39 Pioneer.** This prototype, designed in 1940, was used as a test-bed for the Whittle gas-turbine engine which was the culmination of years of research work by Frank Whittle and his team. The E.28/39 was first flown on May 15th 1941. But by then, the Gloster designers were already preparing plans for a single-seat fighter using two turbojets which resulted in the Gloster F.9/40, first flown in March 1943 and the forerunner of the Gloster Meteor series.

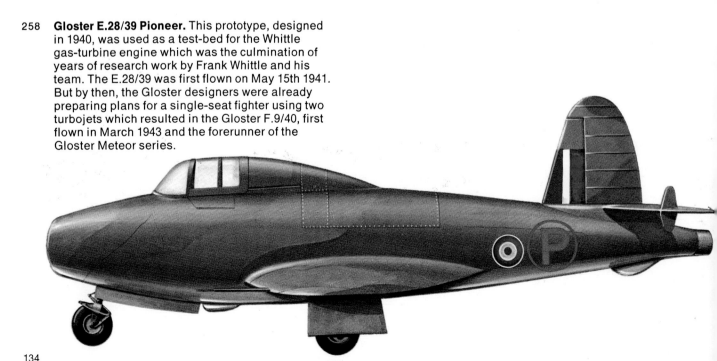

Messerschmitt Me 163 Komet (260), which was ready in mid-1942 but had to wait more than a year for its new engine which used, in addition to T-Stoff, a C-Stoff catalyst of methyl alcohol and hydrazine hydrate. When it entered service in the summer of 1944 the Me 163 was the fastest fighter of the war with a top speed of nearly 600 mph at 30,000 feet and a service ceiling of 39,500. The great advantage of the rocket motor was that its thrust did not decline at high altitudes since it took its own oxygen with it and was therefore not dependent on the outside atmosphere. On the other hand it used fuel at a much higher rate than the turbojet and could only stay in the air for two-and-a-half minutes after its initial climb. Its highly inflammable fuel was also extremely dangerous and many pilots were killed when Komets literally blew up, especially on landing if any fuel was left in the tank. Nevertheless, armed with two 30-mm cannon in the wing roots or up to 24 unguided rockets, the Komet achieved some success against Allied bombers, largely due to its unprecedented speed and the element of surprise.

Towards the end of the war, in a panic move to produce fighters, Heinkel was given a specification for a light, cheap, turbojet Volksjager (People's Fighter) which could be put quickly into mass production. The resulting He 162 Salamander (262) was designed, built and flown in only sixty-nine days, a record in itself considering that it normally took two or three years to develop a new fighter. The He 162 had a top speed of 520 mph at 20,000 feet and a ceiling of 39,500 feet and was armed with two 20-mm cannon. It was constructed largely of duralumin and wood with a BMW turbojet fixed to a pod on top of the fuselage. It was intended that mass production should be at a rate of 1,000 a month but in the event only 100 were built by the time the war ended.

The work of German scientists was so far advanced in the early 1940s that the outcome of the war might have been very different had more attention and facilities been given to them. Spitfires and Mustangs could generally cope with the V–1 flying bombs, even though they were faster, but against the V–2 rockets there was no defence except the destruction of their launching sites. They could carry a ton of explosives more than 200 miles at 3,000 mph and development was under way of a rocket that could even reach New York. The Germans were experimenting with a wide range of new ideas in the field of aviation, including swept-wing designs and VTOL (vertical take-off and landing) machines of which the Bachem Natter (Viper) (263) was the earliest example. This rocket propelled fighter was launched vertically from rails and could climb at the fantastic rate of 35,000 feet a minute. Having reached a bomber formation the pilot would fire a mass of rocket projectiles from the nose of the machine, then use his ejection seat to descend by parachute. The rocket engine would automatically break off from the fuselage and also parachute down. The Natter was still being tested when the war ended and was not used in action. This also applied to the first air-to-air guided missile, the X–4, which the Germans were developing from their earlier unguided rockets. All these and many other technical innovations became available to the victorious Allies after Germany's defeat and provided much of the impetus for the new post-war generation of jet fighters.

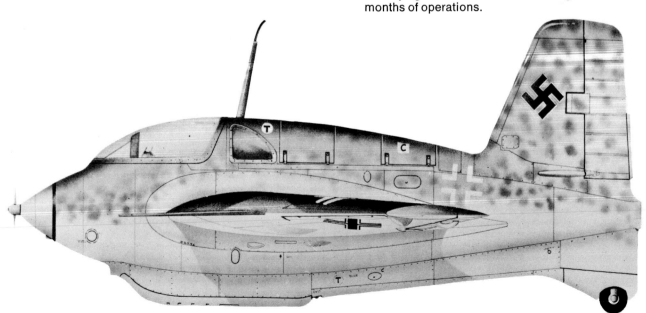

259 **Heinkel He 178.** Span: 23 ft 8 in. Length: 24 ft 7½ in. Engine: 1,100-lb thrust He S-3b turbojet. Max speed: 435 mph. First-ever jet aircraft, with a metal fuselage and wooden wings, which made its maiden flight on August 27th 1939, nearly two years before the Gloster Whittle.

260 **Messerschmitt Me 163 Komet (Comet).** Span: 30 ft. 7 in. Length: 18 ft. 8 in. Engine: 3,750-lb thrust Walter HWK 109-509A liquid rocket motor. Armament: two 30-mm cannon (and provision for 24 unguided rocket projectiles). Max speed: 596 mph at 30,000 ft. Service ceiling: 39,500 ft. Although its duration was only 2½ minutes after climb and it was highly dangerous to fly because of the inflammable hydrogen fuel, the Komet rocket fighter scored heavily against Allied bombers during its nine months of operations.

261 Messerschmitt Me 262A-1a. Span: 40 ft. 11½ in. Length: 34 ft. 9½ in. Engine: two 1,850-lb thrust Jumo 004 turbojets. Armament: four 30-mm cannon (and provision for two 550-lb bombs). Max speed: 540 mph at 19,685 ft. Service ceiling: 37,565 ft. The world's first jet-propelled fighter to go into squadron service, the Me 262 would have been available even earlier had it not been for Hitler's insistence on converting it into a bomber.

A Messerschmitt Me 262 about to be shot down by James Kennedy of 357th Fighter Group, 8th US Air Force, on November 8th, 1944. *R.A.F. Museum*

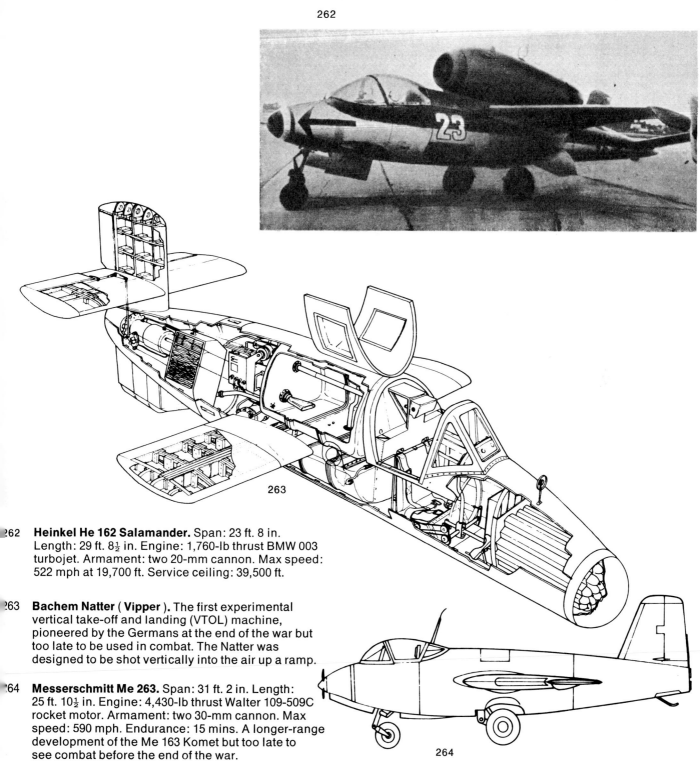

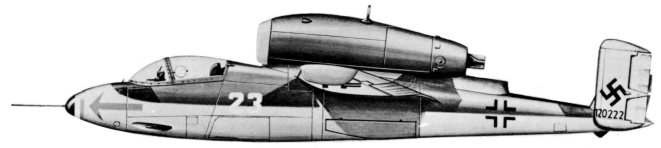

262

263

262 **Heinkel He 162 Salamander.** Span: 23 ft. 8 in. Length: 29 ft. 8½ in. Engine: 1,760-lb thrust BMW 003 turbojet. Armament: two 20-mm cannon. Max speed: 522 mph at 19,700 ft. Service ceiling: 39,500 ft.

263 **Bachem Natter (Vipper).** The first experimental vertical take-off and landing (VTOL) machine, pioneered by the Germans at the end of the war but too late to be used in combat. The Natter was designed to be shot vertically into the air up a ramp.

264 **Messerschmitt Me 263.** Span: 31 ft. 2 in. Length: 25 ft. 10½ in. Engine: 4,430-lb thrust Walter 109-509C rocket motor. Armament: two 30-mm cannon. Max speed: 590 mph. Endurance: 15 mins. A longer-range development of the Me 163 Komet but too late to see combat before the end of the war.

264

The Post-War Years

Although jet aircraft inaugurated a new era during the last year of the Second World War, piston-engined fighters continued to form a large part of many air forces in the world until the 1950s and even into the 1960s in some instances. The Messerschmitt Bf 109 for example, powered by the 1,400 hp Rolls Royce Merlin driving a four-blade Rotol propeller, was built in Spain until the end of 1956 as the main fighter-bomber in service with the Spanish Air Force. The Supermarine Seafire served as a carrier-borne fighter with the Fleet Air Arm until 1954 and took part in the Korean War. The Mustang P–51 also saw service during that war and remained operational with the US Air Force for longer than any other piston-engined type. It was in fact ordered back into production in 1967 as the Cavalier F.51D for counter-insurgency duties when it was found that high-speed jet aircraft were often too sophisticated for fighting in small localized wars. War-surplus Mustangs were bought by the air forces of many countries and the type was built under licence in Australia for the Royal Australian Air Force.

A number of piston-engined fighters developed towards the end of the war arrived too late to see combat but represented the ultimate peak of their technology. An outstanding example was the de Havilland Hornet, a single-seat long-range fighter-bomber powered by two 2,030 hp Merlin engines with four-bladed propellers rotating in opposite directions, its monocoque fuselage built of wood like that of the Mosquito. The prototype Hornet first flew in July 1944 and achieved an incredible speed for that time of 485 mph. It was intended for use in the Pacific 'island-hopping' campaign against the Japanese but the war ended before production models came into service early in 1946 as the RAF's last piston-engined fighter. A later development for the Fleet Air Arm was the Sea Hornet with folding wings, the first single-seat twin-engined fighter to operate from British carriers. A two-seater variant was the standard Fleet Air Arm night-fighter from 1949 to 1954.

The US Navy also introduced in the immediate post-war years two Grumman piston-engined fighters which were too late to see combat. The F7F Tigercat was, like the Sea Hornet, the first twin-engined fighter to operate from American carriers and was also the most heavily armed, with four heavy machine-guns in the nose, four 20-mm wing cannon, and provision for bombs, rockets and torpedoes. The F8F Bearcat was a development of the single-seat Wildcat/Hellcat line and equipped a number of naval squadrons until 1949. Meanwhile the excellent Vought Corsair remained in second-line service with the US Navy until the mid-1950s and with the French Navy until the early 1960s.

But these were the last types of an age that was already passing. In their search for higher speeds, engine and airframe designers had done wonders in the war years. But the point was reached where, even with the strongest and lightest materials available, the piston engine could be taken no further. Power could only be increased by larger cylinders or more of them, but the extra weight was ultimately self-defeating. The use of superchargers proved to be the answer for a while but here again, as they increased in size, they were consuming as much power as they added. There seemed little possibility of extending engines upwards of 5,000 hp to provide the power needed by future aircraft. Another problem was with the traditional propeller which was found to suffer a sharp fall in efficiency as the tips of its blades approached the speed of sound. From 1949 to 1957 the US government made a great effort to develop a supersonic propeller but without success, except for short distances and at the price of creating an excruciating noise. It appeared that speeds of about 520 mph represented the absolute limit for piston-engined aircraft.

No such limits applied to jet-propelled aircraft of course. The turbojet engine revolutionized the whole aviation industry in the post-war years but especially fighters which were the first and most obvious aircraft to make use of this new form of propulsion. The first turbojets were installed in fighters very similar in design to piston-engined types but as a result of research, much of it based on German wartime experiments which had become available to the victorious Allies, new configurations appeared which could best take advantage of the potential offered by jet propulsion, a potential which today has brought fighters to speeds of 1,600 mph and more with an acceleration that can reach twice the speed of sound in as little as three minutes. Although simpler in some ways than the piston engine driving a propeller, in spite of such aids to increased power as water injection and after-burners, the turbojet called into being a whole new technology requiring more sophisticated materials and a vast range of electronic equipment, as well as a new approach to aerodynamics resulting in many unorthodox designs.

The first big difference was to sweep back the wings and tail surfaces and to reduce their thickness/chord ratio, that is the ratio between the thickness of the wing to its width. It had been known in the 1930s that a thin-wing improved an aircraft's speed but had poor lifting ability, while a thick wing had better lift but poor speed. Design was a matter of choosing the best ratio between the two for the qualities most required. The immense power of turbojets removed much of the lift problem at high speeds while thin wings made supersonic flight possible. Their poor lift at low speeds was compensated to some extent by fitting elaborate edge slats and flaps but faster take-off and landing speeds had to be accepted, to the point in fact where they are equal to the maximum speed of most aircraft of the early 1930s. Longer runways became necessary, which in turn has led to an increasing interest in VTOL (vertical take-off and landing) and STOL (short take-off and landing) machines for use in combat areas where such runways might not be available. But in any event range is no longer the problem it was with the development of air-to-air refuelling from 'flying tankers', a technique pioneered by Britain in the immediate post-war period.

As fighters became faster, air combat in the former style of the two world wars was no longer possible. Targets were simply too fleeting for a pilot to have time to bring his guns to bear on them. The answer was radar, which already in the Second World War had pointed the way by detecting enemy raiders and guiding interceptors to attack them, a vital contribution to winning the Battle of Britain. Its most advanced use during the war was by night-fighters. It was now developed to the point where ground control radar could automatically vector a fighter to its target while radar installed in the nose of the aircraft, operating through a fire-control system, automatically selected the best moment to fire its weapons and then turned the aircraft away to avoid return fire. The weapons themselves changed from heavy-calibre guns and rockets to guided missiles, operated either by radar or by infra-

265 North American F-86 (A-5) Sabre. Span: 37 ft. 1 in. Length: 37 ft. 6 in. Engine: J47–GE–1 turbojet. Armament: six 0.5-in machine-guns (as well as provision for bombs or rockets). Max speed: 675 mph at 2,500 ft. Service ceiling: 48,300 ft. The first swept-wing fighter to be built, based on German plans (not adopted) to sweep back the wings of the Me 262.

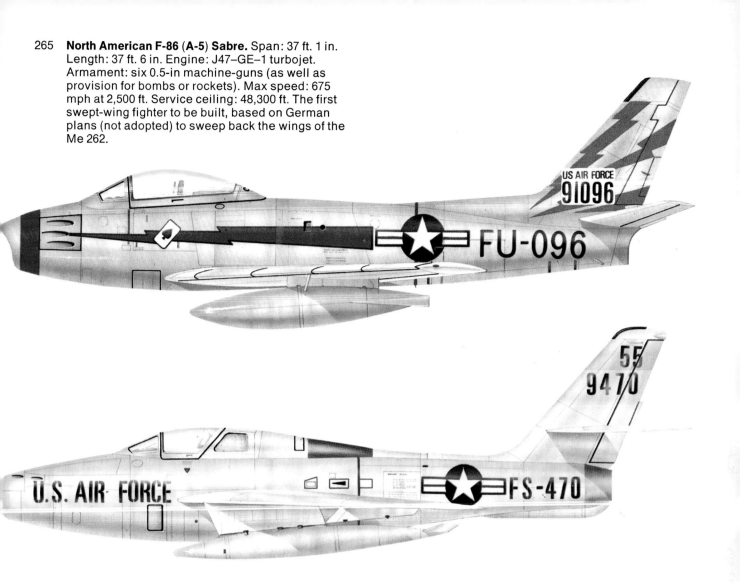

266 Republic F-84 F-G Thunderstreak. Span: 33 ft. 7 in. Length: 43 ft. 5 in. Engine: Wright YJ65–W–1 turbojet (licence-built British Sapphire). Armament: various bombs and rockets, including provision for carrying a nuclear bomb. Max speed: 658 mph at 20,000 ft. Service ceiling: 46,000 ft.

red sensing to home on the heat emitted by the target. In fact the pilot has become little more than a passenger during combat, with all the major decisions taken and put into effect by electronic control systems. It seemed at one time that manned combat aircraft might become redundant but experience has shown that the human brain is still the best insurance should anything go wrong with automatic controls or if they are jammed by anti-radar devices. In the same way, cannon is still the most effective armament in certain circumstances.

The vastly complex equipment carried by fighters today has made them among the most expensive pieces of engineering ever built. Their weight has increased about four times since the Second World War but their cost is many times more than that, running into millions of dollars. Conversely the development of the atomic bomb has negated the need for vast bomber formations of the kind that blasted Germany in 1944 and 1945. A single aircraft

today, carrying a nuclear weapon, can have a greater destructive power than all the piston-engined bombers that ever flew. But it also must have speed to avoid interception, so that while fighters have become larger and more complex, bombers have become more compact and faster. In fact the main type which has emerged today is the fighter-bomber, able to carry out a dual role, while the light fighter as such no longer exists. Its place, together with that of the night-fighter, has been taken by a new class of all-weather fighter which by the use of radar control systems can intercept an enemy that is invisible, whether because of darkness, bad weather, cloud, or sheer speed.

The only major combatant power which had not produced a jet-fighter by the end of the Second World War was the Soviet Union. Even Japan had developed a simple type of jet engine in which the compressor was driven by a small piston-engine, similar to earlier Italian experiments on the same lines. This was installed in the Yokosuka MXY–7 Ohka (Cherry Blossom) piloted bomb used on suicide missions towards the end of the war. But Russia was not slow to take advantage of Germany technical expertise that became available in 1945. Two fighters were developed that year using captured German turbojet engines, the Yak–15 (274) and the Mig–9. Both flew for the first time on April 24th 1946. But whereas the Yak–15 was basically a Yak–3 airframe modified to take the Junkers Jumo turbojet, the MiG–9 was an entirely new all-metal mid-wing monoplane, powered by two BMW turbojets mounted side-by-side in the nose. Fuel was carried in the thin-section wings. Although with a speed of 560 mph at 16,500 feet and a ceiling of 42,600 feet the MiG–9 could stand comparison with most foreign fighters of its day, the United States felt confident of its lead in this field, based on more years of research. Britain continued to develop some of the best turbojet engines but in the austerity post-war years carried out little effective research into supersonic fighter design, gambling on there being no international crisis for at least ten years. The shock came in 1950 when, during the new air war over Korea, the next Mikoyan-Gurevich designed fighter showed itself to be superior to any then available to the Allies. This was the MiG–15 (270), the first to take advantage of German research by using sweptback wings which enabled speeds in excess of 660 mph to be achieved and initially powered by Rolls-Royce Nene turbojets which the British government had made available for export in 1946. This engine was later copied by the Russians for their own production.

The first jet to become operational with the USAAF had been the Lockheed P–80 Shooting Star, developed towards the end of the Second World War and delivered for service with front-line pursuit groups from December 1945 onwards. Its thin-section laminar-flow wings were straight and not sweptback, a main factor in it being completely outclassed by the MiG–15 in the Korean War to the extent of being over 80 mph slower. This also applied to a lesser degree to the Gloster Meteor Mark 8s of the Royal Australian Air Force which were the only British jet-fighters to see action in Korea. Nevertheless the balance was partly redressed by the superior combat experience of the Allied pilots to that of the Chinese. In the first-ever air combat between jet fighters on November 8th 1950, an

F–80 (the designation P for Pursuit was changed to F for Fighter in 1948) shot down a MiG–15. The Americans hurriedly brought their own first swept-wing type into service, the remarkable North American F–86 Sabre (265) which was more than a match for the MiG–15 and prevented the Chinese from establishing air superiority over Korea. By the time the war ended in 1953 the US Air Force had established a kill ratio of nearly ten to one in its favour against the Chinese air force.

The F–86 Sabre was eventually developed into one of the best combat aircraft of all time. One big advantage of the early A and E series, which helped them to defeat the Chinese air force in Korea, was in having radar ranging gunsights for their six heavy machine-guns, a device introduced by the RAF towards the end of the Second World War as the most notable advance in air gunnery since the also-British gyro gunsight. This was to prove essential when air combats were being fought at speeds of 600 mph and more. The major production day-fighter version of the Sabre was the F series which was introduced in 1954, both for the USAF and the air forces of many other countries including Nationalist China, Spain and Japan. The F–86H was a fighter-bomber, armed with four 20-mm cannon, while the type produced in most numbers was the D (Sabre Dog) series all-weather fighter. This had, in place of cannon armament, a retractable pack of twenty-four Mighty Mouse unguided air-to-air rockets which could be lowered from the underside of the fuselage. The type was widely used in many countries, as well as equipping USAF squadrons in Europe and the Far East, and was also produced in Canada and Australia.

More Sabres were built in the 1950s than any other type of jet-fighter, almost 7,000 in fact, and they remained in front-line service until the late 1960s, noted for their excellent all-round performance and ease of handling. The F–86 was however a subsonic aircraft, as was the US Navy's carrier-borne version of the type, the F–1 Fury. A completely new design, in which the wing sweep-back was increased to 45 degrees with a low-mounted slab tailplane, resulted in the F–100 Super Sabre, the first level-supersonic fighter to enter service, late in 1953. By coincidence the designation F–100 in the American fighter numbering system, ushering in what became known

269

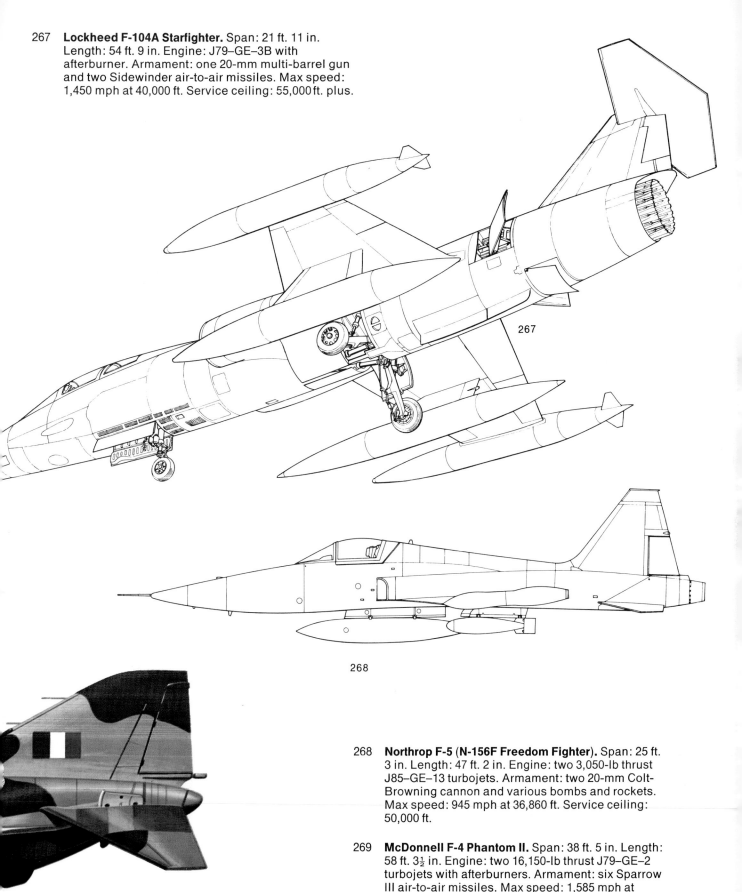

267 **Lockheed F-104A Starfighter.** Span: 21 ft. 11 in.
Length: 54 ft. 9 in. Engine: J79–GE–3B with
afterburner. Armament: one 20-mm multi-barrel gun
and two Sidewinder air-to-air missiles. Max speed:
1,450 mph at 40,000 ft. Service ceiling: 55,000 ft. plus.

267

268

268 **Northrop F-5 (N-156F Freedom Fighter).** Span: 25 ft.
3 in. Length: 47 ft. 2 in. Engine: two 3,050-lb thrust
J85–GE–13 turbojets. Armament: two 20-mm Colt-
Browning cannon and various bombs and rockets.
Max speed: 945 mph at 36,860 ft. Service ceiling:
50,000 ft.

269 **McDonnell F-4 Phantom II.** Span: 38 ft. 5 in. Length:
58 ft. 3½ in. Engine: two 16,150-lb thrust J79–GE–2
turbojets with afterburners. Armament: six Sparrow
III air-to-air missiles. Max speed: 1,585 mph at
48,000 ft. Service ceiling: 62,000 ft. Originated by the
US Navy as a two-seat attack fighter for carrier-borne
operations, the Phantom was subsequently adopted
by the US Air Force and also by the RAF and Royal
Navy.

270 Mikoyan-Gurevich MiG-15. Span 33 ft. 1 in. Length: 36 ft. 3½ in. Engine: 5,450-lb thrust RD–45 turbojet, based on the Rolls-Royce Nene. Armament: one 37-mm and two 23-mm cannon (and provision for two 1,000-lb bombs *or* load of rockets). Max speed: 668 mph at sea level. Service ceiling: 51,000 ft.

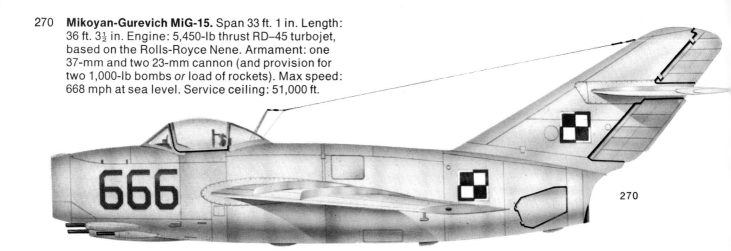

270

271 Mikoyan-Gurevich MiG-19PD. Span: 32 ft. Length: 37 ft. 6 in. Engine: two 5,500-lb thrust RD–9F axial-flow turbojets with afterburners. Armament: four beam-riding missiles. Max speed: Mach 1.3 at 20,000 ft. Service ceiling: 58,000 ft. Night-fighter version code-named 'Farmer-D' by NATO.

272 Sukhoi Su-7. Span: 30 ft. Length: 56 ft. Engine: reported to develop 22,050-lb thrust with afterburner. Armament: two 30-mm cannon (and provision for 2,550-lb bomb load *or* nineteen unguided 55-mm rockets). Max speed: 1,056 mph at 36,000 ft. Russia's first experimental swing-wing aircraft, intended for close-support ground-attack and code-named 'Fitter' by NATO.

as the 'Century series', also saw the introduction of the first truly supersonic fighters, the Super Sabre being followed by the McDonnell F–101 and the Convair F–102. These immensely powerful aircraft represented the tremendous achievement of American research into advanced propulsion systems and new forms of structure. Powered by the Pratt & Whitney J57 turbojet with afterburner, fed through an oval intake in the nose, the single-seat Super Sabres remained in service with the Tactical Air Command of the USAF until 1965, both as a tactical day-fighter with four 20-mm cannon and as a fighter-bomber with stiffened wings to take an assortment of rockets, missiles and nucelar weapons. The final production version included a second seat for combat training.

Although North American continued to produce fighter designs in the 1960s, none were built in any quantity and the company's place as a major builder of fighters has largely been taken by McDonnell, part of the giant Mc-Donnell Douglas Corporation. The McDonnell FH–1 Phantom, ordered in 1943, was the US Navy's first pure-jet fighter which was brought into limited service in 1947 after making the first jet take-off and landing on board an American aircraft carrier the previous year. This was a straight-wing airplane, as was the F2H Banshee which followed with fixed wing-tip tanks to accommodate more fuel and which saw service in the Korean War. With their third series, the F3H Demon, McDonnell adopted a single-engined layout with swept-back wings and tail unit but many problems were encountered because of the failure of the Westinghouse J40 engine programme. Then in 1954 the company really made its mark with the outstanding F–101 Voodoo, second of the USAF's supersonic Century fighters with two afterburning turbojets giving a maximum speed of 1,100 mph at 42,000 feet and a service ceiling of 48,000 feet. This was developed variously as a long-range escort fighter (with a combat range of 1,700 miles), a low-level fighter-bomber with provision for carrying air-to-air missiles and tactical nuclear weapons in addition to a fixed armament of four 20-mm cannon, and a two-seat long-range interceptor armed with three Falcon

air-to-air missiles and two Genie unguided rockets with nuclear warheads. These versions served in a number of USAF and Tactical Air Command squadrons until the early 1960s.

The Voodoo was followed by an even better McDonnell fighter, in fact one of the most successful fighters of all time. The Phantom II (269) was originally developed for the US Navy and from the beginning of its flight trials in May 1958 showed outstanding promise. With its long drooping nose and two very deep ducts projecting from either side of the fuselage this massive two-seater looked anything but gainly. It showed the extent to which aerodynamics had changed with the arrival of supersonic flight for its performance was superior to any other fighter at that time and it is still the fastest fighter in the West with a speed of Mach 2-plus and a service ceiling of 70,000 feet. It is not only immensely strong and powerful, with two General Electric J79 turbojets with reheat, but also has excellent manoeuvrability and one of the highest rates of climb. Such was its versatility that it became the first Navy fighter ever to be adopted by the USAF for a major role, with the designation F–4. In 1964 it was chosen by the Royal Navy to equip its fighter squadrons instead of continuing with the development of the Hawker Siddeley P.1154 VTOL fighter for a Navy role. British machines are fitted with two Rolls-Royce Spey turbofans, a type of engine mid-way between a turbojet and a propeller turbine in which an internal fan drives the air rearwards, one advantage being fuel economy. Armament includes a selection of Sparrow and Sidewinder guided missiles and the Vulcan 20-mm cannon housed under the nose. The F–4 Phantom II is equipped with the most effective search radar yet developed in the West, the Doppler fire-control radar system, and will remain in production until McDonnell Douglas (the two companies were merged in 1967) start building their next generation USAF fighter, the F–15.

Third of the Century fighters was the Convair F–102 Delta Dagger, the prototype model of which was the first powered aircraft to use the delta wing developed in Germany during the war by Dr. Alexander Lippisch. A

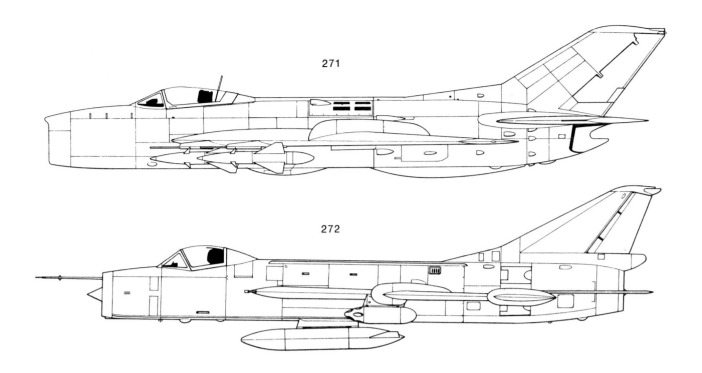

271

272

new specification was drawn up by the USAF in 1950 for an all-weather interceptor but the resulting prototype did not come up to the Mach 1.5 performance required. Major re-design work was carried out, introducing a waisted fuselage which was to become common to most high-speed fighters, and in December 1954 the F–102 achieved supersonic flight and was put into production as the USAF's first operational delta. It was also the first fighter to discard gun armament completely in favour of guided and unguided missiles. An improved version was developed into the F–106 Delta Dart with the more power-ful Pratt & Whitney J75 turbojet which became operational in 1959.

Other American companies meanwhile had also been developing supersonic fighters. Lockheed followed its two subsonic types, the F–80 Shooting Star and F–94 Starfire two-seater, with the controversial F–104 Star-fighter (267) which first flew in 1954 and was one of the most widely operated fighters in the 1960s. Its most remarkable feature is its very short wings, placed well back on the fuselage. Instead of being sweptback as with most other fighters they are straight, exceptionally thin, and have a downward slope of 10 degrees, giving the aircraft its distinctive dagger shape, accentuated by a very long pointed nose. The J79 engine was designed by the American General Electric Company and fitted with an afterburner, apparent from the large diameter of the jet tailpipe. Although little used in America the Starfighter was developed as a close-support strike-fighter for the re-formed *Luftwaffe* and was manufactured in a number of other countries including Canada, Italy and Japan. It was over its high accident rate in German service that con-troversy arose. Apart from various missiles, the Star-fighter was the first fighter to be armed with the Vulcan 20-mm 'revolving cannon', based on the old Gatling gun principle with a rotating group of barrels and able to fire over 1,000 rounds of ammunition in one fifteen-second burst. For in spite of the introduction of air-to-air missiles and rockets, a need is still felt for heavy machine-guns and cannon which can shoot straighter and faster and are more suitable in some circumstances. Most fighters still carry 20-mm and 30-mm cannon.

The first fighter to test-fire the Genie nuclear-tipped missile, developed by the Douglas company as the first such weapon designed for launching from a fighter, was the Northrop F–89 Scorpion in July 1957. The Genie has a range of six miles and is launched automatically, the nuclear warhead being armed a few seconds before firing and detonated by a fire-control system in the aircraft. It is intended for use against not just one aircraft but a whole formation. Because of the extent of the resulting explosion, precise accuracy is not necessary and the Genie has no guidance system. The first air-to-air guided missile taken into service by the USAF was the Hughes Falcon, later developed into a whole range of weapons including one with a nuclear warhead. Another missile originally developed for the US Navy but also used by the USAF, the RAF and the Royal Navy is the Raytheon Sparrow, with a range of over eight miles and a speed of Mach 2.5. But the simplest and most widely used type is the Sidewinder, designed by the US Ordnance Test Station in 1953 with either a radar or infra-red homing guidance system. This was carried by the Grumman F11F Tiger which first flew in July 1954 and in 1957 became the US Navy's first carrier-borne fighter that could exceed the speed of sound, replacing two other Grumman types, the F9F Panther and the F9F Cougar which was the first swept-wing jet fighter designed for the US Navy. Grum-man's latest fighter for the US Navy is the F–14, an ex-tremely sophisticated fighter-bomber of which deliveries and flight-testing began in 1972. The cost is over sixteen million dollars each, but even at that price Grumman have said they are losing about $1 million on each airplane.

Two other American manufacturers who followed suc-cessful Second World War fighters with turbojet types are Republic and Vought (now in association as Ling-Temco-Vought). The three Republic fighters which followed the excellent Thunderbolt, the last radial-engined fighter to serve with the USAF, continued the prefix Thunder. They were all primarily ground-attack aircraft; the P–84 Thunder-jet straight-wing type of 1946, the sweptwing F–84F

Thunderstreak (266) of 1950, and the F–105 Thunderchief of 1955 which was supersonic and the heaviest single-seater ever to enter USAF service, weighging 54,000 lbs in its latest torm. The Vought Corsair was followed by the Chance Vought F6U–1 Pirate in 1946, a straight-wing turbojet and the first Navy fighter to have an afterburner, and the sweptwing Chance Vought F7U Cutlass in 1948. The LTV F–8 Crusader which first flew in 1955 became the US Navy's standard fleet fighter and is unique in having a variable-incidence wing to give it a reasonably low landing speed.

Although better known for its bombers and airliners, the Douglas company built two jet fighters for the US Navy in the early post-war years before supersonic types became generally available. The F3D Skynight was a straight-wing two-seater, intended as a night-fighter, which served with US Marine squadrons in Korea and destroyed more enemy aircraft than any other Navy or Marine type. This was followed by the small single-seat F4D Skyray which was distinctive for its delta wing with rounded tips. In 1953 a Skyray set a World Air Speed

Record of 752.9 mph; only eight years later a McDonnell Phantom II became the first airplane to fly at over 1,600 mph, giving some indication of the tremendous advances made by the American aircraft industry. It is not surprising that development problems occurred in breaking such new ground. The outstanding example of this is General Dynamics, F–111, originally intended to meet all the fighter and bomber requirements of the US Air Force and the US Navy. Work on this project started in 1960 and the outcome was the world's first combat aircraft to incorporate variable-sweep wings which can be spread out for low speeds and folded back for maximum speed. The two-seat F–111, powered by two Pratt & Whitney turbofans side-by-side in the rear fuselage which gave it a maximum speed of 1,650 mph at 40,000 feet, first flew at the end of 1964 but difficulties were met from the outset, especially from engine mismatching. The Navy version was abandoned in 1968, when fifty ordered by the RAF were also cancelled. A much smaller number than originally planned have been bought by the USAF and the type is now under development as a long-range bomber.

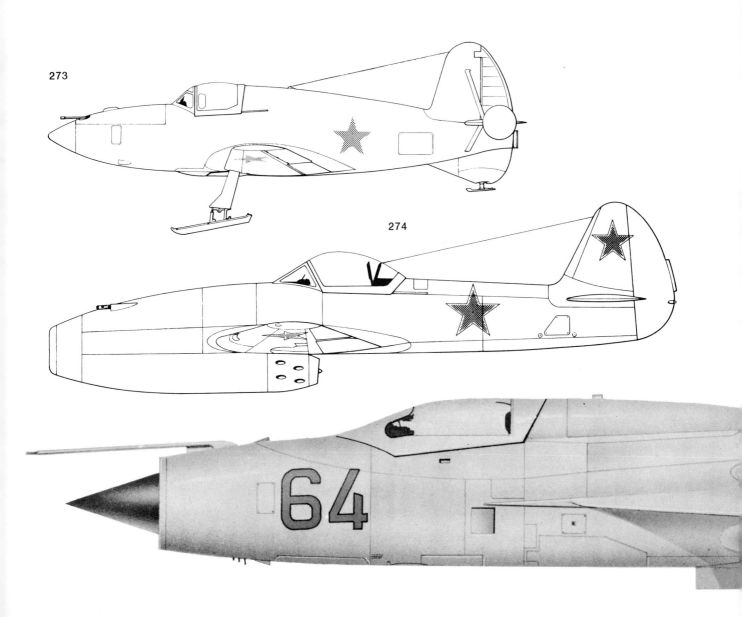

273

274

64

Although Britain pioneered the turbojet and continued to make some of the best engines, often built by American companies, research into airframe design was hampered in the early post-war years by a lack of government funds. The Gloster Meteor had been outclassed even at the end of the Second World War by the Messerschmitt Me 262 and this was certainly the case in the Korean War, by which time the Mark 8 had been developed for high-altitude interception or ground-attack with rocket projectiles. The Meteor was later converted into a two-seat night-fighter, the last operational variant being the NF 14. Meanwhile, Britain's second jet-fighter, the de Havilland Vampire, had entered service just too late to see combat in the Second War. Powered by de Havilland's Goblin centrifugal-flow turbojet its most distinctive feature was its twin-boom layout, designed to keep the jet pipe as short as possible. The Vampire was an excellent aircraft for its time and in 1948 became the first jet to fly the Atlantic. It served to initiate pilots into the high-speed jet age and was used by many countries for that purpose. The Venom was a later development of the Vampire, with the higher-powered de Havilland Ghost engine and long-range fuel tanks on the wing-tips. The wings were moderately swept-back on the leading edge which helped to give increased speeds of up to 640 mph. This type was used as a single-seat fighter-bomber and a two-seat night-fighter, while the Sea Venom was brought into service as a two-seat carrier-borne all-weather fighter. After de Havilland had merged with Hawker Siddeley, this was replaced by the twin-jet Sea Vixen, some of which are still in service, having lasted longer than the Supermarine Scimitar which was a single-seater and also powered by two Rolls-Royce Avon turbo-jets. The Scimitar was the first swept-wing aircraft to be produced for the Fleet Air Arm but in spite of its high cost it was still subsonic, except in a dive.

The previous Supermarine jets had been the straight-wing Attacker, which went into service in 1951 as the first carrier-borne jet fighter for Fleet Air Arm first-line squadrons, and the Swift, which was the first British swept-wing jet fighter to enter RAF service. Many problems were encountered with the Swift however, and it was withdrawn from Fighter Command in 1955.

273 **Beriev BB-1.** Span: 21 ft. 3 in. Length: 20 ft. 11¾ in. Engine: Dushkin D1–A liquid fuel rocket. Armament: two 20-mm cannon. Max speed: 610 mph at 16,400 ft. Rate of climb: 59 seconds to 32,810 ft.

274 **Yakovlev Yak-15.** Span: 30 ft. 2½ in. Length: 27 ft. 10½ in. Engine: 1,980-lb thrust German Junkers Jumo 004B turbojet (designated RD–10 by the Russians). Armament: two 23-mm cannon. Max speed: 503 mph. Service ceiling: 41,000 ft.

275 **Mikoyan-Gurevich MiG-21.** Span: 25 ft. Length: 55 ft. Engine: 9,500-lb thrust TDR Mk R37F turbojet with afterburner. Armament: two 30-mm cannon and two 'Atoll' air-to-air infra-red homing missiles. Max speed: 1,320 mph at 36,000 ft. Code-named 'Fishbed–C' by NATO.

275

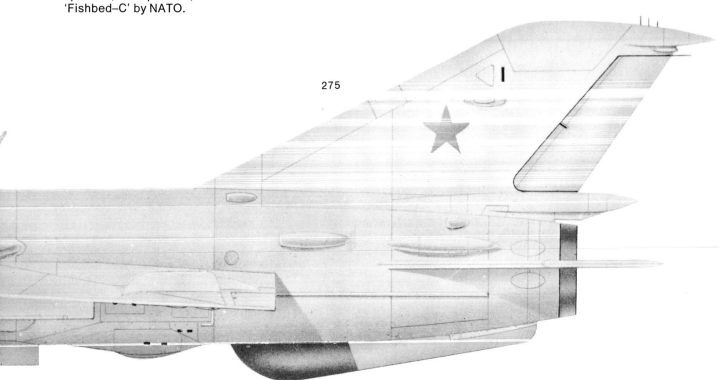

The famous Hawker line of fighters was continued after the Second World War with the piston-engined Fury and Sea Fury, the latter being the Fleet Air Arm's principle single-seat carrier-borne fighter until 1953 and the last piston-engined type to serve with the Royal Navy. It was followed by the Sea Hawk, developed from a proposal to install a turbojet engine in a Fury airframe. This fighter saw combat during the Suez Campaign in 1956 and had excellent manoeuvrability although it again was subsonic. The same speed limitation applied to the swept-wing Hawker Hunter (278) which went into service with the RAF in 1954 as a single-seat day fighter. Early problems were encountered with the Rolls-Royce Avon engine, the flame of which tended to blow out when the guns were fired at high altitudes, but these were overcome when improved Avons were fitted. Although not supersonic in level flight, at a time when American and Russian fighters can achieve twice the speed of sound, the good all-round performance of the Hunter and its quickly replace-able armament pack of four 30-mm cannon has ensured its continued use by many air forces of the world. It has been more successful in many ways than the massive two-seat Gloster Javelin, the first twin-jet delta-wing aircraft to fly and which, as an all-weather fighter, served to introduce air-to-air guided missiles into the RAF. Four Firestreak guided missiles were carried under the wing, in addition to armament of two 30-mm cannon. The Javelin was intended for supersonic development but the programme was cancelled because of cost. It was with such costs in mind that an attempt was made by the Folland company to introduce a relatively cheap lightweight fighter. This is the single-seat high-wing Gnat, only one-third the size and half the weight of a conventional jet fighter. Although extremely agile it has found little acceptance because of its inability to carry the complex equipment necessary today and is being used by the RAF as an advanced two-seat trainer.

Although Britain has fallen well behind in the production of modern jet fighters since the Second World War, most of her advanced projects such as the TSR-2 having been cancelled, there is one field in which British design has led the way and that is in V/STOL. Tests were begun with an experimental Meteor in the early 1950s on the possibility of diverting the exhaust from a jet engine downwards so that the aircraft would take off vertically, thus making front-line fighter squadrons independent of vulnerable runways. From the experimental P.1127 of 1960, designed by the late Sir Sydney Camm, has been developed the Hawker Siddeley Harrier (280), its Pegasus turbofan engine fitted with four rotating exhaust nozzles. It is in limited service today as a strike fighter, but it is more important as an experimental machine whose potential is still being evaluated in both Britain and the United States. Meanwhile, the only supersonic fighter to be produced in Britain is the BAC Lightning (279), the RAF's first single-seat all-weather fighter to have gun, rocket and guided weapon armament and a speed of Mach 2. With its sharply swept-back wings and twin Rolls-Royce Avon turbojets with reheat, the Lightning can rank with most foreign fighters although it has been in service since 1960. It can carry 30-mm cannon, rockets in retractable packs, or guided missiles of the Firestreak or Red Top type, both developed by Hawker Siddeley.

Two other countries of Western Europe have produced supersonic fighters in the Mach 2 range. In France the excellent Dassault Mystère (284) series of jet fighters which came out in the 1950s has been followed by the outstanding delta-wing Mirage III (286), successfully developed as a fighter, fighter-bomber and reconnaissance

aircraft and sold to a number of other countries as well as equipping the French Air Force from 1961. In addition to its SNECMA Atar turbojet the Mirage can be fitted with a rocket propulsion engine to give increased thrust. When the liquid fuel is exhausted after eighty seconds, the pack containing the rocket engine is jettisoned. A speed of Mach 2.2 (1,450 mph) at 50,000 feet was achieved by an improved prototype which first flew in 1958. As a high-altitude interceptor the Mirage can carry a Matra R.530 radar-guided missile under the fuselage, two Sidewinder infra-red guided missiles under the wing, and two 30-mm cannon in the fuselage. Experiments have included the fitting of a turbofan engine, VTOL capabilities, and variable-sweep wings.

The SAAB company in Sweden also built a number of excellent jet aircraft in the post-war years. Its SAAB-29 (281) in April 1951 became the first swept-wing jet fighter to enter production in Western Europe. The SAAB-35 Draken (Dragon) (283) introduced a remarkable double-delta wing design which gave both good manoeuvrability and short take-off and landing performance without hindering maximum speeds which were eventually increased to 1,320 mph at 40,000 feet, with a service ceiling of 70,000 feet. The Draken is still in service with the Swedish Air Force, powered by two Rolls-Royce Avon turbojets with afterburners, and has been sold successfully abroad. Meanwhile, after ten years of design work and the most expensive engineering project ever undertaken in Sweden, the SAAB-37 Viggen (Thunderbolt) (282) has been produced and will replace the Draken in Swedish service in the mid-1970s. This is also of unconventional design with a foreplan ahead of the main delta wing, so that although its top speed is more than Mach 2, it can operate from runways only 500 yards long.

In spite of these developments in Europe, the only country which is likely to be able to compete with America in the production of super-fighters of the future is the Soviet Union. The MiG-15 which so shocked the Western powers with its appearance in Korea remained in production until the mid-1950s and equipped the air forces of many of Russia's allies. It was improved with the MiG-17, in which an afterburner was fitted to give increased power. In 1953 the MiG-19 (271) appeared as the first supersonic Soviet fighter, with two turbojets and swept-back wings. This type came into service two years later, armed either with one 37-mm and two 23-mm cannon or four beam-riding guided missiles. The axial-flow turbojets are also fitted with afterburners. Then in 1956 the MiG-21 was seen for the first time and its delta-wing form showed the Americans and their allies just how far the Russians had advanced in aircraft design. The MiG-21, which is now in service with the Russian Air Force as well as with allied and friendly countries like Cuba and Syria, has a maximum speed of 1,520 mph at 36,000 feet and carries an armament of two 30-mm cannon and two 'Atoll' air-to-air infra-red homing missiles similar to the American Sidewinder.

But in the summer of 1967 a new multi-purpose fighter began entering into Russian service which seemed to outclass all Western fighters of that time, certainly those of the British. This was the MiG-23, a twin-jet single-seater with cropped delta wings, huge sloping air intakes, and a unique twin-finned tail unit. One of the records it set up that year was the 500 kilometres circuit at 1,852 mph.

Naturally far less is known about Russian fighter development than that of Western countries. The last Yakovlev fighter which has been publicly seen is the Yak-28, a twin-jet two-seater armed with 'Anab' air-to-air missiles which appeared in 1961 as a development of the Yak–25, Russia's first twin-jet all-weather fighter. A single-seat twin-jet all-weather fighter, the Sukhoi 'Flagon–A' (272) with delta wings, came into service in 1967 with a maximum speed of Mach 2.5 at 40,000 feet. It also carries air-to-air missiles with radar or infra-red homing devices. What Russian designers have been doing since these aircraft were first built is largely unknown to the West but it is hardly likely that they have been inactive. This is the kind of problem that faces the NATO countries today as they try to develop the strategic and tactical aircraft which might be required in a future war. Intercontinental ballistic missiles with nuclear warheads at one time seemed to render bomber aircraft obsolete, but with the development of anti-missile missiles there is still a place for bombers and, therefore, for interceptors as well.

The supersonic fighter of today is called upon to perform many roles, including bombing, ground-attack and reconnaissance, but this was also true in the past. Air combat has changed to the point where a pilot will seldom see his enemy. But paradoxically, while these costly and complex aircraft have helped to create the stand-off situation that has prevented a possible third world war, it is the slower and even older piston-engined type of aircraft that has been most successful in the small limited wars of recent years, often using old-style tactics. However much it might have changed over the past sixty years, from the Morane-Saulnier Type N to the F–4 Phantom, the fighter is an essential requirement for any military force and will remain so in the foreseeable future.

276 **de Havilland Vampire Mk 5.** Span: 38 ft. Length: 30 ft. 9 in. Engine: 3,100-lb thrust Goblin DGn2 turbojet. Armament: four 20-mm cannon and up to 2,000-lb load of bombs or rockets. Performance details of the Mk 5 fighter-bomber version of the Vampire are not known but the refined FB Mk 9 which followed had a maximum speed of 548 mph at 30,000 ft.

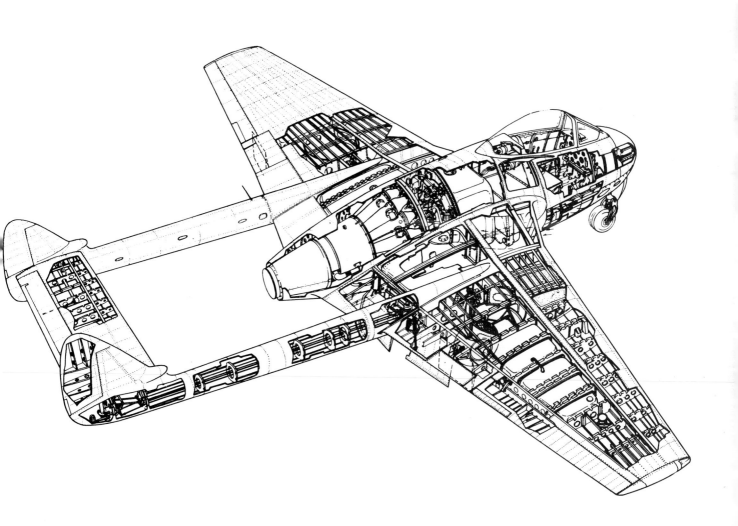

277

277 **Gloster/Armstrong Whitworth Meteor Mk 4.** Span: 37 ft. 2 in. Length: 41 ft. 4 in. Engine: two 3,500-lb thrust Derwent 5 turbojets. Armament: four 20-mm cannon. Max speed: 585 mph at sea level. Service ceiling: 50,000 ft. The Meteors were the only Allied jet fighters to be used operationally during the war.

278

279

280

278 Hawker Hunter Mk 6. Span: 33 ft. 8 in. Length: 45 ft. 10 in. Engine: 10,500-lb thrust Rolls-Royce Avon 200 turbojet. Armament: four Aden cannon in detachable packs (and provision for two 1,000-lb bombs, rocket batteries *or* 100-gallon Napalm bombs; can be adapted to carry two Sidewiner air-to-air missiles). Max speed: 715 mph at 36,000 ft. Service ceiling: 55,000 ft. Still in front-line service with some air forces, the Hunter represents the peak of subsonic jet development.

279 BAC Lightning. Span: 34 ft. 10 in. Length: 55 ft. 3 in. Engine: two 11,250-lb thrust Rolls-Royce Avon 210 (RA 24R) turbojets with variable-area nozzles, developing 14,430 lbs thrust with reheat. Armament: two 30-mm Aden cannon and two Hawker Siddeley Firestreak missiles (and provision for 48 two-inch rockets in retractable packs). Max speed: 1,500 mph. Service ceiling: 60,000 ft. plus. This was the first fully supersonic aircraft to go into service with the RAF.

280 Hawker Siddeley Harrier. Span: 25 ft. Length: 46 ft. Engine: 19,000-lb thrust Pegasus 6. Armament: various rockets and bombs. Max speed: 680 mph at sea level. The world's first combat aircraft with the ability to take off and land vertically, developed from the P.1127 prototype. Known also as the Kestrel for evaluation by a joint Anglo-American-German squadron.

281 SAAB J-29. Span: 36 ft. 1 in. Length: 33 ft. 2½ in. Engine: 4,400-lb thrust de Havilland Ghost turbojet. Armament: four 20-mm cannon (and provision for twenty-four 75-mm Bofors air-to-air rockets *or* up to 1,100-lb bomb load). Max speed: 658 mph at 5,000 ft. Service ceiling: 50,850 ft.

282 SAAB-37 Viggen (Thunderbolt). Span: 34 ft. 9½ in. Length: 53 ft. 5½ in. Engine: 26,450-lb thrust RM8 afterburning turbofan, a Swedish development of the civil Pratt & Whitney JT–8D–22. Armament: four 30-mm cannon and air-to-air or air-to-surface missiles. Max speed: 1,320 mph at 39,370 ft. Service ceiling: 60,000 ft. plus. The biggest and most expensive engineering project ever undertaken in Sweden, the Viggen fighter is designed to take off and land on 500-metre sections of Sweden's trunk-road system.

282

283 SAAB-35 (J35F) Draken (Dragon). Span: 30 ft. 10 in. Length: 51 ft. 10 in. Engine: 17,635-lb. thrust RM6C turbojet with afterburner (Swedish-built Rolls-Royce Avon 300). Armament: four radar-guided or infra-red Falcon air-to-air missiles. Max speed: 1,320 mph at 40,000 ft. Service ceiling: 70,000 ft. The double-delta wing provides manoeuvrability and excellent STOL qualities.

283

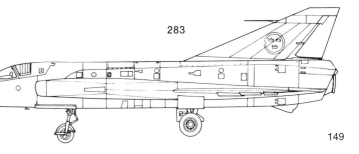

284 **Dassault Super Mystère B-2.** Span: 34 ft. 6½ in. Length: 46 ft. 1 in. Engine: 9,700-lb thrust SNECMA Atar 101G turbojet with afterburner. Armament: two 30-mm cannon and pack of 55 air-to-air rockets (and provision for a 1,100-lb bomb *or* a further 38 rockets *or* two Sidewinder missiles). Max speed: 743 mph at 38,000 ft. Service ceiling: 55,750 ft.

285 **Dassault MD 450 Ouragan.** Span: 43 ft. 2 in. Length: 35 ft. 2½ in. Engine: Hispano-manufactured Rolls-Royce Nene turbojet. Armament: four 20-mm cannon (and provision for two 1,000-lb bombs *or* sixteen rockets). Max speed: 585 mph at sea level.

286 **Dassault Mirage III-E.** Span: 27 ft. Length: 49 ft. 3½ in. Engine: 14,110-lb thrust Atar 9C turbojet with 3,700-lb thrust SEPR 844 auxiliary rocket engine. Armament: one Matra R.530 air-to-air radar-homing missile *or* two 30-mm cannon and two Sidewinder infra-red air-to-air missiles (and provision for two 1,000-lb bombs and launchers for 72 rockets). Max speed: 1,430 mph at 36,000 ft. Service ceiling: 65,600 ft.

284

285

286

Acknowledgements

Royal Air Force Museum.

Smithsonian Institute Air and
Space Museum, Jon Casey in particular.

Helen Downton,

Tony Bryan,

Arthur Gaye.

Bibliography

Bruce, J. M.   Warplanes of the First World War: Fighters. (three volumes). Macdonald, 1965, 1968, 1969.

Green, William   Warplanes of the Second World War: Fighters. (four volumes). Macdonald, 1961.

Higham, Robin   Air Power – A Concise Histroy. Macdonald. 1972.

King, H. F.   The World's Fighters. Putnam. 1971.

Lamberton, W. M.   Fighter Aircraft of the 1914–1918 War. Harleyford Publications. 1961.

Lewis, Peter   The British Fighter since 1912. Putnam. 1965.

Taylor, John W. R.   Combat Aircraft of the World. Ebury Press and Michael Joseph. 1969.

Taylor, John W. R.   Jane's All the World's Aircraft. Sampson Low Marston & Co. Ltd. Annual.

Wagner, Ray   American Combat Planes. 1960.

Illustration Index

(References in italic are to page numbers)

Anatomy of a Fighter (curtiss Hawk).

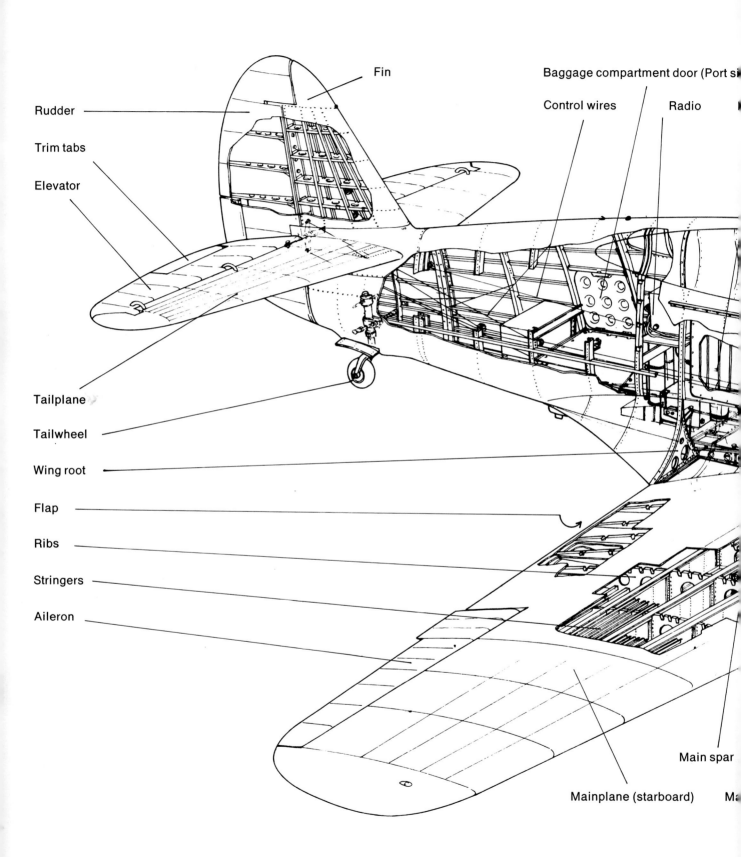

Fin

Baggage compartment door (Port s

Rudder

Control wires

Radio

Trim tabs

Elevator

Tailplane

Tailwheel

Wing root

Flap

Ribs

Stringers

Aileron

Main spar

Mainplane (starboard)

M

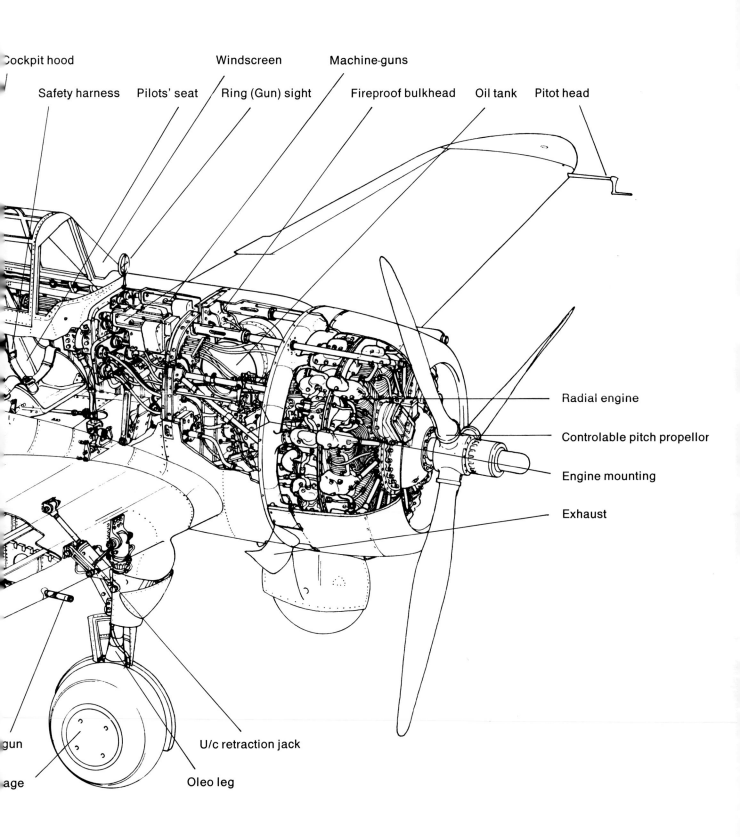

Cockpit hood

Safety harness Pilots' seat Ring (Gun) sight

Windscreen Machine-guns

Fireproof bulkhead Oil tank Pitot head

Radial engine

Controlable pitch propellor

Engine mounting

Exhaust

gun

age

U/c retraction jack

Oleo leg